CREATING A DEMOCRATIC PUBLIC

KEVIN MATTSON

CREATING A DEMOCRATIC PUBLIC

The Struggle for Urban Participatory Democracy During the Progressive Era

The Pennsylvania State University Press
University Park, Pennsylvania

Library of Congress Cataloging-in-Publication Data

Mattson, Kevin, 1966–
Creating a democratic public : the struggle for urban participatory democracy during the progressive era / Kevin Mattson.

p. cm.
Includes bibliographical references (p.) and index.
ISBN 0-271-01722-8 (cloth : alk. paper)
ISBN 0-271-01723-6 (pbk. : alk. paper)
1. Political participation—United States—History. 2. Political culture—United States—History. 3. Progressivism (United States politics). 4. United States—Politics and government—1865–1933. I. Title.
JK1764.M384 1998
323′.042′0973—dc21 96-53211
CIP

Printed in the United States of America
Published by The Pennsylvania State University Press,
University Park, PA 16802-1003

It is the policy of The Pennsylvania State University Press to use acid-free paper for the first printing of all clothbound books. Publications on uncoated stock satisfy the minimum requirements of American National Standard for Information Sciences—Permanence of Paper for Printed Library Materials, ANSI Z39.48-1992.

CONTENTS

ACKNOWLEDGMENTS

I have few acknowledgments to make here. There were no fancy institutions that provided me with large research grants, only individuals who read this manuscript in some form and encouraged me to pursue it further. First, there was Christopher Lasch. Before his untimely death Kit served as my adviser in graduate school. His intellectual guidance was supreme, his humility refreshing. He will be missed. Second, I thank Robert Westbrook, whose commitment to making this manuscript better kept my spirits alive at crucial times. For reading this manuscript and providing insights, I thank Thomas Bender, Benjamin Barber, Margo Shea, and Marie Bernard. Two readers, Scott Bowman and Sidney Milkis, gave me very helpful editorial suggestions at a crucial moment. Margaret Becket, a reference librarian at the University of Rochester, helped me in the primary research that serves as the basis of this book. She did an excellent job at it. Sandy Thatcher has been a marvelous editor, both encouraging and helpful in making this a better book. Thanks are also due Cherene Holland and Cathy Thatcher of Penn State Press. Jeff Boxer and Richard Ford, friends and comrades, read this work and kept me going through the hard times. My other friends know who they are and helped me in ways hard to describe. Finally, my mom's support was constant throughout and helped me in more ways than one.

INTRODUCTION

Creating a Democratic Public

The essential need . . . is the improvement of the methods and conditions of debate, discussion, and persuasion. That is the problem of the public.
—John Dewey[1]

From 1907 until 1912 citizens, many of them recently arrived immigrants, gathered in public schools scattered throughout the burgeoning city of Rochester, New York. During these evening meetings they debated the great issues of the day—everything from local city planning initiatives and school board decisions to American foreign policy in the Philippines and Theodore Roosevelt's call for the federal government to regulate American corporations more rigorously. All city residents were welcome to attend these sessions of public deliberation about pressing matters. One woman remembers a meeting on the "commission form of [city] government" where the president of the Women's Christian Temperance Union and a Polish washwoman found themselves debating a college professor and a day cleaner. The exchanges between these citizens were serious, passionate, and normally quite civil, and many citizens took action based upon what they had learned from one another within these deliberative sessions.[2]

America's current political landscape seems bereft of these sorts of meetings and such vigorous citizen engagement in political talk. In fact, today there seem to be few arenas in which citizens can discuss and deliberate on the political issues that face them. Political debate instead is shallow, relying less on deliberation than on political advertising, shoddy slogans, and imagery. Lacking the means to shape political debate, we distance ourselves from politics, and by distancing ourselves from politics we threaten the foundation of democracy: citizens participating in their own self-government by deciding their political fate.

To say that Americans feel disaffected from politics is nothing new. We have heard the complaint many times before. Most Americans no longer take time to vote, and opinion poll after opinion poll rediscovers deep-rooted political alienation. As one political critic put it, "For most of us, politics is increasingly abstract, a spectator sport barely worth watching." Television has replaced the newspaper as the principal news medium, and campaign advisers have learned to sell candidates and their political agendas just like other commodities—to a disengaged and passive television audience jaded by images and sound bites. Few citizens believe what they hear politicians say any longer, and many conceive of politics taking place far away from their homes in Washington, D.C.—a seemingly sordid place where politicians and lobbyists, disconnected from the realities of most citizens, cut shady deals. Though we still call our system democratic, we see few ways in which democratic debate and democratic decision making influence politics.[3]

It seems that over the last fifty years the word "democracy" has become increasingly meaningless. As one political scientist noted, "A term that means anything means nothing. And so it has become with 'democracy.' " With the advent of the Cold War, political leaders used the term "democratic" synonymously with anything anticommunist in nature. In foreign policy, American politicians upheld political leaders who opposed communism, even if they were authoritarian dictators (an examination of the Vietnam War and American foreign policy in Central America makes that clear). Domestically, democracy became equated with the economic prosperity and consumer ethic of America's abundant post–World War II economy. In the 1959 "Kitchen Debate" with the leader of the Soviet Union, Nikita Khrushchev, Vice President Richard Nixon used a modern-day kitchen with its various appliances as the basis for his argument against communism. Showing off the abundance that a consumer society could offer, Nixon asserted that the American way of life grew out of the plethora of commodities provided by corporations and the freedom to purchase them. Political participation and public deliberation fell out of the equation when consumption and democracy became synonymous.[4]

The equation of consumption with democracy was made not only by politicians but by sophisticated social theorists like Joseph Schumpeter in his now classic book *Capitalism, Socialism, and Democracy* (1942). Believing that politicians and administrators—not regular citizens—should be the central actors in a political democracy, Schumpeter relegated citizens' roles to choosing among different candidates who would advertise themselves in the political marketplace during infrequent elections. Not only did this greatly limit the role of a citizen in a democracy, it made democracy the equivalent of shopping. Democracy was not to be understood as citizens educating themselves into political decision making about public goods (that would get in the way of politicians and administrators getting their jobs done) but as consumers passively enjoying products bestowed by American corporations or occasionally choosing among politicians who were turned into commodities by political advertisers. With the Cold War and a consumer society, the idea of American democracy no longer seemed to include the active participation of citizens in their own self-governance.[5]

The Cold War is over, and many believe that the economic prosperity of post–World War II America is as well. Americans today stand at a very distinct historical juncture. For quite some time we have believed that our country is a leader of democracy in the world. Yet many critics are discovering that America is bereft of the civic institutions necessary to teach citizens the skills of self-government and public dialogue. What political theorists call "civil society"—an assortment of voluntary and intermediary associations in which citizens associate as equals and collectively solve problems—has been on the decline in recent years. Americans are not learning how to participate in social life or building relations based on trust and mutual obligation, as Robert Putnam and others have argued, but are becoming passive consumers glued to their television sets. Many critics are discovering that America has not paid enough attention to nurturing democratic practices among regular citizens, and with the end of the Cold War it seems much less justifiable to use the term "democracy" loosely or to identify it solely with a consumer society and economic prosperity. Instead, we need to set out much more clearly what democracy requires of and for its citizenry if it is to be vibrant and healthy.[6]

In examining the history of ideas in America it is not difficult to find visions of democracy distinct from those that equate it with consumption and abundance. A more rigorous definition begins with the ideas of Thomas Jefferson. Though Jefferson believed, along with the Federalists, that a constitutional balance of power was necessary for democracy, he also argued against an overly centralized government and understood that alongside a Constitution with a Bill of Rights (which were, after all, only paper documents) citizens must nurture democratic practices on a day-to-day basis in local settings. To provide the spaces in which citizens could educate themselves in preparation for political decision making, Jefferson suggested that America be broken down into small wards. By doing this, America could achieve a form of government "where every man is a sharer in the direction of his ward-republic, . . . and feels that he is a participator in the government of affairs, not merely at an election one day in the year, but every day." Jefferson saw that citizens had to be provided with places where they could educate themselves and participate in their own self-government effectively if America was to have a democracy more than just in name.[7]

Though the world of Thomas Jefferson, which was made up of family farms and small towns, has long since passed, intellectuals in the twentieth century have continued to elaborate on Jefferson's ideas. One of America's most astute social critics during the 1950s, C. Wright Mills, analyzed how the mass media has displaced the political role of "primary publics," locales akin to Jefferson's wards where citizens interact face-to-face and decide on pressing issues. Mills thought that something could be done to counter the apathy resulting from this modern destruction of local arenas of political deliberation by developing "two things": "articulate and knowledgeable publics and political leaders who if not men of reason are at least reasonably responsible to such knowledgeable publics as exist." The famous pragmatic philosopher and one of C. Wright Mills's most important intellectual predecessors, John Dewey, had already located the source of these publics. Dewey explained: "Unless local communal life can be restored, the public cannot adequately resolve its most urgent problem: to find and identify itself."

Contemporary political theorists continue this type of thinking about democracy by arguing that the development of "public judgment" among regular citizens should be made the central concern of modern politics. Public judgment, in the words of Benjamin Barber, is a "function of commonality that can be exercised only by citizens interacting with one another in the context of mutual deliberation and decision." The idea developed by Dewey, Mills, and contemporary political theorists of participatory democracy—that community-based forums and discussions play a constitutive role in making the public judgments necessary for a democracy—provides the basis for this book.[8]

What I call a democratic public is central to this work. A democratic public forms when citizens gather together to deliberate and make public judgments about local and national issues that affect their lives. By associating together for public discussion, citizens learn the skills necessary for the health of a democratic public: listening, persuading, arguing, compromising, and seeking common ground. When these skills are nurtured within the institutions of a democratic public, citizens educate themselves in order to make informed political decisions. A political system that offers spaces in which citizens can form such a democratic public and that tries to have democratic decision making influence politics is what I call, following the activists and intellectuals studied here, a "real" or "true" democracy (this is in contrast to a democracy in name only, where citizens are exhorted to participate and engage in public life but are never provided with the institutional means by which to do these things). This "real democracy," it should be made clear, is not direct or "pure" democracy (where citizens make all decisions without leadership or representation), since political representatives remain in the picture while being strongly encouraged to listen to the citizens they represent. Rather, a "real democracy" is one that puts the development of a democratic public at the center of political life.[9]

The key question remains: How can a democratic public form and become effective? This issue requires concrete institutional analysis and historical exploration to be answered. We must understand how citizens have formed institutions that facilitated the processes of public discussion and collective education and how these institutions succeeded and failed. In addition, we need to explore how activists and writers reflected upon their experiences in creating a democratic public. By investigating how American citizens have grappled with this challenge in the past, we can learn more about our present predicaments and possibilities. This sort of historical exploration is the central focus of this book.

Let me be clear what I mean here. I am not interested in the sort of historical research practiced by most academic historians, those concerned with what the historical profession defines as relevant (i.e., what is written about in academic journals and is typically read only by other academics). Instead, I harken back to the work of progressive historians in the past like James Harvey Robinson and Charles Beard. These historians understood history's relevance for the present and for a wider public of fellow citizens. In a classic essay Robinson argued that the "one thing" history "ought to do, and has not yet effectively done, is to help us to understand ourselves and our fellows and the problems and prospects of mankind. It is this most significant form of history's usefulness that has been most commonly neglected." History for Robinson and for Beard helped citizens understand the sources of contemporary problems. Though I do not agree with many of Beard's or Robinson's other arguments regarding history (for instance, that economic principles often outweigh all other principles), I think we must renew their belief that historical exploration should concern itself with public issues and become "useful" for people's self-understanding.[10]

Following the model of historical exploration set out by progressive historians, this book takes contemporary concerns about the state of American democracy and asks how things could have been different. It is both a work of history and social criticism. Throughout the American past, citizens have tried to create institutions that could develop a "real democracy." By understanding those who struggled for this ideal, we perceive that the world we live in today could have been different and that our contemporary institutions and values are contingent on activities and decisions made in the past. What exists now did not necessarily *have to* exist. Thus, we must study the so-called losers in history (those whose visions failed to determine the course of society) to figure out how our society could have been different. Just because people's visions are defeated does not make them wrong. Justice is not on the side of history, and if anyone should understand this, it is historians who have studied the past. History is thus indelibly linked to moral inquiry and criticism of our contemporary values and institutions. In essence, this work is meant to change how we think about democracy by bringing us into critical dialogue with the past and exploring the achievements and failures of activists and intellectuals who had a vision for a better American democracy.[11]

To understand how a democratic public can form I will turn to the time during which Rochester citizens met in public schools to discuss political issues and the time in which Robinson and Beard wrote—the so-called Progressive Era (1890–1920). This era is crucial for a number of reasons. First, and perhaps most important, the central economic, political, and cultural features of the modern American nation formed during this time. Starting in the late nineteenth century, modern corporations centralized their economic power by developing bureaucratic management capable of gaining control of and overseeing a nationwide market tied together by railroads. Partially in response to the problems created by industrial capitalism, American government grew in size, taking on more responsibilities and gradually acquiring regulatory power. Alongside these economic and political developments, intellectuals and artists expanded on the Enlightenment tradition and embraced a secular and increasingly rational culture based on the principles of modernism. Living in the presence of these changes, the activists and intellectuals studied here experienced the transition into modernity and the world as we know it today. But they did not believe that the American nation had to develop the way it did; they saw a different possibility for America's entrance into the modern age. That is what makes these intellectuals and activists so relevant and why they deserve such close study.[12]

These activists and intellectuals not only witnessed the birth of modernity, they lived during a period of time one historian called the "age of reform." Bold political experimentation marked the Progressive Era. Citizens, activists, and intellectuals discussed and debated, with the utmost seriousness, alternatives to industrial capitalism and liberal democracy. The Socialist Party reached its peak during the Progressive Era and influenced mainstream political debates in ways never since seen. The modern civil rights movement, concerned with the plight of Black Americans, formed under the leadership of W.E.B. Du Bois, an activist and intellectual who challenged Booker T. Washington's previous endorsement of racial segregation. Modern feminism arose alongside an increasingly powerful suffragette movement that, after World War I, won women the right to vote. Throughout the Progressive Era, Americans committed themselves to reexamining political institutions and intellectual assumptions guiding Americans into the modern age. This was truly a time when critical social examination and political reform were widespread.[13]

Though these reform efforts might seem disparate, the Progressive Era was united by an overarching awareness that the American political system suffered from corruption (an awareness akin to many contemporary concerns). Big business leaders had gained an influence over local and national political institutions, often encouraging politicians to look the other way as they broke laws while building up their powerful monopolies. Corrupt political bosses bought votes in urban wards by doing favors for local clients. The national political party system had also been corrupted by political bosses who ensured that only certain people would become candidates for public office.

A concerted effort was made during the Progressive Era to expose this corruption and replace it with a more democratic political order. Within the pages of widely read popular magazines (many of which will be cited in this book), "muckrakers"—journalists who exposed the exploitative excesses of big business and documented their increasing influence on politics—encouraged an educated "public" to correct the injustices of industrial capitalism. If people were allowed to know about corruption, these journalists believed, they would do something about it. Muckrakers were not the only citizens who invoked the idea of a public as the basis of reform. When urban activists called for economic reform, they often argued for public control over industry. In addition, state and national political leaders believed a politically engaged public was necessary to save America and that this required creating more direct democracy through the initiative and referendum (this was the period when many states adopted these measures) and encouraging popular education in settlement houses and forums. Reformers understood that a vigilant and perceptive public would have to underpin future political reforms if corruption were to be ended. As the leading progressive thinker, Herbert Croly, explained: "The great object of progressives must always be to create a vital relation between progressivism and popular political education." The idea of a democratic public framed political reform during the Progressive Era and thus makes understanding this period of time extremely important.[14]

Certainly some progressives merely wanted reform, democratic or not, while progressives like Herbert Croly wanted a democratic public to approve progressives' ideas. But there were other activists and intellectuals who believed a democratic public should be a goal in and of itself. They insisted that local publics should become the basis of the American nation. Because of this distinct vision, these activists deserve closer attention than they have yet received. They argued that before any other substantive political reform took place, citizens had to build institutions through which they could educate themselves for the making of binding political judgments. This would be the root of all future political reform. And it was no easy goal. As one social critic recently explained, "The practices of citizenship and self-government, precisely because they run counter to the commercial ethos, do require conscious, collective cultivation to flourish under modern conditions." The activists and intellectuals studied here believed in creating institutions that would, within the confines of the modern world, sustain a democratic public and public-minded values, not just private, commercial motivations. Unlike other activists who spoke only rhetorically about a democratic public, these activists and intellectuals understood the need for institutions through which a public could grow. They thought very concretely and pragmatically about the ways in which modern institutions such as universities, forums, and public schools could help create more democracy.[15]

These activists believed their project to be connected to cities. Urban areas were at the center of modern developments in terms of politics, economics, and culture. Cities also produced a natural sense of public life. Interaction found in city streets, stores, and in new forms of transportation created a sense of a public. As the historian Thomas Bender explains: "What characterizes the modern metropolis is the creation of a significant culture of impersonality, a social world of strangers in continuous . . . association. . . . Cities generate a public culture, made up of life in the streets and other public places, embracing a wide range of institutions of culture that, whether privately owned or not, provide an arena for the making, inscribing, and interpreting of public experiences." The activists studied here believed that the public forming in America's cities must be made fully conscious of its power and capacities for self-government and decision making. To provide their hope with substance, these activists helped create certain institutions that could facilitate democratic discussion and deliberation. This is the starting point of my historical analysis.[16]

My examination will not be strictly chronological. I want at the outset to study the institutions created by various activists in terms of their increasingly democratic organization. In Chapter One, I begin with attempts to beautify urban space in the city beautiful movement and how the debates about the American city found within this movement led to more rigorous thinking about an American democratic public. I then move on to studying the work of Charles Zueblin, who not only worked with the city beautiful movement but also pioneered in university extension. Showing how he failed to make the modern university embrace a civic vision based on its connection to an urban public, I turn to other efforts to create a democratic public under the conditions of modern urban life.[17]

In Chapter Two, I examine Frederic Howe's efforts to build on the civic vision of the city beautiful movement by working with the Progressive Era mayor of Cleveland, Ohio, Tom Johnson. From Johnson, Howe learned how economic issues related to the creation of a democratic public. Expanding on the lessons taught by Johnson, Howe took up leadership of the People's Institute—a central institution in the formation of a democratic public during the Progressive Era. Here working-class citizens participated in public life by attending forums held on the pressing issues of the day. The People's Institute helped initiate a more widespread forum movement across America. I will explain the important ideas of this forum movement but also show how the forum failed to embrace fully the principles of a democratic public.

In many ways Chapter Three, is the climax of the book. Here I set out the work of social centers activists—citizens who opened public schools in the evening for open sessions of public debates and deliberation. In this experiment we witness the highest expression of a democratic public. I show why this movement was so important and why it failed to change the course of American history. Next, in Chapters Four and Five I set out the political thought developed by the leaders of this movement, including that of Mary Parker Follett, to explain these thinkers' profound understanding of the challenges of democracy.

Chapter Six tells a story of decline—a decline in the institutions and ideas developed by activists concerned with enlivening democracy during the Progressive Era. Here a different vision of American politics emerged. This was a vision based on a strong centralized state that usurped local power during World War I. More important, it was based on a growing conception of public opinion as being directed from above—by state propagandists during World War I and by corporate advertisers during the 1920s (the period of time during which modern advertising developed). In many ways the paltry view of democracy that grew out of these historical developments became the basis of our own pessimism about contemporary politics. On the other hand, I will argue that the political thought and work of the activists and intellectuals studied here can still inform our current hopes for a better American democracy.

Before going on I must deal with a few objections that will be raised against this study. Historians have done a good job of dismissing progressives' reforms and hopes. In the first place, it is often argued that progressives tried to make industrial capitalism more "efficient" rather than more democratic. Frederick Taylor's faith in scientific management and technocrats fueled an "efficiency craze" during the Progressive Era. There is much truth to this. Certain of the activists studied here used the term "efficiency," but they believed efficiency and democracy went hand in hand. Democracy was efficient because it did away with the corrupt influence of big business and the meddling of special interests in the political process. When citizens decided what should be done and implemented their decisions, things were accomplished directly and quickly.

This argument reflected both a valid interpretation and misunderstanding of democracy. Democracy is often more efficient than bureaucratic and hierarchical organization or a politics driven by special interests. On the other hand, it is not *always* efficient. It can be contentious and slow in rendering decisions. Nor is efficiency the best grounds for a defense of democracy. As Christopher Lasch has argued, we should "defend democracy not as the most efficient but as the most educational form of government, one that extends the circle of debate as widely as possible and thus forces all citizens to articulate their views, to put their views at risk, and to cultivate the virtues of eloquence, clarity of thought and expression, and sound judgement." Some of the activists and intellectuals I study here understood this point. But even if others placed their hopes in an efficient democracy, we cannot so easily dismiss them as technocrats or elitists. They did not share our contemporary belief that efficiency and democracy are often antagonistic.[18]

Historians have also argued, sometimes eloquently, sometimes crudely, that progressives' hopes grew out of a middle-class desire to tame industrial capitalism's conflicts and merely form a weak version of a welfare state. Progressives supposedly were not intent on democracy but rather on "social control." Besides being a cynical view of middle-class activists, this interpretation ignores many activists' and intellectuals' deeper understanding of democracy and self-government. I will show that these intellectuals and activists very often understood democracy's requirements and committed themselves to its ethic of self-government, not to pernicious forms of social control. I believe middle-class people can be committed to democratic activity and leadership. Privilege need not lead to domination. Our responsibility as social critics should not make us cynical about every democratic initiative.[19]

One last potential criticism needs mention. The intellectuals and activists studied here attacked partisan loyalty. They hoped a democratic public open to all citizens could replace the corruption found within boss-run political parties. Only when citizens deliberated together and made politically effective decisions would the political corruption practiced by party bosses be circumvented. But as political historians have shown, partisan loyalty fueled widespread political participation throughout the nineteenth century. During this time record numbers of citizens (not since surpassed) attached themselves to political parties and participated in public affairs, especially parades and other spectacles, to show their loyalty. The progressives examined here hoped for a modern politics based not on the nineteenth century, boss-controlled party system. But in doing so, some historians would argue, they ironically contributed to a historical decline of popular participation in politics. Though this account carries weight, I hope to show that these activists offered a political and institutional alternative—a democratic public—to partisan loyalty. This alternative failed for historical reasons. Nonetheless, to accuse these progressives of merely fueling political disengagement would ignore both their activism and their ideas.[20]

Yet, it must be acknowledged that the activists studied here made mistakes. In the first place, they did not fully understand the pernicious qualities of national unity. Though they believed in a nation formed out of democratic publics developed by citizens in their local neighborhoods, they ignored the fact that a centralized national government could easily smash this ideal (as happened with World War I). Since these activists argued for local self-government, they had a responsibility to understand the dynamic of state centralization. During their day and age the modern bureaucratic state was no longer a conspiratorial idea held in the minds of political cranks but an actual growing reality. Though it would be unfair to blame these progressives for this mistake, we need to be critical of their misperceptions of developing realities, especially since these misperceptions undermined their own ideas and hopes.[21]

Another central problem these activists faced was beyond their control. This was a different vision of democracy that took hold during the 1920s, a vision that grew out of a consumer economy and the idea that public opinion was manufactured from above (by advertisers), not from below. This new conception of democracy limited the role of citizens who were increasingly perceived as too incompetent for self-government. The activists studied here lost out to this understanding of democracy. In essence, they failed to convince Americans that their hope for democracy, based on the rigorous ideals of citizen participation and the formation of a democratic public, should guide modern political culture. But as I have already argued, this does not make their ideas wrong. By reexamining the efforts and arguments of these activists, this book hopes to make them more compelling in light of recent history and the contemporary challenges American democracy faces.

Let me end here with my own precautionary note. The argument of this book is not that social centers and the ideas of "real democracy" explored here could have saved American politics. If we ask the question whether or not social centers could have redeemed our country, the answer is an emphatic no. But if we frame the question differently by asking if social centers provide us with an institutional basis for thinking critically about how to construct a better democracy, I believe the answer is yes. This is the central argument of this work. Nonetheless, a democratic public does not solve all of our problems. It only provides people with the *opportunity* to act democratically. It is up to citizens to do the acting, and they might choose otherwise.

Finally, this book's idealistic goal to rejuvenate democracy is no small task. Democracy requires a strong commitment by regular citizens and intellectuals. Though it might be a limited role, this work can help us rethink our current political predicament by showing how institutions can help foster democratic practices and values. It would be absurd to think that this is enough. Nonetheless, this work is written in the spirit of what one activist and writer studied here called the "hope of democracy." By rediscovering past efforts to make democracy more vital and real, we can better face up to our present political crisis and renew that great hope of democracy. It is still one of the best hopes we have.

CHAPTER ONE

SEARCHING FOR A PUBLIC

From Beautifying Urban Space to Educating Citizens—The Work of Charles Zueblin

> One can be a citizen only by participation, and that not merely in the annual casting of the ballot, but in daily citizenship.
>
> —Charles Zueblin[1]

Though historians question whether the Progressive Era should be seen as a unified period of time, one overarching theme seems to mark the era. This was a concern about political corruption. The influence business held over political decision making struck many Americans during the Progressive Era as the biggest challenge to democracy. There were a number of responses to such corruption: calls to outlaw monopolies either through stringent taxation policies or direct government regulation, arguments for socialism, beliefs that the "best men" (America's nineteenth-century gentry who were supposedly more "civic-minded" than political bosses) should run political affairs, support for direct democratic proposals like the initiative and referendum that would put power in the hands of citizens, not corporations. Most in line with America's long-standing democratic faith was a vague belief, argued for by many journalists and politicians, that if an educated public could learn about political corruption, this public would be able to end it. Before any reforms were implemented, the "public" had to be educated about them. This view underpinned a great deal of activism during the Progressive Era.[2]

But it was increasingly difficult to understand how a democratic public could form under the conditions of modern industrialism. Throughout the nineteenth century the central institution for democratic self-education was the small town meeting, a fixture in American folklore. In town meetings, it was believed, citizens would gather to discuss and solve the problems in their communities. This romantic notion of the way small towns worked lived on during the Progressive Era, but it became increasingly difficult to cling to this ideal as Americans moved out of small towns and into cities, a pattern that developed rapidly during this time. If a public capable of willing collective decisions was a necessary component of democracy, the question became: How to create such a public within modern urban settings?[3]

The need for a democratic public in industrial cities was especially crucial. Throughout the nineteenth century, political bosses governed American cities. Local ward bosses worked their way up the political machine, doing favors for their local clients in neighborhoods. Though some contemporary historians (and even some progressive activists like Jane Addams) believed these urban bosses were humane toward their clients, none saw them as democratic. "Muckraking" journalists like Lincoln Steffens, Ida Tarbell, and Ray Stannard Baker wrote articles for popular magazines in which they exposed the corrupt paternalism created by this political system. But the muckrakers' hope that, in the words of David Mark Chalmers, "an informed public opinion would make progress possible" never came true. Without the means of deliberating about effective democratic action a public would remain passive in the face of the corruption exposed in muckrakers' articles. If no institutions facilitated popular education and prepared citizens for political decision making and power, then all calls to action by muckrakers degenerated into moral exhortation. Public opinion would be left ineffective.[4]

The modern city certainly offered its citizens many new forms of public association. In different social arenas, including streets, parks, and new transportation networks like streetcars, a city resident was in constant contact with strangers, much more than a rural resident. As the urban historian Thomas Bender explains, "What characterizes the modern metropolis is the creation of a significant culture of impersonality, a social world of strangers in continuous . . . association." But this range of public experiences seemed chaotic and overwhelmingly impersonal. As new immigrants poured into cities, the urban population became increasingly fluid and unstable. In the modern city, areas of residency and work were separated, and people moved throughout the city on a daily basis. Life in urban streets often seemed fast-paced and noisy. As sociologists pointed out, the public association of strangers in the city could seem so anonymous at times as to become disorienting and overwhelming. New and inchoate, the new urban public provoked important questions for those concerned with the state of democracy in the city.[5]

Could this new public become a collective body of self-educating citizens? Or would it become passive and bewildered in the face of the increasingly rapid flux of city life? For anyone concerned about the future of democracy, these questions were paramount. A democratic public was necessary to challenge the corruption of urban politics. And if democracy relied on the growth of an informed and engaged public, then whether the city's modern conditions and its bringing together of strangers could nurture such a public became a pressing problem. To inspire pride and a sense of responsibility in the new urban public was no small task.

With the dawning of the Progressive Era, leaders of the city beautiful movement developed visions of an urban public as an active association of equal citizens. Here progressives began to glimpse the radical potential of a democratic public—an idea whose development during the Progressive Era will be traced in this book. Hoping to counter the domination of America's urban landscape by industrial and commercial interests, city beautiful activists fought against smog-belching factories and tacky commercial billboards. They wanted to supply spaces—especially parks and civic squares—where citizens could gather and feel a sense of civic pride. As they thought about the political meaning of such public spaces, they debated the idea of a democratic public. Activists and intellectuals directly involved in the city beautiful movement, most prominently Charles Zueblin, built upon this idea and started to think about and create institutions through which a democratic public could form.

The City Beautiful Movement, Civic Pride, and the Public

Beginning in the 1890s the city beautiful movement focused on creating and improving urban public spaces—parks, civic squares lined with government buildings, and boulevards—and thereby faced up to the meaning of public space in an urban democracy. Though the movement is often associated with the efforts of famous urban planners like Frederick Law Olmsted (the designer of Central Park in Manhattan and other urban parks) and Daniel Burnham (the architect for many famous urban buildings and for the enormous plans to overhaul downtown Chicago at the turn of the century), it was primarily a movement that relied, in the words of historian William Wilson, on "the work of organized, dedicated and informed laymen." Local citizens played a large role in city beautiful efforts. These citizens not only pressed municipal governments to adopt proposed city plans, they also fought in their cities for paved streets, parks, municipal gardens, monuments, and murals and against the spread of commercial billboards. National organizations tied these citizens' efforts together. The American Park and Outdoor Art Association (APOAA), organized in 1893, and the American League for Civic Improvement (ALCI), formed in 1902, were the two leading organizations of the movement. These two associations merged in 1904 to form the American Civic Association (ACA). During the growth of these organizations, activists had important debates about the meaning of public space, and these debates led to deeper questions about urban democracy. For if public spaces were created, questions still remained: What was their reason for existence and what were citizens to do within them?[6]

At first antiurbanism marked the conferences of the APOAA. Antiurbanism, which cherished the pastoral countryside and saw an ineradicable evil in cities, was a strong tendency in American thought. Since this pattern of thought emphasized the chaos and breakdown in modern cities to the exclusion of any positive values, it limited these activists' sense of what urban public life could be. Activists who hated the city saw in parks a way of reintroducing features of nature and the pastoral countryside into urban areas. They hoped that by doing this they could help "soothe . . . popular discontent" and provide a release valve for pent-up energies, thereby creating spaces in which people let off steam about being trapped in urban areas. There was nothing very democratic about this vision, since in the eyes of these activists an elite would create these safety valves so that the working masses would not boil over. For this group of city activists the urban public was something to be feared, contained, and managed. Public space and the association of citizens in this space had no positive attributes; instead, these early activists saw parks as a necessary evil that aided the processes of social control.[7]

Though certain activists in the APOAA continued to vocalize antiurbanist sentiments, other activists started seeing positive aspects of urban public life. These activists no longer saw just chaos in the city. Instead, they saw a great potential in spaces like parks. Here, these activists believed, a public imbued with civic pride could grow. In the second annual APOAA meeting,

Joseph Wheelock made the connection between parks and democratic public life clear:

> The park belongs to the people. The humblest and laboring man with his family goes out from the hot and dusty street into beautiful parks, and carries with him a sense of ownership. It is his estate, he is lord of it, it belongs to him, all there is in it. It is his, and the condition he respects is the equal ownership and the equal right of every other citizen to the same enjoyment, and it cultivates a spirit of liberalism and equality which I say makes parks a school of Christian ethics.

Instead of just being a relief from urban life, Wheelock believed parks could foster a democratic public and citizenship based on civic pride, political equality, and universal (i.e., Christian) ethics. Gradually, other activists articulated these views on urban life in meetings of the APOAA.[8]

This new line of thought reached its fullest fruition in the last meeting of the APOAA. In his annual address in 1903 the president of the APOAA, Clinton Woodruff, celebrated the open public life found in cities. The city brought people together into full and equal association, especially in its open public spaces. These public spaces, Woodruff believed, could encourage interaction among different people and generate a democratic public. Continuing to develop the obvious conclusion of this line of thought, he argued that the time had come to articulate a thoughtful and clear-cut rationale for the design of new urban parks. Woodruff supported citizens in Iowa's towns who wanted the state to grant them the right "to build town halls and surround them with suitable township parks." These halls could generate a democratic public only if their purpose was perceived correctly by local citizens: "Such halls could be used for township, political and social meetings and made the center of township life. The park would likewise be a convenient place for all kinds of outdoor meetings and a source of inspiration to many." Public meetings would help create a "civic conscience" based on "new communal ideas." The open public life of a city, Woodruff thought, could be a source of good, not evil, but only if it was organized for the distinct purpose of citizens gathering together into a democratic public.[9]

The idea of the public Woodruff talked of was central to the thought of almost all city beautiful activists. In fact, there was something inherently public about city beautiful efforts. The movement focused on designing public squares and public art (typically based on classical architecture and sculpture), and those who wrote on city beautiful efforts believed a sense of a public grew out of appreciating public art. Barr Ferree argued that public sculpture could create a "critical public," and Karl Bitter saw sculpture as "art for out of doors, appealing to everyone as a permanent public possession." In addressing the meaning behind mural paintings, Charles Shean argued that a mural painting could not be a "toy for the rich" but must "command public approval." Public art, like sculptures and murals, forced artists to be citizens and address their public. By working on projects intended for an urban public, city beautiful activists hoped this public would develop self-consciousness and critical capacities.[10]

City beautiful activists hoped that civic pride would grow out of an appreciation of beautiful public monuments. This civic pride would produce wider public concerns. Here was the crux of the argument made by city beautiful activists, for as they believed, the public would develop a proprietary sense when faced with a beautiful city. "Magnificent public buildings, beautiful parks, artistic boulevards, sightly streets, arouse in the individual a keen sense of proprietary pride," one activist wrote. Reflecting on people's pride in parks, H. K. Bush-Brown stated: "Civic pride . . . is that virtue which is born of a community of interest." By inspiring citizens to identify with local examples of beauty, civic pride created public-minded citizens. J. Horace McFarland, the president of the American League for Civic Improvement, explained: "With practical interest aroused in his own dooryard, his own street, his own town, the citizen will almost surely think aright on larger questions." By developing civic pride, citizens would develop a concerned and democratic public and vice versa.[11]

Why did city beautiful activists have so much hope that an appreciation of public beauty led to a more vibrant public life? One immediate reason was that city beautiful activists believed they could re-create the civic pride exhibited during antiquity and the Renaissance. When looking for a valid inspiration to inform city beautiful projects, J. G. Phelps-Stokes, the chairman of the Committee on Civic Centers of the Municipal Art Society of New York City, knew immediately where to turn in history:

> Never has there been more civic pride and more public devotion to the public interest then in the more prosperous days of Athens and Rome, when the beautiful plazas and public buildings of the Acropolis and Forum furnished unparalleled encouragement to the people to come together and mingle, and share in similar thoughts and

> joys and griefs, and become united in common interest in the common weal.

John De Witt Warner agreed since the Acropolis represented for the Greeks "the pride and convenience of her citizens" and "their patriotism and public life." Other activists, like Frederick Lamb, turned to the Renaissance and its city-states. A part of the Renaissance spirit, Lamb believed, was that "art was recognized as a force contributing to the welfare of the community." In both ancient and Renaissance city-states, city beautiful activists believed they found inspiration for a vibrant public life.[12]

Though this argument seemed, at times, very persuasive, it also hinted at elitism. In the first place, in certain Renaissance city-states a wealthy and powerful elite merely commissioned artists to build them palaces of grandeur and pomp. Following this model, some city beautiful activists became apologists for economic inequities. Michele Bogart, an architectural historian, describes the Municipal Arts Society of New York City, a local city beautiful organization, as follows:

> Envisioning themselves as modern-day Medicis, they hired a new generation of professional architects to design opulent Renaissance palaces. Their attempts to create associations with Renaissance culture and civilization extended into the public sphere. Their admiration of the great Italian city-states led them to an unprecedented concern with civic ideals, and prompted the formation of numerous clubs, libraries, museums, and other cultural institutions.

John De Witt Warner, who found inspiration in antiquity and the Renaissance, provides a case in point of how an admiration of past city-state public art could become elitist. Writing on the need to beautify New York City, Warner argued that wealth must display itself in public art. He argued, "There is ample room, not merely to make our city more beautiful than it now is, but, while building here the greatest financial and trade center the world has seen, to make of it such a center of picturesque grandeur as shall stir the pride of every dweller." Warner sounded like a wealthy Florentine explaining how civic beauty could enhance urban, financial wealth. From this viewpoint the urban elite would display its power to a passive public.[13]

Like Warner, city beautiful activists could become mere urban boosters. In doing so their view of the urban public became pernicious. For these activists the beautiful city could impress people and become "absolutely profitable" by facilitating the modern venture of tourism. The city, in effect, could be turned into a commodity and sold to the public. Inspired by the past efforts of "Athens, Florence, Venice, free burgs of Germany, [and] the great trading towns of Flanders," Edwin Bashfield argued that a beautiful city would quickly profit from tourism. George Kriehn believed that "a beautiful city will attract a desirable class of residents" and would "increase [the] value of real estate." Not only did these hopes promote existing economic interests, they degraded the public by turning it into something to be manipulated through surface appearances, a mere purchaser of pretty images.[14]

Though city beautiful activists could become elitist and turn the public into a passive group of people, certain activists understood that ancient city-states offered different visions for those concerned with modern urban democracy. The activists who embraced a more democratic faith did not envision the urban public bowing down to displays of wealth; instead, by examining the past, they discovered an active, engaged, and deliberating public in ancient city-states. For these activists beauty did not promote business interests but inspired a critique of commercialism based on the ancient city-state's conception of a common good. Irene Sargent, one of the most perceptive writers on the city beautiful movement, started to think in these ways. A professor of Romance languages at Syracuse University and a founder of the arts and crafts movement's major publication the *Craftsman*, Sargent expanded upon the more democratic possibilities found in the past.[15]

Sargent began by attacking the rampant commercialism of American cities. For her the spirit found in ancient city-states provided the basis of a criticism, not a celebration, of modern, commercial urban life. When comparing the ancient city to the modern city she wrote, "The city was then the permanent home of the citizen, and not, as now, a chance place of residence fixed by business affairs of which the center of operations may change with every decade or twelve-month." For Sargent the greatness of the past was not wealth but a communal spirit that fostered civic beauty: "In the city republics of Italy it was the so-called 'spirit of the bell tower': that is, the strongly developed communal sentiment, which gave birth to the great monuments of architecture." Sargent argued that Americans should draw inspiration not from the displays of wealth found in Renaissance city-states but from the communal visions found there.[16]

Sargent explained that the public in city-states of the past was not manipulated by an elite and did not fall awestruck and dumb before the monuments of the city. Public life in Athens and the Roman republic was more vibrant and active. By creating open spaces in which a public interacted, the ancient public came alive and took charge of its own affairs. Sargent wrote: "In the ancient cities, intercourse among the citizens was free and uninterrupted, since the temples, colonnades and gardens constituted a kind of open-air clubs [*sic*] at which political affairs and questions of art and literature were discussed from varied, individual points of view." The citizens who gathered publicly in past city-states not only admired beauty but also took their civic pride seriously enough to become engaged in public and political deliberation that determined the future of their polity. Sargent understood that part of the good life in the past entailed a deliberating and democratic public. She made it clear that Americans could not go back to the world of antiquity and the Renaissance but that they could draw inspiration from the past and move forward to create a better city life.[17]

Sargent's defense of a democratic tradition growing out of antiquity and the Renaissance was more profound than the elitism of other city beautiful activists. The idea of citizens gathering in the midst of public monuments and spaces, discussing the issues of the day, rang true for many Americans. Nonetheless, Sargent's ideas suffered from abstraction. How could modern cities realistically capture the public spirit of ancient and Renaissance city-states? So much had changed since antiquity, especially in terms of political and economic arrangements. Besides, Sargent only wrote about ancient city-states as some sort of vague ideal. Stuck in the past, she did not try to figure out what institutional means existed to make the ideals of public life in antiquity come alive in the modern world.

Though she tried her best to argue for a democratic public, the emphasis on public aesthetics and ancient civic virtues severely limited Sargent's and the entire city beautiful movement's grasp of democratic values. It was never clear how to make appreciation of beauty or ancient values transfer into actual public and political engagement among modern citizens. This required much more thoughtful exploration of institutions that could facilitate democratic activity. Though Sargent was right about stressing the democratic side of older ideals of public life, she was not clear on how to make this point relevant in the modern world. Another city beautiful activist, Charles Zueblin, began to embark on this deeper search. Zueblin embraced many of Sargent's ideas but found new ways of thinking and acting upon them.

Charles Zueblin and the Democratic Public

Charles Zueblin was typical of political activists at the turn of the century. Having studied theology at Yale University, he decided against the ministry for a career in progressive reform. Zueblin started out in Chicago at Jane Addams's famous social settlement, Hull House. Here he saw how Addams tried to set up forums where immigrant and working-class citizens debated the issues of the day and related these discussions to problems faced in their local neighborhoods. Undoubtedly, this attempt at creating democratic forums in the modern city had an enormous impact on Zueblin. Striking out on his own, he went ahead to found two such settlements in Chicago—the Northwestern University and University of Chicago social settlements. Soon afterward, he tried to find other ways to educate the mass public forming in American cities.[18]

One of Zueblin's first commitments was to the city beautiful movement. He rose in the ranks of the movement, eventually becoming president of the American League for Civic Improvement. Zueblin contributed to the city beautiful movement in different ways, from helping establish parks to founding municipal museums. Like other city beautiful activists and progressives, he became politically active and wrote on his experiences for a wider public. His activism and ideas were closely intertwined. And like Sargent, he reflected on what could happen when citizens gathered in urban public spaces, but he did not stop there. Although he endorsed city beautification, he also believed in much more. He helped develop institutions that could forge a democratic public.[19]

Like an increasing number of his colleagues in the city beautiful movement, Zueblin argued against antiurbanism and believed the city had many positive features. For Zueblin the city was no more unnatural or artificial than agriculture. He wrote: "The artificiality of the city is both unnatural and inhuman but not more so than the monotony of the farm, and the remedy is present in potential fellowship and the increasing regard for nature [found in urban parks]." Zueblin did not fear the diversity of cities, and later in his life he spoke out against nativist fears of immigrants. Instead of seeing the city as a source of chaos, as early antiurban APOAA activists did, Zueblin saw it as the future site of an American civilization. He explained: "The city is symbolically, as well etymologically, the basis of civilization. It represents not so much the realization of a fuller life, as the opportunity for it." Following Woodruff, Zueblin thought that through public awareness and urban activism—what he called "the new civic spirit"—the city could realize its opportunity and consciously become the central site of American civilization.[20]

Zueblin believed that with a growth in public concern, the city could give birth to a new form of citizenship. He wrote: "The making of the new city will mean the making of a new citizen, and the process is in no sense visionary." Was the new citizen to bow down in front of the beautiful monuments found in the city? Certainly not for Zueblin. Drawing on a line of thought that began with Thomas Jefferson, he argued for a participatory conception of citizenship that was critical of the liberal idea of a private, rights-bearing citizen. As many political theorists have argued, liberalism often stresses negative freedoms such as a freedom *from* government censorship. It does not stress the positive freedom to engage in public speech that can effectively change political decisions. Zueblin wanted freedom to be seen in the act of becoming an effective member of a polity and argued, "One can be a citizen only by participation, and that not merely in the annual casting of the ballot, but in daily citizenship." The new citizen not only possessed rights from persecution (those rights bestowed by liberalism) but also understood the duty and joy of participating in urban public affairs.[21]

The active citizen could be effective only after certain political reforms. To do away with the rule of political bosses, Zueblin endorsed a council form of government for cities, and it is important to understand why. Like other progressives, Zueblin sometimes used the term "efficiency" to explain his endorsement of council government. But efficiency was not enough. He wrote, "Is not efficiency illusory until the goal is the common good?" True efficiency meant making the city into "the laboratory of applied democracy." As Zueblin explained: "The municipality is becoming more efficient in direct proportion to its increasing democracy." Zueblin supported council government only if it was coupled with the initiative and referendum. The council government would only become efficient when it responded to the demands of the public. He explained: "The referendum is not merely a check on representatives; it is a device for sounding and articulating public opinion. This is why it must be accompanied by the initiative. Otherwise the old weakness of American government—reliance on the issues paraded in the heat of a campaign—will exonerate councilmen who plead ignorance of the public's wishes." Zueblin made a crucial point here. A democratic public within the city would have to be constantly active, not just during election times. Periodic deliberation made no sense, for if it was to develop and become truly effective, deliberation needed to be ongoing. Then and only then would city government become responsive to regular citizens, and by becoming responsive to a deliberating public, city government would become both efficient and democratic.[22]

Zueblin made an important connection here. The initiative and referendum entailed a deliberating public constantly educating itself. He wrote: "The citizens should enjoy the use of the initiative and referendum and perhaps the recall, in order that they may be educated to understand government and may inform their representatives of the current state of public opinion." For Americans to create a democratic and deliberating public, Zueblin believed they must extend their conceptions of education. Education could no longer be cloistered in schools; it had to be understood as a continual and infinite process. Zueblin argued that "no diploma can serve as a certificate of a complete education." The continual process of education grew out of the activities of a democratic public.

But unlike Irene Sargent, Zueblin provided concrete examples of ways a democratic public could emerge. Instead of harkening back to an abstract ideal of ancient citizens gathering in public spaces, Zueblin searched for institutions where citizens could reengage in politics within the setting of the modern, urban world. Beyond endorsing the initiative and referendum, he spoke highly of the New York City free lecture system where schools were used after hours for lectures on various issues. Here it was learned that "education never ceases." He praised forums held in the People's Institute of New York City, explaining: "Nowhere else is there a forum where the public questions are discussed as freely, the verdict given as fairly, and the multitudinous voice of the people registered as effectively as in the meetings of the People's Institute." Most important of all, though, was university extension. Zueblin looked upon the urban college as the leader in democratic political education. Since he put so much of his own energy into university extension from 1891 up until 1908, we must understand why he thought it could generate a democratic public and whether or not he was right.[23]

Charles Zueblin and University Extension

The 1890s witnessed the height of university extension. The University of Wisconsin and the University of Chicago led the effort. Chicago's first president, William Rainey Harper, played a large role here. Harper had worked with the Chautauqua Institute of upstate New York, where popular lectures were provided to all who paid to attend. These efforts placed Harper within a nineteenth-century ideal, growing out of lyceums and the Chautauqua Institute. This was an ideal of middle-class civility cultivated through a continual process of rigorous character building and education. Inspired by the Chautauqua Institute's vision, Harper hoped to expand on it while at the University of Chicago. He wanted the university to be connected to the wider urban public through lectures and argued that the university must take part in "the important work of creating in the community at large that demand for the best of everything in the intellectual, aesthetic and moral world which is at once the evidence of, and the surest means toward, the higher civic life." Thus, Harper welded his Chautauqua ideals to the university extension program at Chicago.[24]

By stressing a debt the university had to the public, university extension programs implicitly challenged the growth of professional training in modern universities. During the late nineteenth century the American university embraced the German model of education that stressed the teaching of specialized knowledge to future professionals. But university extension leaders believed professors should not only train future scholars, they had to make their work pertinent to people outside the walls of academe. Professionals within emerging disciplines should not simply address one another but a wider public. In a perceptive article, historian Allen Davis argued that university extension should be seen as "the opposite of professionalism." George Woytanowitz explains this point: "The new university culture—emphasizing research, publication, institutional development, and graduate training—did not provide rewards for those who did extension lecturing." By turning their attention to the public, academics working on university extension refused to focus solely on issues within their professions. Instead of envisioning education as a process located only in the university or ending once an academic degree was obtained, university extension leaders argued that the university had a civic responsibility and rooted education in the continual interaction between adult citizens in local communities and the university. According to a university extension circular of information at the University of Chicago, "Education should be as much one of the serious interests of life as politics, or business, or religion. It is just as absurd for a man to consider his education finished at a certain time as it would be for him to say, after a few years' work in the church, or in politics, 'My work is done as a churchman, or as a citizen.' "

More concerned with the state of the public's continual education, university extension academics challenged the increasing professionalism and hermeticism of the university.[25]

Zueblin darted into the university extension movement. Undoubtedly, he witnessed academics such as John Dewey lecturing at Hull House to working-class immigrants and saw a model for university extension here. In 1891 he helped found Chicago's first university extension organization and served as its secretary. When hired by the University of Chicago a year later, he immediately became a public lecturer, renowned for lectures like "The Structure of Society" and "A Century in the Development of English Social Philosophy." He lectured Chicago's citizens in university centers, established throughout the city, and traveled around America on lecture tours. In the eulogy provided for him at the University of Chicago, Zueblin was rightfully remembered for "presenting the work of scholarship to the larger public."[26]

Zueblin believed that university extension played a significant role in the creation of a democratic public. In his presidential address to the American League for Civic Improvement, he stressed the need for continual education in the life of the new participatory citizen in order to make urban democracy real. By educating citizens, the university helped raise the level of knowledge within the democratic public. In the process the "university and the public are drawn closer together." The university could help breathe more life into the other institutions making up an urban public. Zueblin explained: "It is found . . . that University Extension is proving a decided stimulus to the intellectual life of the communities that undertake it. The clubs, the schools, the churches, even the newspapers, have been aroused to greater intellectual activity." Zueblin hoped that university extension could help create an ever-expanding democratic public based on the principle of continual education.[27]

Though he saw university extension as a necessary component of a democratic public, Zueblin knew it was no easy task. University extension lecturers faced certain challenges. The first challenge was "the degrading, yet ever-extending grasp of the octopus of commercialism." By the 1880s the lyceum lecture system, an important nineteenth-century popular institution that once cultivated middle-class civility, had fully degenerated into commercial entertainment and was starting to collapse. Known once as a serious lecture circuit for intellectuals like Ralph Waldo Emerson, by the 1880s the lyceum had become a carnival of cheap thrills. Zueblin understood that a public relied on much more than commercial entertainment;

it depended on skills like concentration and self-development through continuous education. In Zueblin's words, commercialism "makes it difficult to get an audience for anything but amusement, to secure attention to controversial topics, and, above all, to interest men." The only solution to this problem was for a lecturer to criticize the forces of commercialism. Lecturers became de facto critics of American commercial culture (as did some other city beautiful activists), and the desire to create an educated and discerning public became the basis of their criticism.[28]

Another challenge existed for public lecturers. How should they relate to the public attending their lectures? Zueblin believed the lecturer must always remain connected to this wider audience, speaking a language that the public related to and understood. He worried about "the specialization of the graduate student," which drew the student into the secluded world of a profession (with its own distinct professional language and jargon) and away from public life. More important, Zueblin thought public lecturers must contend with their own condescending attitude toward working-class people. Though he himself sometimes patronized working-class people, Zueblin sincerely believed the lecturer must "learn from the workingmen and workingwomen." The lecturer must remain open to the opinions of the people being lectured to. At the same time, Zueblin explained, "It is not essential that the lecturer should accept the people's standpoint." The lecturer had to understand and speak to citizens' ideas while at the same time remaining critical. The public lecturer thus faced a challenging balance between sympathy with and criticism of the public.[29]

While Zueblin perceived certain challenges for the public lecturer, his career spoke painfully to the biggest institutional barrier for public lecturers—the modern university. Throughout his employment at the University of Chicago, he complained about a lack of support for his work. Communication between Zueblin and the president of the university primarily involved money squabbles. His complaints were legitimate. It was during Harry Pratt Judson's presidency that Zueblin finally quit. Judson had cut back on Harper's earlier support for university extension and instead focused on making the University of Chicago more like other modern universities, concerning itself less with relations to the public world and more with professional knowledge. As the modern university defined its goal in terms of training people for professions, more popular forms of education, such as public lecturing, were maligned as illegitimate.[30]

The modern university also defined knowledge as objective and academic (social "scientists" led this development). University administrators and faculty doubted that knowledge had political implications outside of academia. When public lecturers began politicizing academic knowledge by addressing public issues dealing with social and political conflict, academic administrators made their positions clear. The University of Chicago simply fired Edward Bemis, a public lecturer in economics, when he supported the Pullman Workers' Strike of 1894, and Zueblin faced troubles when he drew media publicity to his criticism of John D. Rockefeller and one of the University of Chicago's lesser-known benefactors. In a letter dated 7 March 1908, Judson made it clear that the public lecturer possessed limited freedom. He wrote: "I have felt that as a member of our faculty it is not expedient for the lecturer on the public platform to attack individuals unless the University has been informed in advance and is willing to put itself in the position of supporting such policy."

The university would not support Zueblin's desire to be both connected to his public *and critical*, especially when that criticism drew bad press or questioned the university's funders. To justify this attack on Zueblin, Judson argued that academic knowledge should not be political. Judson wrote to Zueblin, "In other words, is it the function of the University to enter into present day polemics? Personally I doubt it." Here was a case for knowledge remaining "objective," not partisan. The university could not accept certain features of the democratic public—especially polemical contention and politically charged debate. In addition, the strictures of career and work—the control the university had over his salary—hampered Zueblin's freedom to communicate with a democratic public free from those demands. Facing pressures to become less controversial, Zueblin did the only thing he could: he quit his position at the University of Chicago in late 1908.[31]

The Democratic Public and the Limits of University Extension

After 1908 Zueblin remained involved in the university extension movement. More and more, though, he supported forums generated by citizens outside of academia where citizens themselves discussed issues of the day far from the reach of the modern university's leadership. By 1910 Zueblin was an independent lecturer. He spoke at the Ford Hall Forum in Boston eight times by 1915 and wrote an essay in support of this urban public forum, and he helped out Chicago initiatives to turn schools into lecture halls and social centers. Zueblin continued to search for ways to generate a democratic public that could utilize the initiative and referendum to become politically effective. As he continued his search for institutions that could form a democratic public, he downplayed the role of the university. His political vision and his long-term activism grew together.[32]

Zueblin understood well that the civic pride the city beautiful movement hoped to inspire was very important. But he moved beyond nostalgic celebrations of ancient and Renaissance city-states. He saw that a continual process of education was necessary in order to prepare citizens for public decision making. He also believed modern institutions—especially the university—could create a democratic public. Zueblin asserted that citizens could generate a public that could become politically effective through the initiative and referendum. By solving political problems together, citizens would educate themselves. This process was circular. For by becoming politically educated, political problems would be solved in better ways. The process of continual public education and direct democracy worked together. But this was not an abstract vision for Zueblin as the ancient city-state public was for Sargent and other city beautiful activists. Zueblin had made a crucial break from other activists by believing that certain modern institutions could build a democratic public.

By becoming active, Zueblin learned the limits of university extension. The university could not be the major impetus for a democratic public. Too concerned with generating "objective" knowledge and training people for future professions, the university turned its back on political knowledge and popular education, which were seen increasingly as below academic standards. For these reasons Zueblin did not receive the support he hoped for. He had to search for a better means of creating a democratic public, and other activists joined him in this search.[33]

CHAPTER TWO

FROM TENT MEETINGS TO THE FORUM MOVEMENT

Frederic Howe and the Democratic Public

The city of tomorrow will be a simple democracy, a little republic, like the great cities of the past. It will be an experiment station in government.

—Frederic Howe[1]

Like Charles Zueblin, Frederic Howe placed his hope in the new urban public forming in America's cities at the turn of the century. While Zueblin was participating in university extension programs, Howe was busy discovering other ways to create a democratic public. When writing his autobiography in the mid-1920s, Howe conceived a narrative based on his political self-education. Two major chapters of this education speak to the meaning of an urban public in similar terms to Zueblin's work. The first chapter, which came at the time Zueblin was pioneering in adult education, discussed Howe's work with Tom Johnson, the mayor of Cleveland, Ohio, during the Progressive Era. Here Howe saw a public forming around pressing urban, economic issues. The second chapter examined Howe's directorship of the People's Institute—the model forum that spawned a national movement up to World War I, a movement that both Howe and Zueblin endorsed. In his work with Tom Johnson and the People's Institute, Howe embraced the ideals of urban democracy. By examining both experiments we can understand Howe's belief and his still limited faith in a democratic public. Howe moved beyond Zueblin's university extension but still faced his own weaknesses.[2]

Tom Johnson's Democratic Civic Ideal

Having grown up in a small town in Pennsylvania, Frederic Howe decided to embrace a seemingly more cosmopolitan life by entering academia in a relatively large city. After training to become a professional political scientist at The Johns Hopkins University in Baltimore, Maryland, and writing a dry book on the history of taxation, Howe turned to issues of city life. He moved to Cleveland to practice law and then became involved in city beautiful efforts to erect a civic center in downtown Cleveland. The mayor of Cleveland, Tom Johnson, had commissioned Daniel Burnham to design a traditional city beautiful civic center with government buildings based around a central open space. As with other spaces like these, planners hoped to inspire noble public values. In an article praising the civic center Howe invoked the legacy of Pericles, the ruler of ancient Athens whose famous "Funeral Oration" called citizens to embrace civic pride. Following other city beautiful activists, Howe believed Cleveland would show its own civic pride and its "more intelligent interest in . . . common things" by erecting these public buildings. In this praise for Burnham's work, Howe celebrated both the city beautiful movement and its hope in a wider public life. More important, by lauding one of Tom Johnson's efforts, Howe began his long involvement in Johnson's city government—what Howe himself called "the greatest adventure of my life."[3]

Breaking with his Republican past, Howe endorsed Tom Johnson—a Democrat—for Cleveland's mayor in 1901. Howe believed Tom Johnson embodied a glowing faith in a more democratic city. He explained: "Tom Johnson has an ideal of a free city; such a city as flourished in ancient Greece, in Italy during the Renaissance, or in Germany." Johnson himself talked of an "ideal city" and of making Cleveland into a "city on a hill." But he was most known for his actions as a mayor, actions that made his faith in democratic ideals more concrete. Johnson offered new lessons about a democratic public just as the city beautiful debates about public space and Zueblin's university extension in Chicago had done. From these actions Howe learned much about the deeper meaning of a democratic public.[4]

Tom Johnson was born into a wealthy Kentucky family in 1854. Moving out of the "New South" after his childhood, Johnson quickly became a rich, Midwestern businessman. In Indianapolis he began his climb to economic power, creating a monopoly for his street railway company. Spreading his economic tentacles, Johnson built up street railway monopolies in Detroit and Cleveland. In an excellent dissertation William Suit describes Johnson's early years as a time when a "budding capitalist and self-proclaimed monopolist honed his business skills, concerning himself with politics only at the municipal level and only in connection with advancing his business interests."[5]

In 1883 Johnson had a "conversion" experience. Reading Henry George's *Social Problems* on a train, Johnson became convinced that George was right: monopoly, especially land monopoly, was evil. Through a single tax on land, George argued that land speculation could be impeded and local and free competition could flourish once again. Though some might think that George was an agrarian or antiurbanist, he was committed, in fact, to urban politics. Tom Johnson helped George run for mayor of New York City in 1886. George lost, but Johnson became convinced that he himself had to enter politics to fight the economic evils of the day. Elected to Congress for two terms, Johnson allied with populists like Jerry "Sockless" Simpson and fought unsuccessfully for single-tax reforms. Then more closely following George's political vision and career, Johnson ran for mayor of Cleveland and won.[6]

As mayor, Tom Johnson became "one of the most picturesque and interesting figures in American public life." In certain ways Johnson was a typical progressive mayor who worked on social reform. Lincoln Steffens, the famous muckraker known for his exposés of city bosses, wrote: "Tom Johnson is the best Mayor of the best-governed city in the United States." Steffens had his reasons for admiring this new mayor. Johnson beautified the city by building the civic center Howe had praised, he improved parks and took "Keep off the Grass" signs down (so children could play freely), and he made the criminal justice system more humane. Following Henry George's teachings, he tried to tax real estate speculators heavily, and following the populists' call to public ownership of communal goods, he obtained control over the city's water power. But all these struggles paled in comparison to Johnson's fight over streetcar railways.[7]

Johnson's battle for municipal ownership of street railways in Cleveland became his biggest struggle and biggest loss. Believing city franchises granted companies monopolistic privileges, Johnson sought ways to challenge the high prices set by the companies granted a franchise. In 1902 his demand that railway companies charge no more than a three-cent fare was found unconstitutional by the courts. Following this defeat, Ohio's state government further limited Johnson's power to determine streetcar and other political issues. Johnson finally decided to create his own private company, the Municipal Traction Company, which could run trains that charged a three-cent fare. In 1907 his first three-cent car ran. But Johnson found himself embroiled in another conflict. This time workers at his company went on strike in 1908, and after a long-drawn-out battle, citizens voted in a referendum against Johnson's plan. In the resulting compromise Johnson did not achieve a three-cent fare, to say nothing of municipal ownership.[8]

Howe joined Johnson's struggle, first as a member of city government, then as a state senator. As a member of city government, he supported many of Tom Johnson's policies, and as a state senator Howe tried to aid Tom Johnson in his fight for home rule over Cleveland. But Howe failed to achieve any substantial reform. Much more a visionary activist than a politician, Howe's real success was in providing Johnson's administration with an intellectual vision. Howe began to write articles and books about the meaning of Johnson's rule as mayor. In doing so he set Johnson's work within a wider political and philosophical context and argued that Cleveland's mayor was helping to make the city the "hope of democracy." In Johnson's struggle Howe began to see new ways in which a democratic public could become a reality.[9]

Howe drew out two major themes of Johnson's political struggle and made them central to his philosophy of urban democracy. The first was municipal "home rule," that is, providing cities with legal powers of self-government. In trying to achieve certain political goals Tom Johnson discovered that without home rule, cities would be pawns of often conservative state governments that were growing in power. Johnson also argued that home rule was an end in itself since it taught city residents "about self-government" and responsibility. Home rule would re-create a sense of "a city republic with full powers within itself." By providing citizens with a well-defined and focused arena of politics, home rule could partially re-create the feel of ancient city-states where political responsibility and self-government were decentralized and made real.[10]

Johnson's ideas and Howe's further development of them were not new. Municipal home rule had always been connected to democratic initiative. Already in 1894 Joseph Dana Miller, a political theorist, argued that "absolutely self-governed cities would be the best sort of primary schools for the study of political principles. Every act of a city so controlled would contribute to popular education in the principles of government—would be a factor in molding and shaping public opinion." Connecting this view to a new sense of citizenship, Miller went on to say, "Were our cities self-governing units, the citizen would become at last . . . in truth a citizen." Miller believed that only true responsibility—which entailed decentralization of power so that it rested in cities—could inspire real self-government and participatory citizenship.[11]

Following this line of thought, Frederic Howe argued that home rule could solve two major problems in America's political culture: public apathy and political centralization. Apathy was at the root of contemporary problems, Howe believed. Sounding like other political critics of the Progressive Era, he wrote: "A sense of helplessness has settled down on the community, which has become the football of partisan legislation and spoils politicians." Only by granting citizens true responsibility in the city's affairs could apathy be checked. This entailed challenging the general, modern trend toward political centralization: "These tendencies to centralization would be checked by a return to local self-government, to municipal home rule, in which the city would be responsible to itself alone."

Though many historians believe all progressives embraced a centralized state, Howe clearly wanted power rooted in cities, not the national government. For Howe democratic self-government and decentralization went hand in hand. "Everywhere the tendency of democracy is toward decentralization." By providing cities with home rule, the dreams of City Beautiful activists of an engaged public would be made real. "Home rule would create a city republic, a new sort of sovereignty, a republic like unto those of Athens, Rome, and the medieval Italian cities, a republic related to the state as the states are now related to the nation at large. . . . It was freedom that inspired in these cities local love and patriotism as in no other communities the world has seen." Home rule re-created the power, self-government, and active citizenship found in ancient city-states, all within a modern context.[12]

Howe's faith in home rule led to a distinct understanding of municipal ownership. Though Johnson attacked economic privilege in his battle against private ownership of streetcars, Howe believed there were also political and social reasons for municipal ownership. Like home rule, municipal ownership created a civic and "public sense" in the minds of citizens. Howe saw this in Cleveland and in the origins of British municipal socialism (a tradition of socialism that eventually became less decentralized and more technocratic). Describing a citizen of a British city, Howe wrote: "The man on the trams . . . owns the trams; therefore he is interested in them." Municipal ownership developed vigilant citizens concerned with the city's public affairs by providing something close to the lives of ordinary citizens that was under their control. This deeper meaning of municipal ownership transcended economic arguments. Howe explained: "The real test of municipal ownership is not a monetary one; not the relief of taxation; not a profit or loss account; not even cheap water, gas, or electricity. It is rather one of higher civic life." Municipal ownership, like home rule, was a first step toward creating a city republic in which citizens ruled themselves. This was its central political importance.[13]

Howe celebrated and elaborated on Tom Johnson's faith in urban home rule and municipal ownership. Both ideals energized Howe's growing faith in democracy. But this was only one side of Johnson's battle. Johnson believed not only in political and economic reform but also in building a democratic public capable of running the affairs of the city. Without a democratic public, political reform lost its meaning. Writing at the beginning of his first term as mayor of Cleveland, Tom Johnson explained: "In the ideal municipality the people will be very close to the government." Sounding like Charles Zueblin, Johnson went on to claim: "Vital questions will not be left to the decision of the executive and council alone. They will come directly before the people." Johnson's faith in a democratic public deliberating on "vital questions" was an important part of his mayoral rule and political philosophy. Once again, Howe learned a great deal from Tom Johnson's political experiments and continued, intellectually and politically, to push them even further in his own experiments and thought.[14]

Tom Johnson and the Democratic Public

> Mayor Johnson was, indeed, a leader in what we can now see to be a revolution effected. The old conception of an indifferent public on the one hand, and scheming and overbearing companies on the other, has passed away almost completely.
>
> —*The Nation*[15]

Tom Johnson believed he acted in the "public's interest" and in the name of "the people." "Public interests" contrasted with the private profit pursued by monopolistic corporations. Using these terms, Johnson spoke a political language common to many progressives. The general problem with this language was its vagueness and tendency to moral exhortation.

Thus, whereas muckrakers believed "public opinion" must wage war on industrial capitalism's excesses, these writers offered no institutional resources by which a public could empower itself. Similarly, when they were at their best, city beautiful advocates marveled at the active public found in ancient city-states but remained stuck in nostalgic remembrance. In contrast, Johnson, like Charles Zueblin, did not rely *only* on moral exhortation but in fact created institutions through which he hoped a democratic public could will itself and help solve pressing political issues.[16]

Much like the agrarian populists before him, Tom Johnson set up tent meetings that were open to the public and addressed political issues. It was here that a democratic public could conceive of itself. Johnson's explanation of the significance of the tent meetings is worth quoting at length:

> In a tent there is a freedom from restraint that is seldom present in halls. The audience seems to feel that it has been invited there for the purpose of finding out the position of various speakers. There is a greater freedom in asking questions too, and this heckling is the most valuable form of political education. Tent meetings can be held in all parts of the city—in short the meetings are literally taken to the people.

Johnson also believed that these meetings went beyond the public opinion generated by the mass media. These meetings drew citizens and politicians together into a dynamic give-and-take process of discussion and argumentation, not the passive activity of reading newspapers. Johnson explained:

> The greatest benefit of the tent meeting, the one which cannot be measured, is the educational influence on the people who compose the audience. It makes them take an interest as nothing else could do, and educates them on local questions as no amount of reading, even of the fairest newspaper accounts, could do. I do not believe there is a city in the country where the electorate is so well informed upon local political questions, nor upon the rights of the people as opposed to the privileges of corporations, as it is in Cleveland.

Johnson believed tent meetings could help form a democratic urban public that could then make intelligent political decisions about pressing municipal issues.[17]

Johnson's tent meetings hold important lessons about how to create a democratic public. Being a thoughtful political leader, Tom Johnson devised ways to ensure a democratic atmosphere in these meetings. When speaking at a tent meeting, Johnson made sure that his opponents had equal speaking time with no interruptions, and he always held question-answer sessions after speeches. From all reports, these meetings—unlike the older lyceums (see Chapter One)—never degenerated into entertainment but maintained a serious level of discussion. They drew large numbers of working-class people, Johnson's major supporters, and though the meetings were orderly they were also lively—full of heckling, arguments, and searing questions. Thomas Campbell argues, "The frontier-like egalitarianism of the atmosphere encouraged unlettered citizens to participate in the give-and-take of these meetings." Johnson introduced Cleveland's citizens to the pleasures of democratic public life—to its liveliness, its give-and-take processes, and its open nature. In doing so he showed how a democratic public was not only politically necessary but also a source of leading a good life since it could be exciting and encouraged commitment and concern for a common good that went beyond one's individual self.[18]

Johnson understood that the democratic public created in tent meetings was a political necessity. Democratic action relied upon a deliberating public: "The greatest obstacle to overcome in any fight in which moral issues are involved is not opposition but the indifference of the public." Johnson believed only political education at the local level could counter public indifference. It is important to understand what he thought the result of political education would be. Johnson wrote: "The chief part of our program in Cleveland was to educate the people never to be indifferent." Through tent meetings citizens learned not only about individual political issues but also about the general requirements of a democratic public—to be ever vigilant and critical and never to succumb to indifference. Through political education at the local level, a democratic public became self-conscious of its own importance and power. By being constantly active, this democratic public could possibly save American politics. For by being vigilant and active this public could become the major element in an end to the central enemy of progressives—the corruption of politics by business and special interests.[19]

Johnson always expressed a deep faith in a democratic public's ability to make its own decisions. He did not fear open discussion and never turned down a debate with an opponent. He allowed radical speakers like Emma Goldman, who were normally hounded by policemen, to speak freely in

Cleveland's public square (where a statue was dedicated to him and the cause of free speech). But Johnson's clearest endorsement of a democratic public came after his biggest defeat. Citizens rejected Johnson's hope for municipal ownership of streetcars through a referendum. Like Charles Zueblin, Tom Johnson had endorsed the initiative and referendum as a means to empower a democratic public to enforce its decisions and had connected the initiative and referendum to collective discussion. But now he found citizens using the referendum to defeat his own plans.

Instead of rejecting referendums, however, Johnson embraced the hard lessons of the democratic public. He explained: "People learn by their mistakes and the good effects that have come and will come from the referendum will largely outweigh any temporary disadvantage." Johnson's endorsement of the initiative and referendum stemmed not from a desire to win on certain issues but from a belief that a democratic public had to wield power and make effective decisions. He accepted the price of this faith—his own ideas could be defeated sometimes. A democratic public could never ensure Johnson's personal victory as it possessed its own initiative and dynamic. For a politician with an agenda, Tom Johnson had made a profound statement on his willingness to play by the often tough rules of democracy.[20]

But Johnson's understanding of a democratic public still faced limits. His critics attacked him as a charlatan, and though these claims were false, Johnson at times made his political struggles into personal ones. In a balanced account of Johnson's political career, Carl Lorenz argued that the battle for municipal ownership of streetcars "swallowed [Johnson] up like a maelstrom." Consumed with the cause, Johnson occasionally ignored the democratic public he helped initiate and made his fight a purely personal and legal one. By his own account he often "spent more time in the courthouse than . . . in the city hall." Worse yet, he tried to block the referendum that eventually defeated him. As we have seen, in the end Johnson learned that this move was foolish. But by turning a public and political struggle into a personal one and trying to prevent a democratic public from making its own decision, Johnson betrayed his faith in this very same democratic public. At times like this Johnson put his personal political agenda ahead of his abiding faith in a democratic public. This was a dangerous precedent—one that would live on in Howe's work.[21]

Howe's own ideas about a democratic public reflect Johnson's influence. After having worked with Johnson, Howe embraced "a belief in democracy yet to be born." Taking up Johnson's faith in political education, Howe argued in 1913 that "there is no training school comparable to politics for the promotion of social and political ideals." Howe believed people learned about politics by *doing* politics. He also held to Johnson's belief in the initiative and referendum after he left Cleveland. Reflecting on his own political experience from 1901 to 1914, Howe argued: "The initiative, . . . referendum, and recall have carried democracy still further and made the city the most democratic instrument in America and in many ways the most democratic agency in the world." Referendums were especially important since they helped produce a democratic public. Howe believed referendums "lead to constant discussion, to a deeper interest in government, and to a psychological conviction that a government is in effect the people themselves." He concluded: "In fine, I believe that government should be responsive to public opinion and free to reflect that opinion in legislation when expressed." Following Johnson, Howe embraced the political importance of a democratic public.[22]

Running alongside this faith in a democratic public was a belief in experts and well-managed administration. Though he never concerned himself with the federal bureaucracy, Howe hoped experts could run city government and thereby replace the power of corrupt city bosses. But, like Zueblin and Johnson, Howe saw no conflict between democracy and efficiency. In fact, Howe argued, "Not until the city is equipped with home rule, with the initiative and referendum, with power to frame policies and determine how great questions shall be settled, will it be possible to do away with the crusader type and introduce the expert into the machinery of administration." Howe wanted competent civil servants serving a democratic public. This faith in a democratic public utilizing an efficient administration came out most clearly in his praise for the state of Wisconsin. Here he believed administrative efficiency was combined with democratic deliberation in schoolhouses and meeting halls. No conflict existed between democratic deliberation and the rule of experts. For Howe, democracy and efficiency were one.[23]

Though an understandable belief, Howe's faith in the compatibility of efficiency and democracy weakened his political thought. Experts grounded in specialized knowledge would not necessarily be able to talk to a democratic public, and a democratic public, with its long debates and conflicts, could easily threaten administrative efficiency. Howe did not understand this; he simply held democracy and efficiency in a symbiotic balance. Seemingly, his move to the People's Institute of New York in 1913 was a tilt away from efficiency and toward democracy, for the People's Institute was the most important democratic forum in America at the time. But Howe retained his belief in expert administrators and a democratic public working together. The limits of this belief showed up both in Howe's leadership while at the People's Institute and in the more general national forum movement that grew out of this institution.

The People's Institute, the Forum Movement, and the Democratic Public

> Broadly considered, there is no greater educational need within a democracy than training for participation in public life. For, while in an autocracy the responsibilities of government are centered, in a democracy no one may delegate to another his share of authority without the community suffering to an appreciable extent. Theory and practice will never accord here, but the nearer the latter approaches the former, the fuller the participation of the entire citizenship in public life, the more perfect will be the result.
>
> —Charles Sprague Smith, founder and director of the People's Institute[24]

The People's Institute of New York started in 1897 in order to "furnish the people continuous and ordered education" and "afford opportunities for the interchange of thought upon topics of general interest between individuals." Founded by Charles Sprague Smith, a university professor who, like Charles Zueblin and other adult educators, tired of the hermeticism of academic life, the People's Institute became famous for its "People's Forum." Here a lecturer spoke typically to about one thousand people, and a question-answer period followed. In the beginning most lecturers spoke on the humanities and literature, but during the second year the People's Institute transformed itself. As Smith explained: "The social-educational work of the Institute developed in the second year into active participation in public, especially legislative, questions." Decisions made during discussions on the floor of the People's Institute were voted on. Resolutions were then sent to city council representatives to protest unfavorable political decisions (New York never achieved the initiative and referendum). Sometimes politicians directly addressed the People's Forum. In these ways democratic deliberation could affect political decisions. Eventually, activists at the People's Institute, including Howe, started up other local forums throughout New York City.[25]

The People's Forum brought intellectuals, activists, and politicians in contact with a democratic public. It forced these speakers to be cogent, articulate, and aware of what they were arguing. Jacob Riis, the famed muckraker and supporter of the People's Institute, explained: "If the speaker has touched in any way upon the social issues of the day, he must be well fortified in argument, for his questioners are in touch with them in their practical working out, and some of them are . . . masters in debate." Question-answer periods encouraged clarity from intellectuals and articulateness from questioners—skills necessary for democratic deliberation. In this and other ways the dynamic of the People's Forum were akin to that of Tom Johnson's tent meetings. Working-class immigrants formed the majority of the audience, and forums produced a lively floor dynamic, with sharp questions interspersed with booing and heckling. Speakers addressed a variety of important issues. Before Howe arrived the People's Institute tackled municipal ownership, imperialism and American foreign policy (with a majority voting against intervention in the Philippines), tenement housing, socialism, and other issues. If the forum was similar to Johnson's tent meetings, the difference was that Tom Johnson often called tent meetings sporadically around pressing issues or at election time, while the People's Forum took place regularly, and thus more adequately developed the skills of a democratic public.[26]

Having experienced many of Tom Johnson's tent meetings, Howe must have been comfortable with the dynamics of the People's Forum. Here he found a place to express his commitment to urban democracy. As John Collier, another activist deeply involved with the People's Institute, explained in 1912: "Mr. Howe has elected to join a movement whose aim is to help a little in the clearer and more earnest formulation of . . . public opinion, which is the soul of American democracy. He has chosen this work because his own interest in American democracy is, at its fountainhead, a spiritual interest." Howe saw himself following in Smith's footsteps and argued that Smith "believed that the great city of New York should have an open platform for discussion in which progressive, ethical, political and social views can be voiced." Continuing in this tradition, Howe sponsored a series of lectures on a "Better New York," the development of World War I, labor issues, and feminism. Howe understood the composition of his audience when he explained to one potential speaker, "Our audience consists largely of workingmen of the most intelligent type, many of them socialists and radicals, and after the addresses they may ask many shrewd questions." In this observation and elsewhere, Howe saw that through question-answer periods an active public formed on the floor of the forum. In the *Eighteenth Annual Report of the People's Institute*, Howe announced the true and remarkable meaning behind the People's Forum: "In a city of surging and changing population, of complex nationalities, of furious political antagonisms, of radicalism and idealism as brought by the immigrants from the oppressed nations of Europe—in this city an open forum, with absolutely free discussion, the audience itself free to act as it sees fit on public questions, has been conducted year after year with orderliness and with a continuity of public opinion, as expressed by the audience, which is impressive." The People's Forum thus produced an independent democratic public, made up of different immigrant groups, that willed its own processes and did not remain subservient to academic teachers. Here the forum made a crucial move beyond Zueblin's experiments in university extension. For once, regular citizens were given a chance to hear one another deliberate as public actors and see themselves as equals to intellectuals.[27]

After leading the People's Institute for almost three years, Howe became the Commissioner of Immigration in 1915. Afterward he remained active with the People's Institute on an informal basis only. While Howe moved on, though, a forum movement spread throughout the United States. Clearly connected to Howe's leadership, the first and most important forum to emerge outside of the People's Institute was the Ford Hall Forum in Boston. George Coleman, who founded Ford Hall in 1908, modeled his forum after the People's Institute, with lectures followed by lively question-answer periods and "town meetings" where citizens—predominantly immigrants and working men—discussed pressing political issues. While becoming a regular speaker at Ford Hall, Charles Zueblin argued in support of the forum and set it within the wider public culture developed by Boston's nineteenth-century civic gentry:

> Certainly there is nowhere else in Boston such an eager, restless desire to compass knowledge and human welfare,—not in the venerable Lowell Institute, not in the mausoleum of books on Copley Square, not in the society of Orientalists and antiquarians at the Museum of Fine Arts, nor even in the aggregation of antagonistic specialists that throng Huntington Avenue from the Mother Church to the Young Men's Christian Association and the Harvard Medical School. Ford Hall is not therefore scientific or a seat of culture. It is rather an intellectual and emotional power-house, sending out

> currents to vitalize the wireless service of the municipality. Ford Hall is not unbiased, but it is tolerant; it is self-conscious, but at the same time open-armed; cosmopolitan, but still organic.

In Ford Hall, Zueblin found an institution that transcended older forms of public culture in Boston. He believed that here was born a democratic public.[28]

Coleman soon became the leader of the national forum movement, and he drew his inspiration from Ford Hall. He set up the Cooperative Forum Bureau that acted as a clearinghouse by sending speakers to forums dispersed throughout the country. Retaining its faith in local democracy while going national, leaders in local forums decided what was to be lectured on and who would do the lecturing. It was up to Coleman to recruit speakers for the growing number of local forums, and he attracted many intellectual heavyweights, including Charlotte Perkins Gilman, W.E.B. Du Bois, and Walter Rauschenbusch. By 1916 there were about one hundred forums, most of them in Massachusetts, Connecticut, New York, and New Jersey (others existed in western and southern America). These forums had question-answer periods and addressed interesting political issues. Though Coleman led the forum movement, the People's Institute rightfully took credit for its inception. Howe himself had supported the growing movement as director of the People's Institute, but as he turned his attention to national policies surrounding immigration, it was up to others to provide the forum movement with a working philosophy.[29]

What was the forum's relevance to America? Certain writers pondered this question by drawing on Frederic Howe's experiments and providing interesting ideas about a democratic public. Like university extension programs, the forum held out a certain vision of intellectual expression. But where university extension lecturers often played a teacher's role, the forum forced intellectuals to answer questions from citizens and thus rooted intellectuals in a give-and-take dynamic. Knowledge was thus seen as growing out of communal deliberation—not just out of the minds and mouths of intellectuals. Rather than allow intellectuals to speak *to* fellow citizens, the forum ensured they spoke *with* them. Stanton Coit explained that when he spoke at Ford Hall, "I addressed not pupils but judges." Intellectuals brought their ideas to a court of judgment, the judgment of a democratic public.

The intellectual who spoke at a forum, therefore, had to be connected to forum participants in a meaningful way. Glenn Frank, who wrote the most insightful article on forums, "The Parliament of the People," explained how a forum speaker, much like the university extension teacher, found a balance between telling the truth and speaking a common and popular language. Frank wrote: "To be true to oneself and to the truth, and yet keep the sympathetic attention of the crowd, demands the best a man may have of mind and morals." Rooting a speaker in a democratic public produced a new type of intellectual dedicated to truth and criticism that could develop only out of collective deliberation.[30]

While the forum transformed intellectuals, it also transformed the public. Writers once again focused on the question-answer and discussion periods of the forum. Percy Grant, the director of the Public Forum in New York City, argued: "The forum is a device by which people become articulate." Glenn Frank explained how the forum provided "discussion in which the rank and file of the people participate." In forums people learned the necessary skills of a democratic public: how to listen, how to argue, and how to deliberate. People became a public in a forum—not a passive audience. According to Frank: "We are a press-reading and lecture-hearing people, but our genius for debate has gone long unused. We are a chronic audience, and the *audience habit is death to the political creativeness of a people.*" In saying this, Frank made the most important connection of all: without a deliberating and debating public, democracy would stagnate.

George Coleman and others drew out the political implications of this idea by linking the deliberation in forums to the initiative and referendum. Citizens could deliberate in forums and then make binding decisions through initiatives and referendums. As Joseph Walker, a supporter of the forum movement, explained: "If the people are to assume the responsibility of voting upon measures, as well as upon men, it is obvious that some effective means of public discussion must be devised . . . . The initiative and referendum and the open forum must go hand in hand." The forum seemed the perfect institution for a deliberating, democratic, and politically effective public.[31]

By seeing intellectuals and citizens as equals and by developing a much stronger conception of the public, the forum movement went beyond university extension in terms of developing a democratic public. Nonetheless, the question remains, Did the forum truly empower a democratic public or did it face certain limits? Without a doubt the forum's floor produced its own uncontrollable dynamic, as witnessed in the booing and heckling.

Nonetheless, Charles Sprague Smith, Frederic Howe, and George Coleman directed and steered their respective forums, often losing sight of the freedom necessary for open deliberation.

When Howe took over as director of the People's Institute, his control could become antidemocratic at times. Although he believed in a democratic public, Howe's role as a political activist occasionally caused him to envision the forum as a *tool* for political reform. Writing to a trustee of the People's Institute in 1912 he explained part of his attitude toward his forthcoming work: "I sincerely hope that you will feel that we have an institution here that we can build *in any way we want* as a democratic agency for a lot of things" (my emphasis). At times like this Howe admired the forum less for its democratic initiative and more for its use-value for reformers.

This tendency became more apparent in Howe's account of a political conflict that occurred while director of the People's Institute. Here Howe made the forum appear subsidiary to his own initiative: "When the subway contracts were being put through by the Gaynor administration, I organized a campaign for their rejection; they were a betrayal of the city's interests and the pledges on which the administration had been elected. Meetings were held, the [People's] Institute took the lead in opposing the contracts." In this instance Howe envisioned the public following the lead of political reformers, an interpretation of the democratic public that he learned from Tom Johnson, who put personal struggles ahead of his faith in a democratic public. Howe went on to display these limits while at the People's Institute. At times political leaders like Johnson and Howe could trust a democratic public; at other times they subordinated it to their own goals and agendas.[32]

Though this was a shortcoming of Howe's understanding of a democratic public, it also reflected an inherent limitation of the forum itself. Even though lecturers faced questions, they still led the discussion. When the forum speakers were well-known intellectual "stars," the role of citizens was probably even more limited. Certainly booing, hissing, and heckling could be lively and to a certain extent an expression of democratic dissent. At the same time, however, these actions illustrated just how subordinate the forum floor was to the leadership of speakers. People on the floor could only introject, they could not redirect discussion. The possibility of asking a few questions at the end of a speech was not enough to produce democratic deliberation; the speaker and the chairperson who took questions from the floor still controlled the forum's discussion. The forum could not give full birth to a democratic public, and this signified its biggest institutional shortcoming. Howe's flawed understanding of the democratic public (his too-trustworthy attitude toward experts and political reformers, for instance) meshed with the institutional limitations of the forum. Both hampered the development of a truly powerful and effective democratic public.

On the other hand, the forum's freedom moved beyond university extension. Forum leaders understood that public life and its questions offered a model of intellectual life different from and superior to academic life and its growing concerns with professionalization and objectivity. The question-answer periods and the lively floor activities found in forums also offered a glimpse into the dynamics and radical potentials of a democratic public. The challenge remained this: How to turn these activities over to citizens themselves so they could have more control over the means of democratic deliberation? The People's Institute developed some ideas along these lines. Some activists here thought forums held in schools after hours could provide citizens with more freedom to determine political debate. In 1912 Howe belatedly endorsed this possibility. But by 1912 the movement to form school centers had already reached a climax, and its leaders had taken the next and most important step in the formation of a democratic public during the Progressive Era.[33]

CHAPTER THREE

"BUTTRESSING THE FOUNDATIONS OF DEMOCRACY"

The Social Centers Movement

> Yes, I see it. The foundation of this development in Rochester is the right of free discussion and democratic control.
>
> —F. B. Dyer, a school superintendent remarking on Rochester's social centers[1]

When Frederic Howe endorsed the social centers movement in 1912, the idea of using public schools as places for forums and debates had existed for some time. An effort associated with Rochester, New York, in 1907, the movement gained national recognition and praise, and by 1912 was endorsed by America's two major political parties and the Progressive Party. From 1912 to America's entry into World War I the movement continued to grow nationwide and offer Americans a vision of how to create a "real democracy." Though short-lived and transformed by World War I, the social centers movement was clearly the most important attempt to create a democratic public during the Progressive Era, and its relevance lies not only in the institutional reform it accomplished but in the democratic ideals it generated. Both building upon and going beyond the accomplishments of university extension and the forum movement, social centers became one of the most interesting political experiments in the early twentieth century and the truest expression of a democratic public.

Early Experiments and Ideas

The original impetus behind using public schools as adult evening centers was quite benign. The simplest reason grew out of a concern for efficiency.

It seemed wasteful to leave schools standing dormant for long periods of time, especially in the evenings and during the summer. Charles Eliot, the president of Harvard, made this argument most succinctly in 1903. Endorsing the use of the schoolhouse for "recitations, plays, readings, and illustrated lectures" in the evenings, Eliot drew out a cost-benefit analysis to legitimate the wider use of the school: "The present inadequate use of schoolhouses is wasteful precisely in proportion to the costliness of the grounds and buildings." This idea held sway for a long time afterward, and certain progressives endorsed using schools as social centers solely because it was an efficient use of what they called the "school plant."[2]

Drawing from this language of efficiency, certain reformers argued that schools must become more utilitarian for local communities, and they started connecting social centers to wider concerns about the state of American politics. Expanding greatly during the early twentieth century, the public school system was marked by two features: it was funded by the public (through taxation) and decentralized (schools were based in neighborhoods). Because of this, certain reformers argued, citizens should have the right to use their schools for other community purposes. Turning the school into an evening social center would help to legitimate the cost in the eyes of the taxpayers and in addition it would provide a focal point for community life thereby generating social solidarity—"that old town sentiment and social sympathy and power of cooperation among good people." Sometimes this hope for community cohesiveness smacked of what certain historians call "social control," a pernicious attempt to generate a false harmony and sense of community in order to conceal forms of social conflict. But many activists saw the democratic potential behind the idea of a "public" in the conception of public schools. For as Eleanor Glueck pointed out when looking back on the movement in 1927, by making schools into evening centers, citizens could also find a place for public, democratic deliberation, not just "social sympathy."[3]

By stressing the community's right to use the school, reformers also hoped that parents could gain control over education. Behind what in our day and age have become Parent-Teacher Associations (PTAs) lay a criticism of the removal of the processes of education from the larger community. Louise Montgomery, a Chicago educator, argued: "The parent has been strangely silent, surrendering his child to the school system with a curious, unquestioning faith. It is difficult to understand this attitude, except in the light of the old idea of education as a purely intellectual process which must be intrusted to specialists and is therefore beyond the comprehension of the average parent." By having parents assemble in the evenings to examine and criticize school policies, Montgomery believed parent-teacher associations would build up a citizen's interest in public life in general. Other proponents of parent-teacher associations argued that by becoming active in community issues such as education, parents would make connections between education and other public issues. Mary Grice believed citizens who involved themselves in the politics of education would become more politically astute and capable of widespread democratic participation.[4]

In 1902 John Dewey, the renowned American philosopher and political theorist, provided the most thoughtful and important reason for evening school centers. He situated all of the ideas discussed above within his developing philosophy of democracy. Having broken with his earlier commitment to philosophical idealism, Dewey retained his hope for democracy but focused on the concrete and everyday issue of education. While at the University of Chicago he had learned from and participated in experiments at Hull House, the famous settlement house started by Jane Addams and her fellow middle-class colleagues in the late nineteenth century (a place where Charles Zueblin drew much of his inspiration). Here Dewey witnessed working-class immigrants gathering in open meetings and discussions in order to solve neighborhood problems and understand how these problems related to the forces of industrial capitalism.

When thinking about how schools could be used as community centers, Dewey took Hull House as his "working model." He situated Hull House and schools within what he called "society" (and what political theorists today call "civil society")—that "less definite and freer play of forces of the community which goes on in the daily intercourse and contact of men in an endless variety of ways that have nothing to do with politics or government or the state in any institutional sense." After setting society apart from the state, Dewey rooted the development of democratic and participatory citizenship in local community discussion. Believing in neighborhood democracy, as found in Hull House, Dewey hoped for "every public school" to do "the same sort of work that is now done by a settlement." By becoming a "social center" where citizens collectively met to solve social problems, the school would fulfill its democratic promise. Dewey situated this hope within the "entire democratic movement" and the hope for socialism—not "material socialism" but rather "a socialism of the intelligence and of the spirit." The social center would facilitate neighborhood democracy and participation.[5]

It was this democratic vision of neighborhoods generating their own processes of collective deliberation that inspired Dewey and many other people who were turning schools into social centers. These democratic ideas continued to spread, and by 1906, four years after Dewey's article on social centers appeared, a number of city neighborhoods across the country made "wider use" of their schools. At this time the New York City free lecture system, which was based in public schools, was at its height of popularity, the People's Institute had formed "People's Clubs" in schools, and cities like Chicago and Cleveland were experimenting with parent-teacher associations, evening schools, and school recreation centers. Then in 1907 the movement for the "wider use of the school plant" took a new turn in Rochester, New York. It is necessary to analyze what took place in Rochester, for here the movement caught sight of its truly democratic possibilities, possibilities that would have national implications.[6]

The Rise, Fall, and Rise of Rochester's Social Centers

At the turn of the century Rochester, New York, was a small city that faced the general processes of so-called modernization and urban industrialization while retaining its own peculiar traditions. Rochester never developed as much heavy industry and never produced the crowded tenement housing found in most cities. Instead, it was known for its light, small industry and for its freestanding homes and large numbers of home owners. On the other hand, Rochester did face those processes of modernization such as spatial differentiation that established certain neighborhoods, that are tied together by public transportation systems, as locations solely for work or residence. Rochester also witnessed a rise, as all cities did, in "new immigration" from areas like Italy and Poland. Most important for this study, Rochester developed its own public culture during this period of modernization.[7]

Before social centers started up in 1907, Rochester developed the types of institutions discussed in the two previous chapters. By 1890 the University of Rochester had a well-established extension program. In addition, privately funded forums spread throughout the city. The Y.M.C.A. sponsored lectures on apolitical topics as well as on more political topics like socialism. Women organized the Political Equality Club, which had public discussions especially on the struggle for suffrage; other women formed the Women's Educational and Industrial Union that brought famous national speakers to Rochester. Socialists created a "Labor Lyceum" that had widely attended debates on many popular topics in a centrally located, government-owned building. Churches throughout the city sponsored lyceums that eventually inspired the People's Sunday Evenings, a popular forum started in 1908 and one modeled after the People's Institute. Here Walter Rauschenbusch, Rochester's famous "public intellectual" who was developing his philosophy of a "social gospel," often spoke. By 1907, when social centers started forming, Rochester had already developed a burgeoning public culture based on university extension and many different privately funded forums.[8]

Although the social centers in Rochester instituted their own lectures, they cannot be subsumed within Rochester's wider public culture without losing sight of their distinctive contributions to the forging of a democratic public. The social centers made a qualitative leap beyond previously organized university extension programs, forums, and lecture circuits. In the first place, within social centers it was the citizens themselves—not university professors or forum organizers—that decided what was to be debated and who was to do the debating. Citizens organized forums and helped oversee them. They also decided on political actions to be taken based on their deliberation. By having citizens themselves set the agenda for democratic discussion, social centers became the truest expression of a democratic public. As the *Democrat and Chronicle* reported, "Rochester is the only city in which the programmes of these meetings are selected by the people of the communities instead of by some official or board." In Rochester, social center activists learned the deeper meanings of democracy and eventually taught the rest of the nation these lessons.[9]

The original drive for social centers started in February 1907 and came from local organizations. These organizations ranged from conservative nativist groups to liberal suffragette groups to socialists. The range of groups illustrated how different organizations could find common ground in order to form a democratic public. These various organizations petitioned the Board of Education to open schools in the evening for popular use, not for any single purpose but for open democratic deliberation. Thus, as Harriet Childs argued, "The opening of the school buildings for social and civic purposes was due to a growth of popular sentiment."

This popular participation continued to fuel Rochester's movement. Although the Board of Education provided funds for the movement, it never controlled what was to be debated or how. That was left to the people. The board stated: "The demand came originally from the people and the people should express their will as to its maintenance and extension." Providing people with the chance to deliberate democratically, the board fully understood the consequence of open, democratic politics:

> If we have any faith at all in democracy or in free discussion as a means of forming intelligent opinion it would seem that we ought not to withhold from non-exclusive responsible organizations of citizens the opportunity for free discussion in a public building because of occasional objectionable utterances of individuals occurring in the midst of addresses or discussions and leading to no partisan or exclusive action on the part of the responsible body.

In order to embrace democracy the board accepted the self-government of social centers by citizens themselves as well as the conflicts that could ensue from this self-government.[10]

The Board of Education continued to rely on petitions in local neighborhoods to open up new social centers, and it intervened in the setting up of social centers in only one way. If attendance at a social center during one evening fell below twenty-five people, funds were cut. This way popular participation became the sole requirement of funding. Essentially the Board of Education provided people with a chance to create a democratic public on their own by helping form a "common meeting place for a neighborhood." Citizens determined the rest.[11]

Administrative details piled up in the beginning days of the movement, and in order to take care of these details the Board of Education hired Edward Ward. Described by one contemporary as an "enthusiastic apostle of democracy," Ward was especially suited for the job. Like other political activists during the Progressive Era (including Charles Zueblin), he had trained for the ministry but eventually became disgruntled with organized religion. Graduating from Auburn Theological Seminary in 1905, he became pastor at First Presbyterian Church in Silver Creek, New York, where he turned the church into a social center for wide community use. Ward became disillusioned with the ministry and decided to teach at Hamilton College where he found himself embroiled in controversy caused by his attack on public service corporations. Edging closer to some sort of Christian socialism (the type espoused by Walter Rauschenbusch and other Progressive Era intellectuals), Ward was hired as Rochester's supervisor of social center and playground development in 1907. As well as being a local organizer, he became a national spokesman for the movement by publishing several articles and books that won him acclaim.[12]

Ward was deeply influenced by Jane Addams's and John Dewey's visions of democracy and participatory citizenship, though he hoped to divorce the social center movement from any residual paternalism that Hull House exhibited. The social centers grew out of popular demand, not from a decision made by middle-class women to move into working-class neighborhoods. Most important, the centers were supported by public institutions and taxation, not by private wealth as was Hull House (Addams always felt uncomfortable with her methods of financial support). At his first public appearance on social centers in Rochester, Ward made it clear that the social centers had nothing to do with charity or philanthropy. Agreeing with Ward, George Forbes, the newly elected president of the Board of Education, argued early in 1908 that "[the social centers movement] is not a charity enterprise and is not organized especially for the poor. It is for the community, it is social, it is democratic and is generally patronized." When analyzing the movement two years later, Ray Stannard Baker agreed with Forbes. Baker argued that through social centers "it is being discovered that neither charity nor 'uplift' will meet the fundamental difficulties [of social life]. Neither is democratic." These sorts of statements were not mere rhetoric, for as Ward pointed out, the neighborhood with the first social center had many different ethnic groups and economic classes. Instead of philanthropy, the social centers movement was based on the politics of democratic initiative and participation.[13]

Though the social centers opened schoolhouses to recreational and evening lecture uses, the movement was essentially political (most of the lectures themselves were political). For soon after beginning, social centers developed civic clubs. One civic club delineated its purpose quite clearly in its constitution:

> Whereas, the welfare of society demands that those whose duty it is to exercise the franchise be well informed upon the economic, industrial and political questions of today; and whereas, by combination of effort the best results may be obtained; and, whereas the public school building is the best available place for such combination of effect; Therefore, we . . . do form a society to hold, in the public school building, meetings whose object shall be the gaining

> of information upon public questions by listening to public speakers and by public readings and discussions.

The civic clubs were intent on developing citizens' public skills of deliberation and what Kenneth Cmiel, a historian of nineteenth-century American culture, called "democratic eloquence." This is clear in another civic club's constitutional preamble:

> Whereas, the world needs men and women, who can think clearly and express their thoughts well; and whereas, each of us has powers of clear thinking and good expression which need only practice for development; and, whereas, by combination of effort the best results may be obtained, we whose names are hereunto annexed, do form a society whose object shall be the cultivation of the powers of clear thinking and good expression by means of debates, essays, orations, public readings and discussions.

For those involved in the movement the civic club, which remained distinct from the recreational aspect of the social centers, was considered the "fundamental element of the Social Center movement." New York State had not acquired the initiative and referendum, as many states did during the Progressive Era, so certain activists tried to make civic clubs politically effective by forming a League of Civic Clubs. As Livy Richard, a Rochester journalist, described it: "The federated civic clubs . . . send delegates to a monthly congress where standing committees closely scrutinize the progress of municipal legislation and, by their reports, as endorsed by the delegated body, exert some influence upon local government." There were hopes that the civic clubs could become even more politically effective, but that hope had to await further political reform.[14]

Even before they gained direct political influence, social centers and civic clubs appealed to a growing number of people. Rochester's citizens, which included many new immigrants, desired a place to meet and discuss the issues of the day. In the first season only three schools were used for weekly civic discussions, but from 1908 to 1909 more centers opened due to petitions made to the Board of Education by citizens in neighborhoods. By January 1910 Edward Ward reported that "[t]he record of the past year . . . is as follows: Nineteen adult civic clubs, using seventeen school buildings in various parts of the city held 305 meetings. . . . All of them [have been] committed to the policy of free discussion of public questions and all of them open to anybody who cared to attend and participate." In 1909 the No. 14 Social Center averaged from 91 to 146 people attending events, the West High Social Center from 75 to 165, and the No. 9 Social Center from 223 to 331. Even though the social centers faced budget cuts in 1910, the numbers continued to grow, and 25 percent of the registration for clubs during 1910 came from working-class immigrants or "non-English speaking persons," as reported in the *Democrat and Chronicle.* At one social center a person reported seeing 200 people turned away due to lack of space. From 1907 to 1911 the social centers and civic clubs grew exponentially.[15]

Numbers do not speak to the significance of this movement. More important here is what was debated and how it was debated. Here citizens learned crucial lessons about democracy and about the importance of open public discussion. Social centers and civic clubs were based on the principle of "free, untrammeled discussion of public questions, . . . even politics and religion not being tabooed." Controversy was not to be evaded, as activists accepted a wide range of debates and discussions. One report in the *Democrat and Chronicle* from 1910 reflects this range: "This week's programs in the social centers and civic clubs is a varied one, with evenings devoted to discussions of business conditions, health, art, social organization, high prices, the liquor question and neighborhood problems." These discussions ranged, as can be seen here and elsewhere, from the local level (the neighborhood) to the national level. Participants in social centers and civic clubs understood that these two levels could be separated only artificially and that the national and the local levels interacted with one another in important ways, ways that had to be understood by an active citizenry.[16]

The key issues of the day were debated in civic clubs and social centers. Local issues included the politics of streetcar development (where tracks were to go, etc.), local housing conditions, real estate speculation, municipal ownership of utilities, city planning (which once spun off into an interesting debate about the politics of the Chamber of Commerce, which was promoting city planning), and the development of a public library (which was achieved). Local educational debates had a tendency also to address national concerns about progressive education. People engaged not only Board of Education budget decisions and the issue of free textbooks but also the merits or problems of vocational training in high schools.

Debates on immigration and national citizenship, many of which were quite controversial, took place constantly. The first debate on immigration sparked "animated discussion" about whether "immigration was partly to blame for existent conditions of [poverty]." State and national issues that had local ramifications were consistently confronted, including direct primaries, "race relations," "ways and means of reform," the "new nationalism," women's suffrage, "public health as a political issue," labor union politics, and America's continued foreign policy in the Philippines. As these activities made clear, social centers activists believed federal policies were not to be accepted passively but rather were to be debated by citizens gathered in local forums if democracy were to be made real. Although we unfortunately have only a few direct reports about these discussions, it is clear that citizens devised important ways to ensure democratic principles.[17]

In the first place, citizens in social centers confronted important political issues by listening to all sides and by having political representatives from all parties speak in their forums. On U.S. immigration policy, three speakers representing distinct policies participated, and debate followed. In 1908 forums included representatives from the Democratic and Republican parties, but equal time was also given to the Socialists and Prohibitionists, breaking down the hegemony of America's two-party system. Citizens invited mayoral candidates to social centers to speak "on the issues of the city campaign."

Social centers provided a venue for political candidates to deal with issues outside of the influence of special interests, thus creating an institutional basis for the Progressive Era challenge to political corruption. An alderman who spoke at a social center in 1907 spelled out the importance of having public leaders, including both candidates and elected officials, come before the public. According to the alderman, "If every member of the common council and every other public servant had frequently such opportunities as this to come before the people whom he is supposed to represent, and discuss with them the things in which he is supposed to represent them it would mean that we would have a better representation of the people's interest and a more intelligent government." Social centers thus provided an institution that made representative government truly representative. By making political candidates and officials face the public, the cycle of official corruption—that great fear of so many progressives—might be broken.[18]

Civic clubs did not evade controversy in public discussions. They understood that a democratic public would be both contentious and reflect the plurality of the city's different members. Tensions and divisions were aired in public debates. For instance, one civic club at West High School debated whether or not textbooks should be issued to all students for free. This seemingly inconsequential issue brought out divisions within the local neighborhood, especially between Catholics (more normally against the idea) and Protestants (more often for the idea). A journalist for the *Democrat and Chronicle* reported that the ensuing debates were quite noisy since religious differences were sharp. There was so much conflict that another meeting was called for the next week, and people demanded a representative from the antitextbook side make a full speech. One can only imagine what the debates on capital punishment, prohibition, and the exclusion of the Japanese from America would have been like. People probably debated with quite a bit of passion. At one meeting a journalist, forgetting his code of objectivity, joined in with considerable fervor. Social centers helped air the tensions and passions created by democratic public life.[19]

But not all debates were so noisy or emotional. Based on an ethic of public dialogue, civic clubs encouraged citizens to listen carefully to differing viewpoints, seek out common ground, and find resolutions for conflicts. A debate was held on the "social value of the saloon" at which a prohibitionist and a defender of the saloon spoke. "The audience was made up of a few men who were decidedly opposed to the saloon, a few who were ardent defenders of the saloon, and a large majority who had no strong feelings either way, who had not given the subject much thought." After listening to both the attack on the saloon and the defense, citizens debated and came to a resolution of sorts. "The idea began to take form as a consensus of opinion, that the solution was to be found neither in attacking nor in maintaining the saloon, but in the development of an institution which should provide opportunity for the man-to-man liberty of comradely association, and the education of free discussion which the saloon now offers (at least, while a man has money), but which would be free from the degrading elements of that institution." Other discussions reflected this sort of give and take, a necessary part of public deliberation.[20]

Debates also developed citizens' sense of fairness and inclusion, values utterly necessary for democracy. At one discussion about the "relative merits of the Republican and Democratic candidates," citizens made sure the debate followed the principle of equality and respect. "In the midst of the discussion in the hall it was suggested that in order to give all sides a fair show they should hold a five-sided debate, with two defendants of the claims of each of the candidates." But since no Independence Leaguer or Prohibitionist attended the meeting, participants "decided to make it a triangular debate, giving the one socialist youth in the crowd a chance to speak twice to make up for the fact that there were two Republicans and two Democrats present." This way citizens created a forum in which all involved received an equal voice in debating.[21]

Most important of all, citizens learned that they themselves could create a deliberating, democratic public. Understanding who debated in social centers illustrates this point. Describing a debate within one social center, Harriet Childs explained: "The topic being the commission form of government, a Polish washwoman and the president of the W.C.T.U. [Women's Christian Temperance Union] were opposed by a day cleaner and a college professor." Social centers taught participants that any citizen—not just intellectuals—could deliberate and debate. By being responsible for debates, citizens learned some of the ins-and-outs of democratic participation. Moving beyond university extension programs and the forum movement, citizens learned that in a democracy the distinction between teachers and students was often blurred. In addition, some realized that if citizens were affected by political decisions, they needed to be involved in making these decisions. For instance, a reverend spoke at a civic club on "Community Problems" and addressed the issue of Italian immigration. He protested the widespread prejudice against Italians, and an interesting motion was passed: "The result of the remarks . . . was a motion to have some Italian speaker address the club and outline what in his opinion should be done to aid in the solution of the Italian problem." By prizing open deliberation, citizens learned that people could not be treated as objects but had to be involved in democratic decision making themselves.[22]

Citizens not only talked in social centers, they deliberated. This distinction is important, for citizens in social centers came together to consider different options and find ways to solve local and national problems. One speaker at a civic club argued that social centers provided a "vehicle for bringing matters to the very doors of the people. The response in Rochester is marked and there is developing a civic pride and interest in the city that is bound to place Rochester . . . among cities of the century." Only by citizens actively discussing and solving local problems could democracy be made real. Due to this, civic clubs often organized around immediate issues, like setting up playgrounds and parks, improving sewage systems, checking into the repercussions of a local dam on the Genesee River, acquiring a public library, putting on plays, improving the quality of schools, curbing real estate speculation, gaining control over newly laid railroads, and setting up cooperative markets. Citizens held open meetings to discuss "What We Have and What We Want in Rochester," thus examining what exactly should take priority among various community concerns. In addition, social centers activists organized libraries and reading rooms where citizens could educate themselves about issues before they deliberated.[23]

By holding public debates in which any citizen could develop skills at deliberation, by facing up to all issues no matter how controversial or passionate debate might become, by encouraging public agreement on pressing matters while not demanding unity, and by having citizens focus on concrete and local issues in hopes of widening their concerns, social centers in Rochester set out new ways in which to revitalize American democracy. Here was an experiment that explored what was necessary to educate citizens for the responsibilities of self-government. For all these reasons citizens in Rochester developed pride and excitement about their newfound political experiment—so much pride that three hundred citizens signed a petition requesting that New York State governor Charles Evans Hughes come to Rochester to witness this experiment. Hughes came quickly on 8 April 1909.

Known for his support of a direct primary bill that suffered defeat the same day he spoke in Rochester, Hughes linked his hope for the direct primary, a popular reform for many progressives, to the democratic and public deliberation carried out in civic clubs and social centers. After seeing a few of the civic clubs in operation, he made a public speech. The *Democrat and Chronicle* reported that Hughes "passed to the subject of direct nominations by lauding the social center idea for the opportunity it affords of discussing public questions in calm and well-controlled meetings." The governor pointed out that democratic deliberation in social centers could replace the older, autocratic means of selecting candidates for a party. He went on to state, "It is a great work that you are doing here—the buttressing the foundations of democracy." It is of no surprise that social centers activists quickly made this statement a slogan for their movement.[24]

Not everyone praised Rochester's social centers like Governor Hughes. In fact, by February 1910 the Board of Education cut social center funds in response to attacks made on them. Organized religion led the attacks. One Sunday a social center held a pageant that was criticized since it was thought to be unchaperoned by parents (which was false) and fell on a Sunday (which was true). As Edward Ward quickly pointed out, those involved in the pageant were Jews, and Sunday was not their holy day. Thus, one controversy and subsequent attacks made on social centers rose out of cultural misunderstandings. But others grew out of general animosity toward social centers on the part of churches, many of which saw social centers leading to "anarchy." More important than the attacks made by churches were the worries of Rochester's political elite. This elite feared citizens educating themselves into the processes of deliberation and decision making. As religious and political leaders attacked the social centers, an important debate about the repercussions of democracy emerged.[25]

In trying to understand the attacks made on social centers Ray Stannard Baker, a political journalist, drew up a conspiracy theory, arguing that Boss Aldridge gathered business and church leaders around him and coordinated their protest against social centers. Although the more conspiratorial aspects of this analysis are false, there is no doubt that Boss Aldridge wanted social centers to cease and desist. Aldridge, a Republican Party boss who built a successful political machine, had direct interests in Rochester's municipal gas and transportation issues, and he clearly hated the open debates in the social centers, especially since they were funded through public dollars. Mayor Edgerton, who eventually closed down the social centers, was essentially Aldridge's pawn. Those who held political power despised open discussion and citizens deciding what needed to be done about municipal issues, and their attacks were fueled by hatred and fear of citizens seeking input into political decision making. In the *Post-Express*, a local Rochester paper, one editor expressed fear that speakers at social centers had an "influence" on "the ignorant and the unthinking." Fearing political and social chaos if citizens were allowed to listen to speakers and make up their own minds, this editor showed a deep distrust of citizens deliberating on their own terms. Most people who criticized social centers feared the repercussions of open, democratic debate.[26]

Though facing attacks and a budget crunch, social centers persevered throughout 1910, but at the beginning of 1911 a new controversy caused havoc. Citizens voted to have Kendrick Shedd, a professor of German at the University of Rochester who was described in 1908 as "extremely popular with the residents of No. 9 District," to speak at the No. 9 social center on 6 February 1911. A socialist, Shedd argued in his speech that the "red flag of socialism" transcended the limits of American nationalism. As can be imagined, criticisms of the speech abounded. Nativist groups like Sons of the American Revolution attacked Shedd's speech for its lack of patriotism, and Catholics reiterated their complaints about the social centers, adding this time that they were promoting anti-American ideas (Catholics and nativists made strange bedfellows in this case). The mayor prevented Shedd from speaking in public buildings, including schools (he also removed the Labor Lyceum from the city council building it met in), and

Rush Rhees, the president of the University of Rochester, eventually forced Shedd to leave his teaching position, since George Eastman made future funding of the university contingent on Shedd's departure. Social Center No. 9 was forced to condemn Shedd's speech. Most important of all, the mayor finally had an excuse to shut down the social centers, and he did. In March the Board of Education declared the movement dead. Protests followed.[27]

Clearly, social centers activists accepted open, contentious debate, but their opposition did not. One reverend who refused to participate in the social center debate on free textbooks explained why he disliked the contention expressed at social centers: "I am convinced that these assemblages tend more to produce animosities than to enlighten the people on the question for discussion." This reverend could only understand public disagreement as producing "animosities." The natural conclusion here seemed to be that animosities were better repressed than aired. Even worse, the assumption was that citizens were ignorant and would succumb to the most pernicious tendencies of these animosities. This line of reasoning ran directly counter to social centers activists' trust in the common people, but it resonated with those who held political power. Although certain social centers activists were convinced that "the strongest guarantee of the character of the Social Center is it's [*sic*] openness to criticism," when attacks like the one of the reverend were coupled with political power in the hands of the mayor, the movement was doomed.[28]

Throughout 1911 different citizens and organizations tried to renew the social centers project. By the end of the year the Jewish community and certain women's clubs made calls to reopen social centers. George Forbes, once president of the Board of Education, made the most eloquent demand for renewing the social centers project. Forbes argued that social centers did not promote radical ideas but brought them to the table to be examined by all. He asserted that democracy could not be realized without social centers:

> The civic clubs were small parliaments which created civic intelligence by developing opinions in a broad, fair way on questions of importance to the city, state, and nation. In order to realize the ideal of democracy the control must not only be put in the hands of the average man but something must be done to make the average man capable of exercising that power. Many of the mistakes attributed to democracy in the past have arisen because little atten-

tion has been paid to the manner in which the powers given to the people shall be exercised by them.

Forbes's defense was eloquent: only if citizens were given the institutional means to develop their democratic skills could they ever become citizens. Here was a clearheaded and thoughtful argument for the principles underlying a democratic public. Forbes showed that democrats did not blindly trust "the people." They did not believe in "chaos" either. Rather, they knew that those who believed in democracy had a responsibility to provide ways in which citizens could become capable of self-government. Nonetheless, even though Forbes eloquently defended the civic clubs, the damage had been done. Some members of the Board of Education tried to get money for the movement in 1912 but failed. After 1912 the social centers movement could not regain its strength.[29]

Why did the social centers movement in Rochester fail to regenerate itself? The simplest and most obvious reason was a lack of funds. If a civic club used a school after March 1911, it had to raise the money to pay the electricity and heating charges, the janitors, and the supervisors who had to stay late. Some groups tried to do this and learned about these difficulties firsthand. One women's civic club that paid their way found themselves locked in the school late at night. More important, by turning civic clubs into voluntary groups who had to pay their way to use public schools, the mayor delegitimized the civic clubs, making them into closed, voluntary organizations—not open, public organizations. Without public legitimacy, funding, and help with the administration (bureaucrats were necessary for some things), the movement ran into many problems.[30]

There were more significant problems than funding. Edward Ward believed that the movement in Rochester died because it failed to build an alliance with the mayor. Known for his independence from Boss Aldridge, Mayor Cutler had approved the movement in 1907, but soon afterward Mayor Edgerton came into office. Boss Aldridge controlled Edgerton, but Ward argued that if the movement had pushed and shown its popular strength to Edgerton, he might have come around to supporting social centers against Aldridge's wishes. Unfortunately, social center activists had written Edgerton off as Aldridge's tool and thus refused to consider building an alliance. Ward's point can be extended, for what the movement should have struggled for was not just political legitimacy in the eyes of the mayor but the initiative and referendum, a reform that would have ensured that the deliberation carried out in social centers could have become politically effective and that social centers could have protected themselves. The social centers needed both more legitimacy and institutional stability while retaining a certain amount of independence from existing forms of political power—a very difficult challenge.[31]

Those with power had attacked the movement for being too politically rancorous, and it was clear that if civic clubs who paid their way after 1911 became politically controversial, they would suffer the consequences. But it was precisely the political content of the movement that attracted people. The numbers of people attending the social centers increased in 1910, and it was that same year that the centers engaged politics head-on. When political and controversial issues were ruled out from 1911 to 1912, the numbers attending decreased. This is no causal argument, but it shows that many people wanted a political forum, not just recreational facilities. George Edwards, who studied the social centers movement for his thesis at the University of South Carolina, argued: "The general popularity of the movement, where it has been tried, shows that folks enjoy coming together to talk and learn about the affairs of the day." George Forbes went further and asserted that social centers without politically charged civic clubs would prove meaningless: "I only insist that while the social center may be an inestimable good, it makes no necessary contribution to the problem of democracy unless it is also a civic center, developing the consciousness of communal responsibility and power." To force politics—both deliberation and decision making—out of social centers (in order to placate those with political power) ensured a lack of popular participation and defeated the purpose and meaning of the movement.[32]

Undoubtedly, those with political power played the major role in shutting down the social centers. Nonetheless, after Ward's departure the leadership of the social centers movement failed to respond to these attacks forcefully. Herbert Weet, Edward Ward's successor, at first seemed to endorse Ward's vision of democracy, but as time went on it was clear that he did not trust the people to act responsibly or democratically. He did not embrace Ward's democratic teachings enough to resist the pressure of a hostile political boss and mayor. He hoped to limit controversy and conflict by regulating all future social centers activities autocratically. Weet contradicted two major premises of democracy: that citizens must be trusted with self-government and that public life thrives on conflict and contention. Forgetting this, Weet destroyed the major reason for social centers. Democracy without a certain amount of trust in the people and without an acceptance of contention is an impossibility, if not a contradiction in terms.

Trying to impose harmonious public activity on social centers constituted automatic failure. After Ward, the leadership of social centers, failed to preserve the deeper meaning of the movement.[33]

By 1911 the social centers movement in Rochester had died. The conflict and debate about social centers was resolved in favor of those who preferred the status quo to the rancorous repercussions of democracy. This set up a dangerous historical precedent, one that would not become completely evident until six years later (see Chapter Six). Ironically, at the time that Rochester's social centers suffered political paralysis, the movement caught on nationally. The movement in Rochester inspired Americans' political imagination, as intellectuals and activists started reflecting on and writing about what social centers taught Americans about democracy. Before studying the ideas that the movement generated, it is important to understand just how the social center idea gained recognition and fueled a national movement.

Going National

Rochester's social centers caught on early. In September 1908 representatives from New York City, Chicago, and Toronto visited Rochester's social centers to see if their cities could draw lessons from the experience. Not only did Governor Hughes come to visit, so did Charles Zueblin, who in December 1908—soon after leaving the University of Chicago and starting his search for other institutions to create a democratic public—argued that the social centers movement had achieved national prominence. Lincoln Steffens followed in Zueblin's path in 1909. By September 1909 Boston, Pittsburgh, and Columbus were experimenting with social centers and "more than a dozen periodicals" had published articles on Rochester while "letters had been received from people in more than one hundred cities" requesting information on the movement. In 1910 a writer confidently argued that "the use of the school building as a social and educational center . . . has become firmly established."[34]

The movement spread westward. Social centers emerged in Oklahoma, Ohio, Minnesota, and Indiana, and the entire Southwest experienced a growth. Lee Hanmer, working for the Russell Sage Foundation, studied the movement and found that "in 1912, 101 cities carried on some form of evening-center work and used 338 school buildings for that purpose." In addition to this, certain states decided to tax their citizens to support social centers. "Ten states have amended their school laws during the past two years so as to provide for the maintenance of this work at public expense." The movement continued to grow after 1912, and five years later, during 1917 alone, nineteen American cities pressed for social centers.[35]

Besides the fact that social centers appealed to Americans' general faith in democracy, there was another reason they caught on: Edward Ward became a national figure. In 1910 Ward decided to take his "big idea . . . from its nursery bed in Rochester to the fertile soil of democratic Wisconsin." Thinking he could gain more legitimacy by linking up with a university committed to public service, Ward was appointed to oversee social centers for the University of Wisconsin's extension project. He remained in Wisconsin until 1915 when he moved into an even more nationally prestigious position as specialist in community organization for the U.S. Bureau of Education. From 1910 onward Ward dedicated himself to promoting social centers and participatory democracy at a national level. But by 1921 he quit his position at the Bureau of Education, never to return to the movement again.[36]

In Wisconsin Ward achieved greater national recognition for social centers. After gaining statewide legislative support for social centers, he convinced Senator La Follette, the national leader of insurgent progressivism in the Midwest, that the senator needed to support social centers if he truly believed in democracy. Renewing the ideal of participatory citizenship that, as the historian David Thelen has shown, lay at the root of Wisconsin progressivism, La Follette stated: "Should this [social centers] movement become general, it would unquestionably result in the establishment of a foundation of intelligent democracy, which would make civic progress not only rapid, but conservative and sure." Following La Follette's endorsement, Woodrow Wilson, the presidential candidate for the Democratic Party, supported the movement that he believed regenerated "the constructive and creative genius of the American people." Before announcing his independent Progressive Party candidacy, Theodore Roosevelt quickly joined in by arguing that the social center should become the "Senate of the people." Ward's activities snowballed and made the social center a part of national political consciousness.[37]

While he pushed for national recognition of the movement, Ward sometimes lost sight of his responsibilities in Wisconsin. His leadership reflected the strengths and weaknesses of any national leader. Though he often neglected his local responsibilities, he made Americans aware that if they wanted true democracy, they needed to change their institutions on a nationwide basis—nothing less would suffice. Whatever his strengths and weaknesses, by 1912 Ward clearly made major political leaders supportive of national reform toward democracy.[38]

But Ward was not the only person working on social centers. Already by late 1911 a national organization, the Social Center Association of America, formed out of a conference held in Madison, Wisconsin. A great optimism marked the conference. One participant described the general mood this way: "It seemed to those present that America was at last to develop a true democracy; that at last the people of the United States were about to direct their own affairs." The Social Center Association of America helped local activists, worked with other organizations, and tried to change Americans' national political consciousness. Re-formed in 1916 as the National Community Center Association, the organization continued to raise awareness of how only in public forums could citizens generate real democracy. Figures like John Collier and Mary Parker Follett entered the movement, giving it fresh life and bringing forth new debates about the direction of the movement. But no matter what issues were debated, the organization always remained committed to community-based democracy.[39]

From 1912 to 1916 the social centers movement established itself nationally. Cities and towns across America followed Rochester's model and set up their own social centers. While the Progressive Era was known for a great deal of *rhetoric* about democracy, the social centers provided an actual institution in which citizens could educate themselves for political deliberation and decision making. From the perspective of these activists it truly seemed that "America was at last to develop a true democracy," as George Ford had put it. If Americans were to develop such a "true democracy," they needed to develop not only democratic institutions but also democratic ideas fit for the twentieth century. As the social centers movement became national, certain activists reflected upon their experiment and began articulating new and radical ideas about democracy. Out of their reflections came very important arguments about what was needed to enliven the political imagination of America.

CHAPTER FOUR

ENVISIONING DEMOCRACY

Social Centers and Political Thought

> There is no better means of securing good municipal government than an interested citizenship, and there is no better agency for securing an interested citizenship than . . . local associations, operating from community civic centers. In the fulfillment of such a plan there is to be gained all the advantages of ward representation without its evils, all the power that is contemplated in the initiative and referendum without sacrificing the principle of representative government, the real kind of municipal reform starting with the electorate, direct contact with the government and a constant, instead of a spasmodic, generation of healthy public sentiment.
>
> —*New Boston*[1]

Social center activists reflected upon their experiences and developed important ideas about the deeper meaning of democracy. Many of these people were not intellectuals or academics, and thus it is often necessary to read their ideas more from their actions and brief public statements than from their books or essays. But there were certain people, especially Edward Ward, George Forbes, and M. Clyde Kelly, who drew out important and sophisticated intellectual lessons from the movement. By reading both ideas and actions, we can understand the lessons learned by those who tried to create a democratic public.

The few historians who have studied social centers activists have been too quick to dismiss their ideas as nostalgic communitarianism. Reflecting on the tradition of community organizing in America, Robert Fisher portrays Edward Ward as a man concerned with creating "community solidarity" and little more. In analyzing Ward's efforts in Wisconsin, Victor Jew asserts, "The social centers were appeals to community, consensus, and democracy, looking forward to a nation built upon neighborhood loyalty while looking backwards to some idyllic New England town meeting ideal." Edward Stevens takes this logic one step further and argues that social centers developed a cynical means of hampering radical, leftist ideals. Straining to make his point, Stevens declares that the Board of Education in Rochester "took the position . . . that radical and unprogressive views could best be kept in check by exposing them to the rigors of debate." Stevens concludes awkwardly (for what is better than the "rigors of debate" to settle conflicts?) that this effort did not reflect democratic intentions but rather technocratic social engineering. The work of Fisher, Jew, and Stevens follows Jean Quandt's earlier and very influential work that dismissed communitarian social thought during the Progressive Era. For Quandt, communitarian intellectuals' "reliance on the curative powers of the local community blunted the edge of their social criticism and drew their attention away from the need for a basic transformation of American society." According to these historians, social center activists and intellectuals either wanted to create stagnant and harmonious communities, social control, or just bad politics.[2]

These contemporary dismissals of the social centers movement's ideals ignore the important work done by democratic theorists who took social centers as their model. Many of the intellectual reflections on social center experiments illustrate a provocative understanding of how democracy can work in the modern world. Hoping to inspire their fellow Americans, the writers who propounded this sort of theory based their work on three central ideas: the idea of a public, citizenship, and democracy. These ideas cannot be easily dismissed as nostalgic communitarianism or regressive, antimodern politics. Instead, these ideas hold important lessons for us. They suggest how we can accept modernity while making democracy more participatory, enlivening, and rigorous.[3]

Creating a Community or a Public?

> The term "political" is one of the synonyms for the word "public."
>
> —Edward Ward[4]

Certainly some social centers activists spoke the language of community spirit and harmony, the type of language examined by Robert Fisher and Jean Quandt. Charles Gilbert, an educational theorist writing in 1906, hoped school centers would promote "the higher intellectual and social life of the community without arousing antagonisms." This sentiment was echoed in the 1920s when Clarence Perry argued that the major goal of the social centers had been the "dissolution of class and racial antagonisms." C. J. Bushnell, a philosopher, believed the movement hoped for "social union." Even Edward Ward sometimes wanted the movement to generate a sense of neighborhood solidarity by renewing the spirit of the "little red schoolhouse" of the past. Though these ideas might be easily written off as nostalgia, when examined more thoroughly, the hope of generating community becomes a much more complex idea than it first appears.[5]

M. Clyde Kelly, a Pennsylvania congressman who wrote an important book in support of social centers, understood that capitalism and urbanization destroyed the cohesion of older communities. In many ways this was a typical finding of Progressive Era intellectuals. Kelly argued: "Skyscrapers have blotted out the village greens and hurrying traffic beats over the commons." Kelly explained that the hope to duplicate the supposed cohesion of the older "New England town" was futile. But there had to be *some* sort of community consciousness created if democratic initiative and collective participation were not to be lost. Kelly asserted that "in city and town alike, we may win back the old spirit of neighborhood and common life and common action by efficient organization of the communities, with democratically elected, publicly paid officials to serve under the people's direction."

The social center, which for Kelly was more political than social, would play the major role in this effort. Kelly expressed a consciousness about renewing—but not duplicating—a sense of community, which he and others believed might have been stronger in the past. Kelly did not nostalgically remember bygone communities. When he talked of the importance of renewing localities, he did not glamorize strong traditions or what German sociologists were starting to describe as "Gemeinschaft." Rather, he saw the locality as providing the space within which open public discussion could grow. The community within the modern city would not emerge organically. Nor would it be a place of traditional or communal obligations. Instead, it would consciously organize itself to initiate a democratic politics of deliberation and collective action.[6]

Few activists were under the illusion that modern social conditions could foster tight hermetic communities, and even fewer social centers activists wanted harmonious communities like the mythical ones of the past. Like

Kelly, Anna Pendleton Schenck understood that "modern material progress has disorganized neighborhood life," but she believed that "our scattered neighborhoods have in them the germs of a finer and more inspiring community ideal." This community ideal would not develop harmony and cohesion but rather civic association and political action. As one writer in the *American City* understood, the future urban community would rejuvenate democracy: "The community which has not arrived at the age of consciousness will seldom do anything as a community. It will have no public opinion that is effective, and its affairs will be managed or mismanaged according to the whims or interests of the clique that happens to get itself into power." It was not that communities at present functioned well. Nor did social centers activists hope to create an idyllic small-town feel in communities, since this could lead to conformity and blind submission to local traditions. Instead, these activists hoped to root discussion in local arenas; only in this way could democracy grow from the bottom up. Politics had to originate in local, face-to-face arenas to be democratic. Neither the small town of the past nor the disorganized neighborhoods of the present could do this.[7]

If the primary goal of social centers activists was not to create hermetic communities, what did they want? Edward Ward celebrated the hope for civic pride that city beautiful activists had placed in public life, and he understood that the local social centers rooted people not just in their communities but in a wider urban public. Only through "the federated interchange and union in the enterprise of politics . . . with other neighborhoods" could a "membership" within the wider city be conceived and made real by citizens. Ward did not leave local neighborhoods and communities unto themselves, for he believed that social centers inspired people to recognize their connection to an urban public life beyond their locales. The debates within social centers reflected this idea; they did not merely engage local problems but city, state, and national issues. By becoming involved at the local level, citizens drew themselves into the wider public world of politics. Communities were not enough; they had to help build up a larger and more inclusive democratic public.[8]

Instead of communal solidarity, social centers developed the skill of collective public judgment. Public judgment required deliberation that evaluated political leaders' decisions and decided on appropriate political action to be taken by citizens. Ward did not want citizens to become conformist members of a community; instead, he celebrated the modern principle of enlightened public judgment:

> The American attitude which says "Come let us reason together," expressed in the old Yankee, "I want to know," and modernized into, "You'll have to show me," is the true political attitude. This is the normal attitude in which acquainted citizens will face the together-problems of government when the one political organization of the whole citizenship is seen for what it is, the common bond of uniting membership in responsibility which implies the common union of citizens for discussion.

This discussion grew out of citizens collectively deliberating together. Social centers thinkers took the ideas of pragmatism seriously and believed that democratic deliberation produced a contingent sort of truth constantly open to further debate. Rochester social centers activists believed that "information regarding the facts" of a political problem was necessary, but that citizens also needed "the interpretation which other members of [our city] hold—especially those whose opinions differ from ours." Public, political judgment required constant interpretation and contestation and was the major goal of the social centers movement.[9]

M. Clyde Kelly fully understood what public judgment meant. Believing in democratic deliberation, Kelly realized public judgment's importance, and his ideas are worth quoting at length here:

> While debate without decision is folly, decision without debate is dangerous. Neither one need be chosen when the community gets together for orderly discussion and mutual decision. No other service is greater than for a man, through practice in fellowship, to be able to analyze the motives of men, to know how to rebuke their worse impulses and at the same time to inspire their best qualities; to be able to puncture sophistry and to encourage truth; to be able to allay strife and promote good will. These are the accomplishments . . . which America needs now as never before.

Edward Ward too endorsed this ideal of public judgment and understood that only when citizens developed the skills of deliberating in public and judging the merits of political leaders could corruption be prevented. Political judgment in public forums was the best check against private interests dominating American politics—the central concern for many Americans during the Progressive Era.[10]

In order for citizens to develop public judgment, social centers activists argued that education could no longer be thought of as cloistered in formal institutions of learning. For intelligence to be democratized, collective education had to be a part of everyday life (a discovery already made by university extension advocates). In his analysis of social centers Irving King argued that they initiated a "broader conception of education." George Forbes drew this argument out to its fullest extent and argued: "All school work is by necessity artificial, isolated from life, even from the life of the family and so ABSTRACT. The school, as such, is not an ETHICAL community. It is not a DEMOCRACY."

Against the "abstract" education of formal institutions, Forbes celebrated the wider educational principle found in social centers: "[The social centers movement] was educational in the sense that where there is human aspiration and joint effort for better things there is education." Forbes understood that in social centers citizens taught and learned from one another through political deliberation. The process of discussing pressing issues was itself educational, and by coming together and taking on the responsibility to make public judgments, citizens understood that education did not end in school. A professor of education at the University of Wisconsin summed it up this way: "If the movement accomplishes nothing more than to attract public attention to the necessity and worth of *education through action*, it will have served no mean end."[11]

Not only did democratic deliberation promote education for making public judgment, it also promoted a more profound sense of political equality. By showing how fellow citizens helped one another to make important decisions, social centers provided substance to the often abstract principle of political equality. Charles Ferguson, a popular philosopher of sorts who made democracy into the highest ideal, influenced Edward Ward and stated most succinctly the idea that democratic deliberation promoted equality. According to Ferguson, in a democracy "every man becomes a teacher—and a learner." The democratic ideal for Ferguson and Ward meant that all citizens contributed to public debate in some way. Charles Evans Hughes, the governor of New York who visited Rochester's social centers in 1909, argued that social centers promoted a strong sense of civic equality: "The social center affords opportunity for intellectual development. Whether born in mansion, flat, or tenement, human beings are all pretty much alike. Only a very rash man would measure brains by the cost of their rearing." Citizens learned in social centers that they needed one another to come to intelligent public decisions. Only by coming together could citizens develop "clear thinking and good expression which need . . .

practice for development." Citizens helped teach one another the skills of public deliberation, and by deliberating together citizens learned to rely on one another. It did not matter what class or racial background a person came from, since a democratic public carved out a sphere in which citizens gathered as equals to listen to one another. What a person contributed to public dialogue was all that mattered. Through the collective process of deliberation citizens came to a deeper understanding of political equality.[12]

The more profound nature of social centers activists' understanding of the democratic public can be understood best by placing their reflections in historical context. The idea that "public opinion" should govern democratic politics climaxed during the Progressive Era, up until World War I. The era rang out with praise for public opinion. Josiah Royce wrote in 1908: "At the present time, our thoughtful public—the great company of those who read, reflect, and aspire—is a larger factor in our national life than ever before." During the early years of the twentieth century a market for an increasing number of national magazines flourished, and as more and more Americans received a high-school education, a general reading public blossomed. Muckrakers, those popular journalists who wrote exposés of industrial capitalism's worst forms of exploitation for this burgeoning reading public, hoped they could initiate reform by "creating an informed public opinion that would make progress possible." Although many of the muckrakers' writings degenerated into moral exhortation, these writers and journalists made clear that "informed public opinion" was a steering force in a healthy democracy.[13]

Social centers activists echoed their era's faith in public opinion yet went beyond their contemporaries' shallower celebration of the concept. They understood that without institutions where citizens could deliberate, "intelligent public opinion" would never develop. To make public opinion and judgment truly effective, citizens had to contextualize and deliberate on the "facts" and stories provided by journalists and muckrakers (as well as on the stories told by politicians). Social centers activists understood that the mass media alone could not produce good public judgment. Without the aid of other institutions promoting deliberation, the media would only generate a *passive* reading public much too reliant on the media's power. As seen already, social centers activists argued that "information regarding the facts" was worthless without "the interpretation which the other members" of society offered. As social centers activists saw it, the media was controlled by the principle of profit, thus making its claim to truth questionable at best. In any case, the print media did not promote the give-

and-take process of public discussion that the social centers promoted. By insisting that public opinion grew out of local forums and face-to-face discussions, social centers activists adopted the Progressive Era's faith in public opinion but created institutions in which public opinion could actually develop and become effective.[14]

Social centers activists also had a much more profound understanding of a democratic public's importance, that is, what values it promoted and what lessons it held. Not surprisingly, certain activists believed social centers promoted the liberal value of tolerance. By talking with different people, citizens came to accept difference. But to stop here would be to miss much of the insight that social centers held. Tolerance was not the ultimate goal of social centers, for when taken to its fullest extent, tolerance becomes mere relativism (the flattening of all opinions to one even level), something social centers activists did not promote. Edward Ward believed that *better* positions could come out of discussions with varied viewpoints, for in the process of discussing and making a decision, citizens would decide what aspects of certain viewpoints could be held to and which could not. To say that Ward preached tolerance ignores his faith that deliberation led to *better* political decisions and judgments.

Though they did not believe in tolerance, social centers activists did promote the idea that people must listen to one another. Anyone who came to a civic club debate understood that they had to respect the merit of people's ideas and that they could not attack people's characters, only their arguments. But instead of labeling this idea tolerance, we should understand it more as promoting the principles of respect, civility, and critical discussion. By entering the public world of politics, citizens treated one another with respect based on equal standards of public dialogue and judgment, standards inimical to mere tolerance.[15]

Social centers activists embraced the important skills generated in a democratic public, and they firmly believed that a democratic public was essential for American politics and could not be fit within a rigid political ideology of right or left. During the Progressive Era critics attacked social centers, calling them "socialistic centers." Today, however, historians like Edward Stevens argue that social centers were antiradical means of social control. These criticisms illustrate how the idea of a democratic public transcends rigid political categories and why it should not be seen in strict ideological terms but rather as a source of political health no matter what one's ideology might be. For in the end, a democratic public assures that all political viewpoints will receive a fair hearing.

With this in mind, certain features of social centers activists' thoughts on a democratic public seem conservative. Drawing upon the political thought of Walter Bagehot, a prominent British liberal during the nineteenth century, Edward Ward argued that deliberation and discussion promote "cautious, all-considering procedure . . . and the prevention of hasty and impulsive action." Thus Edward Stevens argued that Rochester's Board of Education "took the position . . . that radical and unprogressive views could best be kept in check by exposing them to the rigors of debate." Stevens suggests that the "rigors of debate" act as conservative forces. Yet Walter Bagehot, Ward's seemingly conservative hero, also asserted: "The mere putting up of a subject to discussion, with the object of being guided by that discussion, is a clear admission that that subject is in no degree settled by established rule, and that men are free to choose in it." Democratic discussion is neither conservative nor radical but both. It is open to new ideas but requires that these ideas be put to the table of discussion and be thoughtfully analyzed, not acted upon immediately. A democratic public serves as the only source for a healthy political situation in which citizens engage questions and make intelligent—not hasty—political decisions. In their understanding of this, social centers thinkers like Edward Ward moved beyond rigid political ideologies. A democratic public was too important to sacrifice to the outlooks of political dogmatists.[16]

If it is difficult to fit social centers activists and intellectuals into a conservative or radical mold, what traditions did they draw from? Certain contemporary social theorists assert that modern ethical theory and political philosophy must be pluralistic and conflicted, not unified. Social centers activists were, of course, not aware of contemporary ethical philosophy, but they seemed to have discovered these lessons long before present-day philosophers. From a communitarian tradition in American social thought they drew out the idea that politics grew out of locales where political issues could be made real and dealt with in face-to-face forums. Community consciousness was a necessary basis for a healthy politics. But social centers activists also drew from a liberal tradition that celebrated the principle of "public justification" and the idea that political equality and rational deliberation—universal principles that transcended local communities—must shape politics. They understood that politics could not be rooted solely in local communities, for if it was, it could stagnate under the pressure of local traditions and norms. Thus, social centers intellectuals extended their vision to the wider public world. By both evading simplistic celebrations of community but also recognizing the importance of locality, social centers intellectuals created a complex vision of political action. Their complexity was a major source of their insight.[17]

Their recognition of a democratic public's importance not only made them powerful thinkers, it also led them to a critical analysis of the concept of citizenship. A democratic public awakened these activists and intellectuals to a common good beyond individual selves. When individuals entered a democratic public, they recognized a world outside of themselves and no longer remained private beings but instead became citizens. Public life and citizenship grew reciprocally. Social centers activists reflected upon this connection between the democratic public and citizenship in interesting and provocative ways.[18]

Modern Participatory Citizenship

> Now, "good citizenship" is more than obedience. Good citizenship in a democracy is the consciousness of responsibility, not only for obeying the government but for participation in being the government.
>
> —Edward Ward[19]

The idea of citizenship grew out of a republican tradition of political thought. For republican thinkers from Aristotle to Machiavelli to certain colonial Americans, the citizen provided the key to a healthy political community. For republicans, a virtuous citizen bore arms and boldly defended the republic against attacks. He—and the masculine is intended here—had enough property to provide independence from others and thus make independent political decisions with others. As J.G.A. Pocock explained: "A citizen, constantly involved with his fellows in the making of public decisions, must possess an intellectual armory which takes him beyond the perception of hierarchy and tradition, and gives him cause to rely on his and his fellows' power to understand and respond to what is happening to him." The virile and virtuous citizen provided the basis of a republic. According to Gordon Wood: "A republic was such a delicate polity precisely because it demanded an extraordinary moral character in the people."[20]

The republican tradition of political thought was made up of many different strains. As Pocock and others have pointed out, elitist republican thinkers placed their hopes in a disinterested aristocracy while populist republican thinkers believed in the common person and citizen-soldier.

Debates still rage between scholars about the various meanings of republican political thought, and this is not the place to settle these debates. Nonetheless, we have to pay attention to certain features of republican thought, since it provided the major source of thinking about the idea of citizenship. Social centers activists adopted certain strains of this thought but also made an important transition away from republican thinking to what is best understood as modern democratic political thought. It is important to understand the constellation of ideas in republican political thought to figure out what social centers thinkers borrowed and what they creatively ignored.[21]

Republican political thought in America was predominantly an ideology of opposition. American revolutionaries who argued against the corruption of the British throne were the first to adopt republican ideas from their radical British counterparts. Later, members of the newly formed Republican Party, led by Thomas Jefferson, argued against the policies of Alexander Hamilton (especially his support of manufactures and a national bank) along republican lines. Republican ideas were well suited to opposition leaders. In the first place, republican thinkers feared corruption based on a cyclical history that saw republics constantly degenerating into empires obsessed with wealth (the story of Athens and Rome). Due largely to the influence of Puritanism, American republican thinkers were especially fearful of a corruption grown out of man's sinful nature. Republican fears of corruption were also tied to an economic argument that stressed the importance of a citizen's status as an independent producer. The basis of this idea was that a farmer who owned his own land could not be influenced or bribed by a large landowner who would threaten the farmer's ability to make critical decisions for the common good. As well, an independent farmer would be able to bear arms to defend the republic. In essence, property and arms bestowed independence. In America this republican principle became what historians call producerism—a belief that those who created value with their hands (farmers and independent craft producers) were more virtuous than those who did not. Finally, republican thinkers also valued older ideals of government, stressing the British theory, which stemmed from Aristotle, that a constitution should separate powers (the one, the few, and the many personified in the king, the nobles, and the commons). These beliefs were central to American republican thought during the Revolutionary period and the late eighteenth century.

Clearly, the world of social centers activists—the modern world as we know it today—differed greatly from the world of republican political thinkers of the Revolutionary period. Nonetheless, social centers thinkers preserved the central concept of republican political thought—a virtuous citizen concerned with a common good. In certain ways social centers thinkers drew on one strain in republican thought captured partially in the thinking of Thomas Paine but more so in the ideas of Thomas Jefferson. Jefferson continued an important line in republican thought by making the health of a republic dependent on the virtue of its citizens.

What mattered more than this residue of republican thought was the way in which Jefferson began making revisions. Though he believed in the virtue of independent, yeoman farmers (the "chosen people" of Virginia, as he saw it) and balanced government, Jefferson also believed in preparing citizens for universal manhood suffrage. Jefferson clearly placed his faith in the American Revolution, but when the event came to an end, he did not believe the Constitution was enough to preserve the American republic's virtue. Nor did he believe in bearing arms or owning land as the only basis of a future American citizenship. Instead, influenced by Scottish Enlightenment thinkers as much as by ancient political theorists, Jefferson saw critical enlightenment through public education as being the best source for a democratic citizenry. This was a critical transition in republican political thought.

While making this transition, though, Jefferson preserved the idea that participation in self-government should still serve as a display of an educated citizen's virtue. To make the daily participation of citizens in government a reality, Jefferson suggested that America be divided into small political wards. By doing this America would acquire a form of government "where every man is a sharer in the direction of his ward-republic; . . . and feels that he is a participator in the government of affairs, not merely at an election one day in the year, but every day." In essence, to make democratic citizens, Jefferson looked to modern enlightenment principles and political decentralization, not to older republican ideals. Public education and small wards ensured the growth of a modern citizenship capable of democratic self-government.[22]

In certain ways social centers thinkers simply built upon Jefferson's ideas of citizenship. They made the values of enlightenment inform citizenship more than the independent ownership of property. In doing so social centers activists helped develop a strong tradition in American political thought—a modern theory of participatory citizenship and democracy. They did not renew all the constellations of republican political thought but creatively chose what they thought important while discarding the more ancient residues and replacing them with a modern basis. This was the central intellectual move in creating a theory of modern participatory citizenship.[23]

There were certainly some social centers activists who spoke as if their task was to renew the classical world of politics. For instance, Edward Ward compared "the citizenship in America" to "the Roman citizenship in the great days of the republic." But normally those enamored with social centers did not make direct analogies; they thought of America as a republic but certainly not an ancient one like Rome or Athens (both of which, it should be noted, used slavery as the basis of economic production). According to Henry Campbell, the president of Milwaukee's Federation of Civic Societies: "It is no exaggeration to say that in making the schoolhouse the forum of the people lies the chief hope of perpetuating the republic and of perfecting its institutions." William Pieplow, another Milwaukeean involved in the social centers movement, argued, "The existence and perpetuation of American institutions depend upon the intelligence as well as the integrity of the citizenship." A modern republic was to be an assemblage of smaller publics based in neighborhoods. Only here could democratic citizens educate themselves. Nonetheless, modern citizens were not like ancient ones: they depended less on property and more on enlightenment and intelligence—values that are modern, democratic, and inclusive. M. Clyde Kelly articulated this conception of modern republican citizenship when he said, "We must have faith that an enlightened citizenship can be trusted with self-government." Not property or virility (or even balanced government) but widespread critical enlightenment was now the most important source of citizenship.[24]

If social centers activists did not renew the republican conception of citizenship, from what traditions did they draw their ideas? First, social centers intellectuals drew from a viewpoint based on the idea of community, a concept that was central to much Progressive Era social thought. But, as has already been argued, community was not perceived by social centers thinkers in terms of traditions or blood ties. Instead, community denoted social interaction that drew a citizen beyond the private realm of the self. By being tied to local communities, citizens could recognize something beyond their own self-interest and accept responsibility to make their communities better. Henry Curtis, someone normally concerned with the recreational side of the movement, understood that if social centers were established everywhere, "the citizen would become such a vital member of the community that civic pride and loyalty would be developed, and he would not consent that his city or ward should be misgoverned." In local neighborhoods citizens recognized their interconnectedness and found "a sense of civic responsibility, a strong local tradition, a regard for the opinions, rights and privileges of others, and most important of all a spirit of cooperation for mutual welfare." Local communities taught people that they had obligations to others, not only rights and privileges. By bringing people in local communities together and stressing the need for political initiative from below, social centers helped citizens recognize this fact.[25]

Though they stressed community, social centers activists did not want citizens to conform to local community rules and customs. Instead, citizens had to be critical while participating in local political life. M. Clyde Kelly traced the difference between conformity and citizenship: "Good citizenship is vastly more than obedience; it is the knowledge of responsibility, the active participation in the government." The stress here on active participation prevented Kelly from accepting a weak conception of citizenship. For Kelly, "Voting is but one phase of the duty of citizenship." Thus, in addition to citizenship's requiring more than voting or being a member of the community, it required autonomous initiative in community affairs, critical thinking, and commitment to public deliberation. Social centers intellectuals placed their hope in a continual process of collective self-education and critical enlightenment. The balance they drew out between community and enlightenment was difficult but utterly central to their conception of a modern and democratic form of political thought.[26]

Besides being a critical member of a community, a citizen always moved beyond the local community in order to consider the concerns of a wider public. To think purely in local terms about community issues would not be enough. A community was always a part of a larger collectivity—be it a society or a nation. The modern citizen had to enter not just the local community but also the wider public world and thereby develop skills of public deliberation. A constitutional preamble of a Rochester civic club explained that good citizenship required "the cultivation of the powers of clear thinking and good expression by means of debates, essays, orations, public readings, and discussions." Social centers activists believed a good citizen was informed, critical, "enlightened," and capable of deliberation and public judgment. A good citizen thus developed the best side of the modern world's values—autonomy, self-rule, and rationality—while transcending the worst aspects of modernity—self-interest and public apathy. By participating in public life, a citizen developed these values gradually.[27]

Participatory citizenship, nourished by a democratic public, constituted a major component of social centers activists' political vision. This was no renewal of classical republicanism. Social centers activists never spoke of building a virtuous citizenry through bearing arms to protect a city-state, exhibiting male virility, or owning enough property to become independent. Rather, they spoke the language of another strong tradition in American politics—the tradition of enlightenment and democracy. As George Forbes put it: "The very foundation of the movement was built upon the underlying assumption of democracy that the spirit of good-will is in the average man, and that this spirit may become dominant." Drawing on Jefferson's views, social centers activists believed citizens needed to be provided with the means to develop enlightened ideas in small public settings. This was the basis of their democratic faith. But when social centers activists spoke of the tradition of democracy, what did they mean by this? How exactly, to use Governor Hughes's word, did social centers activists "buttress the foundations of democracy"? What sort of democracy were they hoping to create?[28]

What Type of Democracy?

> Congress and the legislatures are no longer deliberative bodies. If we are to secure the benefit of all-sided discussion anywhere, it must be in the assembly of ourselves, the citizens.
>
> —Frank Walsh[29]

Anyone who reflects on the concept of democracy quickly realizes that the term holds various meanings. It can easily become rhetorical and completely devoid of deeper meaning. Social centers activists realized the term democracy could become all too vague, which is why George Forbes argued that social centers created "*real* democracy." *Real* democracy required much more than the *formal* freedoms liberalism promised. For instance, whereas many modern democrats stressed the constitutional right to free speech, social centers activists focused on how to make political speech truly effective. Real democracy did not just uphold the right to free speech; it provided forums where people *used* their right in an active and powerful manner. As this one example illustrates, real democracy grew out of ordinary, everyday practices open to average citizens—not out of abstract values.[30]

Critical of liberal democracy, social centers activists believed democracy entailed more than merely voting for candidates. Forbes wrote: "The problem of democracy can never be solved by merely giving a man the right to vote." Hoping to balance rights and duties, these activists believed the right to vote required the duty to think, reflect, and collectively deliberate. Edward Ward argued that the school should become not only a place for voting (which it has) but also deliberating (which it has not). For Ward this arrangement would capture "the idea that intelligent voting presupposes orderly assembly for *deliberation*, which is today practiced by every subordinate public body." By calling for this balance of rights and duties, social centers activists understood that voting was not, as some liberals argued, a private choice but rather a public act that required collective deliberation. Voting involved a choice about public life, so citizens needed to listen and talk in public about their decisions. Democracy was about much more than private, formal choices.[31]

By stressing democracy, social centers activists resembled other progressives who wanted to make government responsive to citizens, not corrupt interests. But emphasizing the necessity of public deliberation meant social centers activists criticized the limits of certain democratic reforms made during the Progressive Era. For instance, although they agreed that the direct primary took control of political parties out of the hands of bosses and corrupt economic interests, they believed it would be meaningless if not coupled with public deliberation. Governor Hughes made this connection when he came to Rochester (see Chapter Three). Frank Walsh, President Wilson's chairman of the Commission on Industrial Relations, both endorsed the direct primary and argued, "With every schoolhouse a permanent primary, open to all shades of political belief, I hazard the prediction that within two years it will be considered as immoral to attempt by financial contributions to campaign funds to influence the citizens' choice as it now is to attempt financially to influence the acts of legislators." Although, like most progressives, they wanted to end political corruption, social centers activists believed that if citizens could not gather to deliberate in public spaces, the same forces corrupting politics would find new and more covert ways to do the same.[32]

Hoping to make the citizenry "itself a legislature," many argued that social centers should supplement the initiative and referendum, a key part of progressive political reform. George Forbes supported the movement to bring a commission form of government to Rochester in order to acquire the initiative and referendum. But Forbes and others knew that without forums for deliberation, citizens could not truly make use of these political tools. Henry Curtis explained this point:

> The last few years have seen a rapid advance through the initiative, referendum, and the recall, through the presidential primaries and other measures; but the fundamental unit is still unorganized. . . . To secure the popular rather than the boss control of the community or district is our great political problem. This demands that some agora, forum, or neighborhood center shall be provided.

Only by deliberating in forums and then enforcing their decisions through the initiative and referendum could citizens truly fight political corruption. A democratic public provided real substance to progressive reforms.[33]

What was the ultimate goal for social center democrats? They were not as concerned with direct election of senators or commission government as they were with creating more direct democracy based on a wide participation of all citizens. As M. Clyde Kelly put it, "The first basis of democratic government is active participation of the great mass of citizens." But social centers activists did not embrace mobocracy, as certain of their conservative critics thought they did. In the first place, they put emphasis on the thoughtful and often slow deliberation of citizens before political decisions were made. But just as important, they did not call for an end to America's system of representative government. Instead, they wanted to make political representatives truly representative by anchoring them in a democratic public created by citizens. George Forbes called politicians the "servants . . . of the people," and M. Clyde Kelly wanted to provide ways for people to "reach out and express their will to their agents in places of power." Only by making politicians enter into constant dialogue with citizens in public forums, Edward Ward argued, could "a man in office . . . reasonably be expected to be faithful to the public interest." Social centers activists did not believe in absolute direct democracy, but they did believe that only by forcing representatives to explain their actions to citizens gathered in democratic publics could politicians be prevented from becoming corrupt. Through debate citizens could prepare themselves for deliberating with politicians who had more power (and sometimes more knowledge of certain issues) than they did. Only deliberation could equalize political power in a representative democracy and make citizens sense that they could influence political decision making in powerful and intelligent ways.[34]

Social centers activists combined direct and representative democracy.

They hoped citizens would initiate legislation through the initiative and referendum, but they also wanted to retain a certain amount of independence for representatives. They hoped democracy could become more "real" and less abstract not by stressing the negative freedoms of liberalism, like freedom from censorship, but by defining positive freedoms like the right to make citizens' speech truly effective in political decision making by requiring representatives to listen to citizens' claims in public forums. By doing this Edward Ward hoped the social center could become "a place for the free discussion by citizens of the problems of democracy, a place wherein the true government, which is the citizenship, finds expression." This was, in essence, the central idea behind the social centers movement.[35]

Envisioning Democracy

Social centers activists not only tried to create a democratic public, they also understood why their effort was so important for modern politics. They argued forcefully that only a democratic public could create a healthy political situation. Without a forum where public deliberation took place and citizens developed critical insight on political issues, politics would boil down to crude power relations and corruption. A democratic public did not fit a conservative or radical strategy but was much more fundamental. It provided a substantive basis for all future democratic initiatives.

Only a democratic public could promote participatory citizenship. By entering the public world, a citizen discovered a public self that transcended the limits of the private self. Carole Pateman describes the process that social centers activists hoped to foster: "As a result of participating in decision-making the individual is educated to distinguish between his own impulses and desires; he learns to be a public as well as a private citizen." Only by accepting the responsibility entailed by political participation could citizens learn how to develop the skills of public judgment. Citizens became responsible by educating themselves into the process of making important political decisions about their future. Social centers activists understood that to take the promise of American democracy seriously required institutional reform that turned power over to regular citizens and at the same time ensured that they would have the capacity for education that prepared them for the responsibilities of citizenship.[36]

The visions of social centers activists grew out of a long tradition of democratic thought in America—a tradition that began with Thomas Jefferson and continued to blossom throughout the nineteenth century. These activists spoke an American language of democracy, and this partially explains why the movement became so well known during its time. But social centers thinkers also drew from other political traditions as well. From the developing communitarian thought of sociologists they developed the idea that citizenship required an understanding of human beings' interconnectedness. But they went beyond the limits of local communities. These thinkers both learned from and criticized liberalism. If on the one hand they appreciated liberalism's stress on the public world beyond communities and on more universalistic, rational values that stemmed from the Enlightenment project, on the other they understood that liberalism often emphasized negative rights at the expense of positive freedoms. Instead of stressing freedom of speech against censorship, social centers activists explored ways in which citizens' speech could become truly effective in guiding politics. Social centers thinkers drew from many traditions to understand how the American political imagination could be rejuvenated.

Social centers intellectuals faced up to the dynamics of modern life. Though they were critical of the apathy and selfishness that marked modernity, they celebrated the modern values of critical insight and enlightenment. They not only helped create institutions that fostered democratic action, they also taught Americans what values and ideals democratic action required and produced. They came up with creative insights by asking how modern citizens could be educated into the processes of political decision making and what institutions could help in this process. Exploring what ideas were necessary for healthy politics, these thinkers made important contributions to democratic theory. In their ideas and words can be glimpsed a deep and passionate understanding of the requirements of public life, citizenship, and democracy.

CHAPTER FIVE

THINKING DEMOCRATICALLY

The Political Thought of Mary Parker Follett

The essence of democracy is an educated and responsible citizenship evolving common ideas and willing its own social life.

—Mary Parker Follett[1]

Though Mary Parker Follett's social thought is similar to that of others involved in the social centers movement, it deserves special attention. In the first place, because of her experience in social centers Follett underwent important and serious changes in her intellectual development that illustrate how social centers could transform an intellectual's development and how democratic practice informed democratic theory. Beginning as a conformist political scientist, Follett became a radical democrat. Also, Follett, unlike the other writers in the movement, was a scholar and intellectual. She confronted the major political and philosophical thinkers of her day with what she learned in social centers. Follett's work illuminates how democratic theory was part of a wider intellectual context during the Progressive Era. Her political thought was the best intellectual work done on social centers and democracy. John Collier believed Follett provided the "experience and philosophy" of social centers in her writings. For these reasons her life and thought deserve special attention.[2]

The Life of a "Struggling Soul"

Addressing a funeral service for Follett in 1934, Richard Cabot, a professor of social ethics at Harvard University, claimed, "Mary Parker Follett was a struggling soul." Unfortunately, Cabot might have known more details of Follett's struggle than we do today. After her death many of Follett's papers were destroyed, and we still await a definitive biography of this remarkable woman. Nonetheless, with the help of surviving papers, letters, essays, and dissertations, we can reconstruct the most important chapters in Follett's life, tracing her developing interest in a democratic public.[3]

Born in Boston in 1868, Follett both epitomized and broke away from late-nineteenth-century New England culture. The opinion people had of her often reflected their opinion of her cultural background. Eduard Lindeman associated New England with Emerson and Thoreau and thus believed Follett belonged to "the high tradition of New England philosophic thought." Another acquaintance, who believed New England bred prudery, called Follett a "gaunt Boston spinster lady." Whatever people thought of her, Follett inherited New England values (especially the values growing out of small-town meetings) but reflected upon them to develop her own ideas and visions. Like Jane Addams and other middle-class women in the late nineteenth century, Follett received her education at a small academy. Unlike Addams, though, Follett pursued an academic career beyond this preliminary education. In 1892 she entered Radcliffe College, the women's branch of Harvard. For a brief period she traveled and studied in England, immersing herself in British political thought, and in 1898 she graduated summa cum laude from Radcliffe.[4]

Follett published the work she did at Radcliffe in *The Speaker of the House of Representatives* (1896). In this book Follett expressed no interest in a democratic public but instead produced a dull work in line with the emerging profession of political science. The book's obsession with details and painstaking research produced a work akin to Frederic Howe's early study of taxation. After tracing the growing power of the Speaker of the House and his domain (speaker by speaker, rule by rule), Follett argued: "The history of the House of Representatives shows that the consolidation of power has been an inevitable development." Americans, Follett believed, must accept this growing power and hope the Speaker could become more like England's premier (because of this comparison to England many people associated Follett's book with Woodrow Wilson's earlier classic, *Congressional Government*). Follett believed an even more powerful national government could consolidate if the legislature and the executive merged. Accepting this growing power of the government, Follett concluded, "We have long since passed the New England town meeting of all the voters; the democracy most to be desired, then, is that in which the representative assembly shall legislate for those who elect it." Thus, citizens played only a minor role in democratic government. Ironically, Follett articulated here a view of politics that critics of democracy would articulate later during the 1920s.[5]

Follett's work conformed to a developing consensus in professional political science. Accepting the growing power of the national state and the decline of old forms of self-government (town meetings), Follett embraced political realism and argued that federal power should become more unified and efficient. In a perceptive analysis of professional political science, Raymond Seidelman explains: "In place of the creaky and impersonal edifice of the nineteenth-century state, political scientists have sought a national state manned by trained experts and supported by responsible and virtuous democratic majorities." Not surprisingly, reviewers in academic journals (the venues where academic thought gained legitimacy) praised *The Speaker of the House.* Writing in the *Political Science Quarterly,* A. D. Morse called Follett's book a work of "rare excellence." In another review John Quincy Adams explained why the book deserved the scientific stamp of approval. Adams wrote: "This book shows a great amount of patient research. It is the kind of work which gives us an insight into the functional activity of government." By suggesting how the national government could function more efficiently, Follett made a major contribution to academic political science.[6]

The book was a success, but Follett did not pursue a traditional academic career. Not only were the doors to becoming a professor closed to women but calls to service and political activity dominated the time of Follett's graduation. Thus, women like Jane Addams rejected genteel culture for more rigorous work—fighting for social justice in American cities. Influenced by the spirit of her age, Follett also chose this type of activism. Staying in Boston after her graduation, Follett fell under the sway of Mrs. Quincy Shaw, "a daughter of Louis Agassiz and prominent contributor to civic projects." Mrs. Shaw encouraged Follett to become involved in local social-work efforts. Follett thus chose a path very similar to that of Jane Addams. In 1900, two years after her graduation, Follett began a new chapter in her life—urban activism.[7]

Social Centers and Democracy

From 1900 to 1908 Follett did social work in the Roxbury neighborhood of Boston, one of the city's poorer areas. Here she helped young people form a boys' club that provided recreational opportunities. Within the club Follett set up debating teams. Hoping to keep young men off city streets, Follett's activities from 1900 to 1908 smacked of what historians term "social control." For instead of achieving social justice, historians might argue, Follett merely indoctrinated working-class young men into middle-class values, thus creating a safety valve for the conflicts inherent in industrial capitalism. There might be some truth to this sort of assertion (though we can never know Follett's motivations). What can be known for certain is that after 1908 Follett chose a much more democratic form of activism. Joining with the newly formed Women's Municipal League, Follett began to organize social centers in public schools.[8]

Follett's social center activities in Boston mirrored those of Ward and others in Rochester. In 1908 (a year after Rochester's experiment began), she became chairperson of the Women's Municipal League's Committee on Extended Use of School Buildings. She wrote reports calling for people to support the effort, and in 1911 she helped open the East Boston High School Social Center. Citizens who participated in this social center organized a dramatic club, a recreation club, and an orchestra. The social center also served to coordinate other local neighborhood activities. Most important, though, was a "City Council" that, in Follett's words, took "up practical municipal questions each week" and was identical to a Rochester civic club. With the success of this social center, Follett helped out with the formation of many other ones throughout Boston.[9]

As Follett's activism became more democratic, so too did her ideas. Speaking at a Ford Hall Forum in 1913, Follett addressed the issue of "The Social Center and the Democratic Ideal." Taking up other social centers activists' call to "real democracy," she argued, "What we want is to make our democracy effective, telling, an actual fact. . . . Here we have the basis and the essence of effective good citizenship." Follett linked social centers to the larger goal of creating a democratic public. Writing in a committee report for the Women's Municipal League, Follett explained that the most important "step" social centers would take would be "when the different School Centres in different parts of the city find that they can, through chosen delegates, combine for a common end. Thus can be formed an intelligent public opinion expressing itself on all the important civic questions of the day." For Follett social centers and democracy were now inseparable.[10]

But this connection was not so simple to make. Undoubtedly due in part to her academic background, Follett became interested in the intellectual justifications for the social centers movement. Since organizing provoked interesting intellectual issues for her, Follett wanted to address these issues more forcefully. She explained in 1913: "Let us be neither hasty nor careless in our advocacy of the extended use of school buildings, but let us endeavor first to find the true principles upon which such an extended use should rest, and then let us use every effort of which we are capable to secure a public acceptance of these principles." After 1913 Follett became less active at the local level. Though becoming vice president of the National Community Center Association in 1917, Follett turned most of her attention to writing for a wider public about what social centers had taught her about democracy. She was now struggling to find those "true principles" for the democratic public.[11]

A "New State" for the Progressive Era

Follett radically changed her political ideas from those found in *The Speaker of the House*, for social centers had taught her a great deal about democracy. No longer concerned with the major political institutions of America, Follett focused on the activities in social centers. She now assumed that a better politics was to be based not on a stronger House of Representatives but rather on the "organization of men in small, local groups" and the association of citizens and groups together in a wider democratic public. It is remarkable that the same woman who wrote about the need to accept representative institutions in *Speaker of the House* now argued, "Representation is not the main fact of political life; the main concern of politics is *modes of association*." Follett radically resituated politics from the national government to the local community. She wrote: "You cannot establish democratic control by legislation . . . ; there is only one way to get democratic control—by people learning how to evolve collective ideas." Follett's change of mind since *The Speaker of the House of Representatives* speaks to the power of democratic experience. Having witnessed regular citizens organize their own events and discuss politics intelligently in social centers, she herself started to think democratically.[12]

These ideas were new to Follett, and when she set to writing *The New State* (1918), her romantic embrace of these ideas found expression. Whereas reviewers praised the dispassionate research found in *The Speaker of the*

House of Representatives, they complained about Follett's abundant enthusiasm in her new work. But the style was appropriate, since it reflected Follett's discovery that politics could be full of passion—that public life with its conflict and contention could be thrilling. She wrote: "My gospel is not for a moment of citizenship as mere duty. We must bring to politics passion and joy" (340). Follett no longer saw politics as political scientists did—as a set of administrative problems to be solved by bureaucratic institutions in order to maintain order. Instead, she saw in public life its pleasures—its cooperation and contention, its excitement and meaning. This belief in a passionate public life seriously challenged liberal political thinking that conceptualized public institutions as necessary evils to protect private needs like property and ensure social order. Where liberals saw public life as an administrative imperative, Follett saw in it human fulfillment based on the joys of association.[13]

Like other social centers activists, Follett embraced the ideas of participatory citizenship and the democratic public. She believed that any political theory that sought means to bypass citizens only fooled itself. Following the tenets of republican political thought, Follett believed a political body's health relied upon the state of its citizens. She argued that "not upon socialism or any rule or any order any plan or any utopia can we rest our hearts, but only on the force of a united and creative citizenship" (8). For Follett, as with other social centers activists, the democratic citizen was committed to public dialogue (313) and strived to be "ever-active" and "articulate" (184). Though the democratic citizen should be open to new experiences and the contingency of politics (38), this did not entail mindless tolerance. When in a meeting citizens should "not subordinate" themselves but "must affirm [themselves] and give [their] full positive value to that meeting" (26). Follett believed the democratic citizen should be passionate, for "it is not opposition but indifference that separates men" (212). Both passionate and open to difference, the democratic citizen lived a challenging ethic.

Though her ideas on citizenship mirrored those of other social centers activists, the rest of her thought was more original. Follett was not merely an activist but an intellectual and scholar. After her experience in Boston's social centers she found herself drawn back to the world of books and immersed herself in the philosophical and political thinking of her time. There was much to be immersed in. As one reviewer put it, "Miss Follett knows her Hegel, her Duguit, her James, her Roscoe Pound, her Harold Laski. She knows her particularism, her syndicalism, her guild socialism, her dualism, her pluralism." Follett believed she could learn from the social thought of her day, and she believed her experience in social centers had something to teach social philosophers.[14]

Follett provided her readers with a philosophical account of what happened in social centers. She discovered a "group process" in the political discussions at social centers. This idea began with a simple premise of the German philosopher G.W.F. Hegel and with progressive social thought: human beings are social animals and become conscious of themselves only through interaction with other humans. Though the idea was simple, it challenged many presuppositions of Western liberal thought based on individualism. As the intellectual historian James Kloppenberg has shown, the stress on "intersubjectivity" (both as a basis of knowledge and politics) caused an intellectual revolution. Follett was a part of this intellectual revolution that took place at the end of the nineteenth century and continued into the twentieth. Building upon the new emphasis on intersubjectivity, Follett argued that the "group process" found in the "democratic community" would help reinvent politics. Like other Progressive Era intellectuals, she politicized the sociological assumptions of her day and age. But unlike other Progressive Era intellectuals, Follett located the most important manifestation of intersubjectivity in social centers. For here people in local communities came together for "discussion"—an "experiment in cooperation" (97); through this process they became conscious of one another's ideas. They then synthesized their ideas into political decisions. Follett called this process "interpenetration."[15]

"Interpenetration" was central to Follett's social thought. Whereas John Dewey already had rejected Hegelian idealism for pragmatism by the 1900s, Mary Parker Follett embraced both pragmatism and the idealism of Hegel and her own contemporary Josiah Royce. "Interpenetration" was a Hegelian idea through and through, but it was also an empirical process Follett believed she saw taking place in the political discussions held at social centers. She described the process as "an acting and reacting, a single and identical process which brings out differences and integrates them into a unity" (33). Citizens at meetings did not compromise their ideas; instead, they released them into a process of give-and-take that both preserved and changed them. Interpenetration taught that "differences must be integrated, not annihilated, nor absorbed" (39). A new synthesis came out of discussion—one that preserved the original insights of different ideas while going beyond them. This process would repeat itself as new discussions took place. Follett believed this to be the essence of the activities found in social centers and what made them a truly creative force in American politics.

Follett also believed the idea of interpenetration could shed light on contemporary philosophical debates. Writing to a colleague right after *The New State* was published, Follett explained her concern with the debate between idealism and empiricism (or pragmatism). Previous to *The New State,* this debate raged between two American philosophers—Josiah Royce, an idealist philosopher, and William James, a pragmatic empiricist. At the time of Follett's writing, British idealists like Bernard Bosanquet argued with pluralists like Harold Laski, who embraced empirical pragmatism. Though her sympathies were with idealism, she explained: "I am beginning to see the synthesis of idealism and realism so clearly." Whereas idealism celebrated unity, realism stressed plurality and difference. Follett believed interpenetration preserved both outlooks, for the unity achieved by interpenetration derived from pluralism and difference. The way citizens in social centers forged agreements was not by foreordaining them but by letting loose a process that allowed different ideas to clash and work off one another.

Thus, Follett believed that the processes taking place in social centers showed how pragmatism and idealism could be welded together. Though an idealist in many ways, she did not believe in objective ideals (i.e., a universal sense of justice, etc.), as did Plato and Hegel. Nor did she believe philosophers could discover or objectively ground answers to life's basic questions. She prized democratic deliberation too much to subscribe to either of these beliefs. Instead, Follett argued that the dialogue of regular citizens in social centers could reach a higher synthesis rather than just remaining a collection of disparate opinions. This faith in synthesis growing out of a democratic and empirical process was Follett's idealistic moment, so to speak. For Follett the democratic processes in social centers showed philosophers how, in one way, they might evade the endless debate between idealism and realism by synthesizing the best from both approaches.[16]

Follett argued that social theorists as well as philosophers had something to learn from the processes in social centers. She juxtaposed her ideas of the "group process" and "interpenetration" to the "law of the crowd" (23). Social thinkers like Gustave Le Bon and Robert Park had dissected the "law of the crowd" before Follett. They saw in modern social congregations (especially in urban settings) regressive and irrational tendencies based on a mob mentality. Follett merely asserted that the group process involved thoughtful debate and contention whereas the "law of the crowd" was based on manipulation and suggestion. Since the group process and interpenetration grew out of deliberation and a give-and-take process based on discussion, Follett believed they illustrated how social congregations need not degenerate into a mobocracy or mass society.[17]

The "group process" Follett endorsed grew out of continuous, collective self-education of citizens. Unfortunately, modern life compartmentalized daily activities: education took place only inside the walls of the schools, while politics centered in institutions like Congress. Though she had nothing against book learning (indeed, she had done her fair share), Follett, like other social centers activists, believed real education occurred in communities when people learned about political issues and practiced self-government. She argued: "Citizenship is not to be learned in good government classes or current events courses or lessons in civics." After all, these lessons were divorced from everyday life. "[Citizenship] is to be acquired only through those modes of living and acting which shall teach us how to grow the social consciousness" (363). The conclusion about education was obvious: "Life and education must never be separated. We must have more life in our universities, more education in our life" (369). The democratic group process of deliberation rooted itself in everyday life; out of this process grew politics and education.

By stressing the group process found in local arenas, Follett became one of America's first "communitarian critics of liberalism." She lambasted the liberal conception of the individual, arguing that the lone self gained consciousness only by relating to others. Following the revolution in liberal thought led by the British political thinker T. H. Green, Follett believed liberalism's negative rights—those that stressed freedom *from* certain obstacles—were not enough. These rights gave the "individual . . . no large positive function" (164). Only by situating persons within networks of association could they become fully effective individuals. Follett wrote: "A man is ideally free only so far as he is interpermeated by every other human being; he gains his freedom through a perfect and complete relationship because thereby he achieves his whole nature" (69). While liberal democracy based itself on the private act of voting and mass majority rule or what Follett cleverly called the "reign of numbers" (142), the new democracy would stress public deliberation and decision making at the local level. It was not, as liberals believed, out of national legislative bodies that democracy grew but out of local communities.[18]

But Follett was no simple communitarian. Like her fellow social centers activists, she did not embrace communitarian solidarity or shared values. Instead of talking abstractly about community (as contemporary communitarian philosophers often do), Follett held up the urban neighborhood as her example. Here was an important argument that distinguished the idea of a democratic public from the idea of a community (see Chapter Four). For in a healthy neighborhood people who differed from one another interacted. This type of provincialism made local people more interesting than "cosmopolitan" people who sought out homogeneous social situations. Follett explained: "Why are provincial people more interesting than cosmopolitan [people], that is, if provincial people have taken advantage of *their* opportunities? Because cosmopolitan people are all alike—that has been the aim of their existence and they have accomplished it" (195).

In contrast, the neighborhood was not based on shared values nor did it represent what Ferdinand Tonnies, the German sociologist, called "Gemeinschaft"—a tightly knit community of blood and tradition. Instead, for Follett a certain amount of "diversity" characterized the modern neighborhood (199). In a free society no one could entirely *choose* their neighbors; instead, people had to face up to heterogeneity. This was good since "the satisfaction and contentment that comes with sameness indicates a meager personality" (196). Follett argued: "In a neighborhood group you have the stimulus and the bracing effect of many different experiences and ideals" (196). For Follett politics originated with groups of diverse people dealing with the problems of living together. The neighborhood, not the tight-knit "Gemeinschaft," was the right location for politics.[19]

Follett's suspicion of a simpleminded communitarianism also came out in her criticism of the British pluralist thinkers J. N. Figgis, Harold Laski, and G.D.H. Cole. Pluralists feared the power of the national state and proposed that local groups like churches, unions, and voluntary associations provide the basis of a new politics. As Figgis, one of the earliest pluralists, explained: "More and more it is clear that the mere individual's freedom against an omnipotent state may be no better than slavery; more and more is it evident that the real question of freedom in our day is the freedom of smaller unions to live within the whole." Although Follett called pluralism the "most important theory of politics before us" (263), when she closely examined its assumptions, she found that it reached quick limits. Follett put it bluntly: "The imagination of the born pluralist stops with the group" (283). By pitting the local association against the state, Follett argued that pluralists denied the possibility of a public world beyond small groups.

Follett did not glamorize localism, though she believed politics started in local arenas. A number of Follett's ideas distinguished her from pluralist political thinkers. First, the neighborhood was much more open than the public groups (especially churches and voluntary groups) that the pluralists celebrated. Neighborhoods were not based on limited membership or a clearly established goal like voluntary groups. Second, for Follett a wider public life existed and was necessary for a healthy political life. Without a faith in a common good and the wider world of public justification and discussion, politics would disintegrate into an "egoism of the group" (306). Follett explained by using a modern analogy: "When you stop your automobile without stopping your engine, the power which runs your car goes on working exactly the same, but is completely lost. It only makes a noise. Do we want this to happen to our groups? Are they to end only in disagreeable noises?" (285). For Follett the wider public world grew out of local associations federating together. There was to be *both* the local group and the wider world. She argued: "Authority is to proceed from the Many to the One, from the smallest neighborhood group up to the city, the state, the nation" (284). Without the community democracy would be empty; without the wider public politics would be chaos.[20]

Precisely for this reason Follett renewed an old tradition in American political thought—federalism. But she did not renew federalism as a constitutional principle. Instead, she saw in federalism a general way of thinking about politics. Here Follett followed Harold Laski, the most articulate pluralist. She believed federalism preserved the autonomy of the local group while bringing it into a higher unity with other groups. Unlike Laski, Follett saw federalism as a political concept that saw unity growing out of difference: "The federal state is the unifying state" (301). For Follett federation meant groups federating, that is, joining together. But it should be noted that Follett did not celebrate American federalism as it existed in her own time, for, as she stated, "we have not indeed a true federalism in the United States today" (299). To found a federalist government, the starting point had to be the local neighborhood—not the states. In this way Follett was much more concrete than Laski when addressing what federalism required. "Every neighborhood must be organized; the neighborhood groups must then be integrated, through larger intermediary groups, into a true state" (245). Neighborhoods would federate into a city, cities would federate into states, and states would federate into the nation. In doing so the local group would maintain its autonomy and power yet not lose sight of a wider public world to which it belonged. Follett rediscovered the essence of federalism—"the process of the Many becoming One." Without legitimacy working itself up from the local associations of citizens practicing self-government, there was no legitimacy.[21]

By combining insights from different thinkers and her experience in social centers, Follett developed a coherent political vision that she believed could revitalize American public life. Local neighborhoods would be relatively autonomous to deal with their own problems, but they would also federate together and integrate into a wider city government and eventually into a nation. Trusting neither the state bureaucracy nor the power of the market, Follett placed her faith in a public generated from below by regular citizens. This was a concrete vision. As a sign of hope Follett could point to social center activities and the growth in the number of social centers across America from 1907 onward. If relevant deliberation in school centers could be tied into the spread of the initiative and referendum, "real democracy" might flourish. The state of public deliberation and democracy itself would be saved from below.

It was Follett's stress on democratic deliberation that distinguished her political vision from that of other Progressive Era intellectuals. At the time Follett wrote, Herbert Croly, Walter Lippmann, and John Dewey, all of whom were associated with the magazine *The New Republic*, were the leading liberal intellectuals of the time. Follett corresponded with Croly and was clearly influenced by John Dewey's social thought. All of these thinkers drew on similar intellectual traditions and innovations. But in many ways Follett's ideas shed light on a weakness and important oversight in the thought of her contemporaries. Certainly, Croly understood the importance of democracy in relation to progressive reform. In his most important work, *Progressive Democracy*, he explained: "The great object of progressives must always be to create a vital relation between progressivism and popular political education." Nonetheless, Croly rarely set out how this vital relation would actually operate. Though Croly and Lippmann talked about democracy, they rarely explained how progressive reform would enhance citizen participation. In some ways the weakness in their thought was due to their conception of the role of the intellectual. Croly and Lippmann became enamored with the idea of becoming political consultants to politicians working on national policies (be it Roosevelt or Wilson). Follett, instead, committed herself to building a new state from the bottom up and had gained most of her experience from working with regular citizens at the local level. Unlike Croly and Lippmann, Follett believed the association of citizens in local publics could transform the American political system and American conceptions of democracy. She paid far more attention to "popular political education" than did Croly, and she set out a theoretical and institutional vision for making "popular political education" actually work.[22]

When Croly did briefly turn to the issue of political education (Walter Lippmann never did), he failed to see that this educational process had to be democratic itself. Croly argued for the formation of a "National School of Political Science." This school would train educators who would then take their progressive ideas to the general public. There was nothing terribly democratic about this vision of political education. It conceived of the public as a passive receptor of ideas generated by intellectuals. The public's role, as far as Croly seemed to conceive of it, was to exchange one set of older ideas for another.

Follett, on the other hand, understood that political education had to be democratic and grow out of the activities of regular citizens. In this way Follett followed John Dewey's theory of democratic and participatory education, but instead of putting an emphasis on school reform, as did Dewey, she believed that democratic reform efforts should focus on political associations of adults, not young students. Follett argued that political reform would be useless unless citizens played a major role in political deliberation. To ensure citizens played such a role, she called for political decentralization and the neighborhood serving as the core unit of political education. In these ways Follett went far beyond Croly's feeble discussion of political education. Follett might have embraced Croly's general vision of "progressive democracy," but she also explained how collective and democratic education could take place and improve the political decision making of average citizens. This was Follett's most important move beyond her intellectual contemporaries, and it explains the significance of her political thought for the Progressive Era in general.[23]

Reevaluating Follett and the Radical Nature of the Democratic Public

Despite Follett's interesting political vision, the few historians who have examined her ideas have dismissed them. The work of Jean Quandt has already been discussed in Chapter Four. Following Jean Quandt's belittling of communitarian social thought as uncritical nostalgia, R. Jeffrey Lustig takes on Follett's social thought. Of all the "group theorists" Lustig dismantles Follett comes out the best. "Mary Parker Follett came closest to a truly democratic vision with her emphasis on neighborhood participation," Lustig correctly explains. But Lustig then skims over Follett's stress on democratic deliberation and her difference from other Progressive Era intellectuals. Instead, he asserts that she concerned herself more with "unity" than with the political processes of contention and conflict. Misunderstanding Follett's conception of group unity, Lustig dismisses her too easily. Once again historians reject the thought that grew out of social centers.[24]

It should be clear that Follett neither plotted a subtle form of social control nor turned away from radicalism. In fact, she argued, "People often speak of 'self-expression' as if it were a letting off of steam, as if there were something inside us that must be let out before it explodes. But this is not the use to which we must put the powers of self-expression; we must release these powers not to be wasted through a *safety-valve*, but to be used constructively for the good of society" (209; my emphasis). For Follett self-government and free political deliberation—which were both open processes—were for the good of society. Instead of planning a scheme of social control, Follett and other social centers activists explored the *radical* potential of democratic deliberation and how it necessitated serious political reform. It is of no surprise that New Left historians like Lustig ignore this. Follett's writings illustrate how very often the idea of participatory democracy can provide a more radical starting point for social criticism than does socialism.

The term *radical* means going to the root and being dissatisfied with superficial change. Contrary to other Progressive Era intellectuals like Herbert Croly and Walter Lippmann, Follett insisted that a democratic public came before all other reforms. In her introduction to *The New State* she argued:

> The first reform needed in our political practice is to find some method by which the government shall continuously represent the people. No state can endure unless the political bond is being forever forged anew. The organization of men in small local groups gives opportunity for this continuous political activity which ceaselessly creates the state. (11)

Though Follett believed in direct democracy, she understood that without a deliberating public capable of making collective decisions about key issues, direct democracy would be a farce. She wrote: "We all know, and we can see every year if we watch the history of referendum votes, that the party organization is quite able to use 'direct government' for its own ends. ... Direct government can be beneficial to American politics only if accompanied by the organization of voters in nonpartisan groups for the production of common ideas and a collective purpose" (178). Without ensuring the institutional means through which citizens could educate themselves about the issues of the day, direct democracy would remain a myth. Thus, the democratic public had to be developed first and become a constant feature of politics, not something generated only at points of crisis. The idea of a democratic public went to the root of the problems of direct government. In Follett's own words: "Those who are working for particular reforms to be accomplished immediately will not be interested in neighborhood organization; only those will be interested who think that it is far more important for us to find the right method of attacking all our problems than to solve any one" (202).

Part of Follett's radicalism stemmed from her ideological flexibility. Follett did not believe any political ideology could provide airtight plans for the future and instead celebrated the contingency and open-endedness of democratic deliberation. Lustig errs in arguing that Follett concerned herself more with unity than with democracy, for, although she embraced idealism, Follett was also a great admirer of pragmatism—the philosophy of contingency and open possibilities. Certainly Follett believed in a common good and achieving unity through discussion and interpenetration of ideas (her idealist moment, as it was called earlier); however, this was no *static* unity but a unity constantly in the making. She wrote: "That the relation of each to the whole is dynamic and not static is perhaps the most profound truth" (66). Since in Follett's mind "life is creative at every moment, ... democracy must be conceived as a process, not a goal. We do not want rigid institutions, however good" (98–99). Follett believed that when citizens solved problems together there was a contingency not controlled by set programs and policies of the right or left. Thus, the radical nature of democracy stemmed not from clear-cut political programs but from unleashing a process by which regular citizens solved and re-solved their political problems in a continuous, open-ended manner.

Understanding the radical nature of democracy, Follett argued that state socialism—the major alternative to Western capitalism throughout the twentieth century—would not generate democracy. Writing shortly after the Russian Revolution (during which time the socialist left defined itself in increasingly Leninist and statist terms), Follett was prophetic. She criticized socialists in a straightforward manner, arguing that transferring power from the old aristocracy to the new Leninist Party would not alter political relations. State socialism produced new forms of hierarchical power, not democracy. Follett wrote: "The wish for socialism is a longing for the ideal state, but it is embraced often by impatient people who want to take a short cut to the ideal state. That state must be grown—its branches will widen as its roots spread" (73). Follett concluded that state socialism was not radical: "The socialization of property must not precede the socialization of the will. If it does, then the only difference between socialism and our present order will be substituting one machine for another" (73–74). Follett believed democracy to be more radical than socialism since it did not rely on top-down processes. Follett's thought made her sympathetic to certain critics on the left (especially guild socialists like G.D.H. Cole) who spoke out against state socialism and Leninism. What Follett taught these leftist critics as well as a general audience was that without a democratic public, political change would always take the form of imposition from above.[25]

In summary, Follett introduced Americans to the idea that democracy required a reorganization of social and political life. She connected her ideas to actual democratic practices carried out in social centers—linking her theory to practice. But instead of stopping with an explanation of social centers, Follett made connections to the wider intellectual context in which she worked: debates about pluralism, pragmatism, idealism, intersubjectivity, and progressive reform initiatives. She drew on ideas inherent in the American intellectual tradition—especially the ideas of federalism and democracy—to make her ideas speak in significant ways to a wide audience. She explained why her vision of democracy was more radical than the state socialist alternative offered to capitalism and liberal democracy. While putting her faith in local groups (as did the political pluralists like Harold Laski), she merged these groups into a wider urban public in order to move beyond the limits of localism. All of these ideas made Follett's theory innovative and interesting. What she saw taking place in social centers made Follett believe that democracy could be something more than just an abstract ideal. Instead, as far as she was concerned, it would have to become a lived reality and a vigorous daily practice.

Follett's Mistakes: Looking Ahead

Follett's political thought did suffer from certain weaknesses. She was at her best when she celebrated the contingency of political deliberation and the need for public contention. Against interpreting her work as being obsessed with harmony or conflict, we should understand that Follett's major enemy was not disunity but public apathy. She explained: "I always feel intimate with my enemies. It is not opposition but indifference which separates men" (212). But when Follett criticized political pluralists, she argued for an objective "law." She wrote: "That very same force which has bound the individuals together in the group . . . goes on working, you cannot stop it; it is the fundamental force of life, of all nature, of all humanity, the universal law of being—the outreaching for the purpose of further unifying" (285). Against Lustig's interpretation, it should be understood that Follett upheld not a static unity but a dynamic, ever-changing process of democratic deliberation. Follett erred not in her celebration of unity but in her supposed discovery of an objective and universal law. Simply put, no such law exists. People cannot always achieve unity. To uphold unity as a social good and attainable ideal is fine; to believe unity is based on an objective law ignores reality. By creating a fictional law Follett weakened her more powerful and interesting ideas on the contingency of politics.

Another one of Follett's weaknesses was her misunderstanding of developing social realities. Follett had no solution for the increasing disorganization and destruction of local neighborhoods. She wrote: "The fluctuating population of neighborhoods may be an argument against getting all we should like out of the neighborhood bond, but at the same time it makes it all the more necessary that some organization should be ready at hand to assimilate the new-comers and give them an opportunity of sharing in civic life as an integral, responsible part of life" (201). James Tufts, the most cogent reviewer of *The New State* and an old colleague of John Dewey's, argued that here Follett's thought weakened. He wrote: "Where people are nearly all renters, and shift from year to year or even from month to month, it is almost impossible to get any group consciousness." Follett had few responses to criticisms like these.[26]

Tufts no doubt held the upper hand in this argument. Neighborhoods have been harmed by industrial capitalism and social mobility. But Follett could have pointed out that in Rochester, new immigrants (especially those from Italy) came in large numbers to social centers. This would have illustrated that social centers appealed to a major urban constituency. Moreover, many contemporary critics point out that local communities have not collapsed as we might think. Even if she did not make these arguments (she never directly responded to Tufts's review), Follett's implicit argument against critics like Tufts still holds: the threat posed to local communities by destructive social forces should not lead us to turning our backs on them but to finding innovative ways to re-create local communities as the basis of democracy. Without a locality as the starting point for democracy, democracy would become a vague ideal. The challenge, as Follett saw it, was to rejuvenate the modern community and make it capable of being part of a wider urban public. This idea makes Follett's work still vital today.[27]

Nonetheless, Follett's work suffered from one overwhelming weakness. Having stressed how the American nation must be built out of the federation of democratic publics, Follett's arguments emerged at a dangerous time—during America's entry into World War I. Follett's major intellectual failure came when she endorsed the federal government's use of social centers to mobilize public opinion during the war. Though some might say that this mistake grew out of her theory of social centers building a unified nation, this was less a theoretical weakness and more a bad political judgment. After all, the building up of a democratic nation was a fine ideal and was not the problem. The problem was how political leaders would conceive of social centers when they made them a part of America's mobilization for war. Though Follett had reservations about endorsing the federal government's use of social centers during the war (see her comments on pages 248–49), she still hoped that by nationalizing social centers for the war effort, local neighborhoods would benefit. She argued: "Our national government clearly sees and specifically states that neighborhood organization is both for the neighborhood and for the nation" (250).

Follett was wrong. In the first place, the social centers had not had enough time to constitute themselves as truly democratic arenas. The movement, after all, was only eleven years old when America entered World War I. Second, despite Follett's wishes, the national government had no concern for the neighborhood—only the nation. Follett's poor judgment here was a mistake she made with other social centers activists, and to understand it we need to return to history, not political theory. Follett's mistake was an enormous one, and it caused the death of the social centers movement.

CHAPTER SIX

THE WANING OF THE DEMOCRATIC PUBLIC

World War I, Social Centers, and America

> A large part of pre-war radicalism dealt with political machinery intended to make the mass power of the uninformed common man apply to problems which he was incompetent to decide. This program is no longer appealing. There is less interest in these so-called democratic methods than ever before. . . . You cannot have a general lack of interest in politics and public questions and have a particularly vital radicalism.
>
> —George Alger, 1926[1]

By 1912 the social centers movement lost its primary locale in Rochester, New York, and became a nationwide movement. National organizations emerged, and political parties endorsed social centers. By creating a national vision, the movement showed that large-scale political change was necessary if democracy was to be made more "real." Thinkers like Mary Parker Follett developed interesting and important political theories to inspire their fellow Americans. Many Americans now debated the deeper meanings of democracy. Yet just as the movement was gaining national recognition and was acquiring intellectual support, the drive for military preparedness and America's entry into World War I transformed the social centers movement and its ideas about democracy.

Between 1912 and 1916 many activists brought social centers to America's national attention. By 1914 the attention reached all the way to the national legislature. Senators and congressmen debated funding Washington, D.C., public-school forums (the initiative was known as the Hollis-Johnson Community Forum Bill), but controversy immediately stifled this initiative. Legislators debated how to carry out the plan, and, in 1916, during the height of America's drive for military "preparedness," Helen Keller advocated pacifism at a privately funded school forum in the nation's capital. Keller's speech, which angered Edward Ward, played a major role in the defeat of the Hollis-Johnson Community Forum Bill in 1917.[2]

In that same year America entered World War I. Politicians now saw in the social centers an opportunity—an opportunity to make the "war to save democracy" appear democratic. Social centers activists, naively or otherwise, hoped that by throwing their support to the war and making citizen input essential to home-front politics that they could inject democracy not only into the war but into the American political system long after the war was over. Their gamble had enormously high stakes, and the risk they took resulted in a long-term defeat of both democratic institutions and ideas. In the debates about social centers during World War I and into the 1920s, many of our contemporary, pessimistic ideas about democracy emerged. The remainder of the chapter details this historical defeat of the social centers movement and its ideas about democracy.

World War I and National Mobilization

President Woodrow Wilson believed that World War I required more than military mobilization. In April 1917 Wilson stated, "It is not an army we must shape and train for war, it is a nation." If America was to win the war, the government had to organize all sectors of national life for this purpose. The War Industries Board, set up in the summer of 1917, coordinated the economy to ensure that unregulated market forces would not divert production for war. The Lever Food and Fuel Control Act (1917) "authorized the president to regulate the output, distribution, and price of food and to control every product, including fuel, that was used in food production." Along with economic and food production the federal government oversaw intellectual life, making sure that every educational institution, from primary schools to universities, served the war cause. Primary schools often became training grounds for the military, and university professors taught courses in support of the war. The federal government organized all sectors of society to ensure wartime unity.[3]

Most important of all, the federal government had to mobilize American public opinion for war. World War I was, in the words of David Kennedy, a "war for the American mind." Since activists had moved public opinion to the center of American politics during the Progressive Era, the federal government knew it had to mobilize this public opinion so that it would firmly support the war. Organized in 1917, the Committee on Public Information (CPI) took up this challenge. Headed by George Creel, a progressive muckraker who endorsed social centers and the initiative and referendum, the CPI worked to unify public opinion around the war. George Creel explained: "It was in this recognition of Public Opinion as a major force that the Great War differed most essentially from all previous conflicts." To galvanize this "major force," the CPI orchestrated a massive propaganda blitz by organizing public speakers and writers, working with newspapers, putting on war exhibits at state fairs, creating advertisements, and putting together movies (the primary institutions of the newly forming mass media). Creel clearly stated his goal: "What we had to have was no mere surface unity, but a passionate belief in the justice of America's cause that should weld the people of the United States into one white-hot mass instinct with fraternity, devotion, courage, and deathless determination."[4]

To weld such a "white-hot mass instinct" and to have the war appear truly legitimate in the eyes of most Americans, the war effort had to come from below. Although the federal government grew in power throughout the Progressive Era, many Americans still did not accept federal intervention in their lives. Realizing this, the federal government made mobilization for the war appear local in nature. For instance, local agents ran the military draft, one of the most obvious federal interventions into people's lives. Barry Karl explains: "Management and selection [of soldiers] by local boards helped smooth the transition from the old nineteenth-century system of locally recruited units to the establishment of a national army." The federal government believed public opinion could be unified only if the war seemed a local, democratic effort. As Neil Wynn points out, the level of government involvement in America's prosecution of World War I pales in contrast to the " 'war socialism' of the European type." The United States "consistently involved the states, local communities, and private individuals in one national purpose, and throughout depended upon voluntarism and self-regulation, cooperation, persuasion, and the force of public opinion shaped by official propaganda."[5]

Both of these wartime imperatives—the need to mobilize public opinion and to appear local in nature—attracted the federal government to working with schools and other institutions in local communities. The federal government encouraged communities to carry out food drives, and schools provided places to disseminate propaganda and practice military training. Where local community institutions did not exist, the federal government established them, going so far as to create its own communities based around newly located war industries. Here federal bureaucrats set up community centers to coordinate local life. The federal government consciously nestled its way into localities to make the "war to save democracy" appear democratic. In doing so the national government did not embrace the localism of the social centers movement but only used localism as a means of spreading the preordained idea that the war had to be won.[6]

The Community Councils of Defense, an aspect of the war overlooked by many historians, became the most important and ambitious effort in the federal government's attempt to make the war seem local and democratic. The Council of National Defense organized the community councils, and the CPI and the Bureau of Education supported the effort. In 1918 J. P. Lichtenberger described how community councils emerged: "At the request of the Council of National Defense, the state councils are now engaging, and in many states have completed, the creation of community councils of defense in the school district or a similar local unit of such small size that all the citizens in that locality can be reached through personal contact." The *Survey* celebrated the Community Councils of Defense as "a new piece of democratic machinery for the conduct of war." The magazine believed these local councils could "make available the efforts of the whole people in recruiting, in enlisting labor for agriculture and war industries, in increasing the food supply and decreasing the waste of food, in soliciting subscriptions to the Liberty Loan and to war savings, in relief and Red Cross work, in health education, soldiers' aid and training camp activities."[7]

This list of efforts explains the Council of National Defense's slogan for the community councils: "Every School District a Community Council for National Service." Normally located in schools, the community councils, in part, extended out of the social centers movement. Seeing its ideas being paid attention to, the National Community Center Association (NCCA) itself argued in favor of the community council idea, and Edward Burchard, a promoter of the plan, asserted that the Community Councils of Defense represented merely a "nationalization" of the community center movement. The *Community Center*, the national magazine of the NCCA, explained in paternalistic language: "Now our schools become suddenly recognized, under the messages of our schoolmaster President and under the appeals of our nation's immediate needs, both to teachers and pupils, as national centers—centers through which these national needs may come to the knowledge of all the people." Organized in community councils, public opinion in support of the war would still come from above (as did the military draft) but would appear to be growing directly out of local neighborhoods.[8]

Although rarely discussed by historians, these community councils certainly helped the federal government mobilize public opinion. By 1918 forty-one states organized community councils. Social centers activists, including Edward Ward, John Collier, and M. Clyde Kelly, threw their energy into community councils and thus provided them with legitimacy. They believed that the nation they wanted America to be—a nation growing out of local democratic publics—was now emerging. By doing this these activists lost sight of their more localistic democratic visions. They ignored that with the war, the nation came first, the neighborhood only second. What these activists could not fully understand was that a new way of organizing and shaping public opinion would emerge now, and this new historical experiment would create an enormous challenge to the principles of a democratic public.[9]

Localist Progressives and the War

The story has often been told how a certain group of "nationalist progressives" endorsed the war. Stuart Rochester writes: "Lured by the prospect of large-scale human cooperation and social reorganization that the war promised, many otherwise disinclined liberals decided to throw in with the interventionists." Since the war was fought in distant lands, liberal intellectuals like Herbert Croly, Walter Lippmann, and John Dewey envisioned the war less as a catastrophe and more as an opportunity to generate social reform through a strengthened federal government. As one writer in the *New Republic* put it cynically, nationalist progressives used the war as a "pretext to foist innovations upon the country." They hoped to direct economic production toward more rational ends and create the basis of a future welfare state. Although partially successful, these nationalist progressives quickly faced a postwar situation in which the reforms achieved were quickly dismantled (allowing corporate power to reassert itself) and a "Red Scare" hampered radical, political debate. As the story goes, these nationalist progressives became disillusioned after the war and seriously questioned their political beliefs.[10]

The story of "localist" and democratic progressives like Edward Ward, John Collier, and Charles Zueblin (who supported the war through the forum movement) follows a similar course. Placing their hopes in the national government, these activists gave up too much to the state while getting little in return, especially in terms of long-lasting reform. Faced with America's entry into war, these activists did their best to make the war effort reflect their vision of a nation formed out of local democratic publics. They hoped that if citizens made their participation crucial to home-front policies during the war the federal government would be restructured to reflect participatory and democratic principles.

To many this hopefulness about the war might seem perplexing, and why social centers activists pledged themselves is still unclear. But while we have no diaries or private correspondence to help explain their decision, we can speculate as to why they supported the war. First, in opposition to autocratic Germany, America was clearly a democratic nation-state. The federal government constantly made this point through grand rhetoric about the "war to save democracy," a rhetoric that undoubtedly influenced social centers activists as it did other Americans. But this explains how *any* American would support the war. For social centers activists there were more specific reasons.

By 1917 Ward and other leaders desired legitimacy and influence regarding political power. Stung by his defeat in Rochester, Ward moved to Wisconsin and later into the federal government to gain more power for the social centers movement. It would have been political suicide, from his perspective, to do anything but endorse the federal government's use of social centers during the war. Besides, Ward and Follett believed in the formation of an American nation, and it seemed to them that community councils could actually build a long-lasting democratic nation—not just a vehicle for propaganda during the war. What they failed to see was that a wartime nation could destroy democratic hopes. Ward and others had little sense about what endorsing the war could mean, in the long run, for their movement. But considering the desire for political legitimacy and a democratic nation, Ward's gamble seemed the right thing to do at the time.

Whatever hopes the social centers activists had about the war were quickly dashed by the top-down, hierarchical organization that marked the entire war effort. The imperatives of wartime "emergency" quickly displaced the social centers activists' hope for a democratic nation forming out of community councils. The director of the Council of National Defense, Grosvenor Clarkson, explained the hierarchical procedures of community councils: "Educational propaganda necessary for the proper emphasis of war measures essential to victory was prepared in Washington and through the Council of National Defense forwarded at once to the State Councils of defense and to the State divisions of the Women's Committee, where immediate decentralization of the message to be conveyed or of the work to be done took place." The federal government thus used community councils to further decisions already made. There was little if anything democratic about this. In the starkest language possible the National Councils of Defense proclaimed: "Priority should be given by the Community Council to all work expressly requested by the National Government, National, State, County Councils, or Branches of the Women's Committee in order that a uniform national response may be quickly obtained. The keynote of efficient decentralization is promptness and accuracy by the local agents in carrying out the requests from a central source."

Here it was in bold and plain language: community councils would not be democratic forums. Reflecting on the community councils and their success, L. J. Hanifan, a superintendent of West Virginia schools, explained how the federal government efficiently utilized community councils: "The success of all these campaigns has demonstrated beyond question that the school is the surest, cheapest, and speediest means the Government had of reaching all the people, and of securing their cooperation in prosecuting its program of helping to make the world safe for democracy." Although Hanifan might not have thought so, by making the war appear democratic, the federal government ironically destroyed democratic initiative. As social centers activists should have known, true democratic initiative relied on open debate—not disseminating propaganda—and organization from below—not above.[11]

Since the federal government concerned itself only with mobilizing local public opinion for the war, it quickly dismantled community councils during the postwar period. In his memoir John Collier explained what happened to community councils after the war:

> We . . . answered the [national] call [for war], and when the National Community Councils of Defense were organized, we organized, in Greater New York, Community Councils of Defense into which we merged the School Community Centers. . . . Then the war ended. Almost instantly the National Councils of Defense died. The

> need for them had ended. And the School Community Centers never entirely re-emerged and re-formed.

By 1920 the Community Center Division within the Bureau of Education ceased, and community councils died out. The federal government had no desire to support politically autonomous community councils, and having been organized from the top down (unlike social centers in Rochester), community councils could not easily become democratic, self-governing units. The movement for community councils simply failed to sustain itself as it passed away with the "crisis" of the war.[12]

By merging with the federal government, community councils lost sight of the original vision that John Dewey held out for social centers in 1902. Dewey argued that social centers should be based on a division between society (or what some today call "civil society") and the state. During the war the state controlled society. Losing sight of its own responsibility to generate public opinion independent of state directives, society lost out to the political power of the state. To be sure, a certain amount of connection between society and the state was necessary if more direct democracy was the goal, for society needed an institutional hold over the state. The crucial problem for social center activists was that the federal government conceived of the public only as a passive object to be manipulated in order to help create national unity during wartime.[13]

When Woodrow Wilson endorsed community councils, he claimed the plan would "result when thoroughly carried out in welding the nation together as no nation of great size has ever been welded before. It will build up from the bottom an understanding and sympathy and unity of purpose and effort which will no doubt have an immediate decisive effect upon our great undertaking." During the war activists ignored their democratic ideals and stressed the need for national unity. In the process the public was conceptualized by statesmen as a pawn of the government.

In December 1915, extending his desire to make social centers legitimate and politically effective, Edward Ward linked military preparedness to social centers. In the words of the *New York Times*, Ward wanted "preparedness that will mean the development of 'a nation with a backbone,' rather than an 'oysterlike country—a military shell protecting a citizenship of mollycoddles.' " In simpler language, Ward hoped preparedness would strengthen citizenship. He explained in alarming terms: "We may use this hardening fear as means of our internal construction. Under its unifying compression we may—if we will, and have sense enough—develop a skeleton inside, instead of a shell outside, and become a vertebrate nation—liberated instead of enshackled—and as much more powerful than a people cowering behind mere external fortifications, as a man is than an oyster." It must be stressed that Ward still believed in strong, participatory citizenship (the source of a "vertebrate nation") and democratic deliberation, and he hoped to gain credibility for these ideas by supporting the war. But now he connected these ideas to "the real unity of national interest." What Ward did not foresee was that national unity would take precedence during the war and would make the public less an active group of citizens than a mass object to be controlled by administrators and politicians. The imperatives of wartime emergency would drown out democratic deliberation and citizen participation.[14]

By making national unity the new goal for community centers, Ward became caught up in the frenzy of preparedness and forgot that the principle of democratic deliberation always challenged a simple, preordained unity. Social centers activists believed in building up a democratic nation—in wartime and in peacetime. They failed to see how wartime unity differed greatly from peacetime unity. Ward might have hoped that if he endorsed the war, social centers could gain long-lasting legitimacy and thus transform postwar America. Nonetheless, Helen Keller was more true to the social centers vision of democracy than Ward was in 1916. By arguing against the war in a local community center, she understood that democracy required debating the nation's motives, especially during a military buildup. The principles of a democratic public stressed deliberation, not mindless action. Ward had learned certain lessons from Rochester but not one of the most important ones: that when centralized power—be it of a city boss or the federal government—demanded political unity and harmony, a democratic public could no longer exist. During the war social centers activists lost sight of this important political lesson. This time the stakes were high, and the lesson wound up destroying the movement.[15]

The stress on national unity not only corrupted the democratic principles of social centers activists, it also transformed their conception of citizenship. The American idea of citizenship has always been dualistic. Drawing on republican political thought, social centers activists had stressed a participatory, democratic, and open conception of citizenship based on values like responsibility, deliberation, and self-government (see Chapter Four). At the same time, nativists concerned with immigration emphasized citizenship based on a "100-percent Americanism" that upheld conformity to preordained national ideals and unquestioned patriotism.

Although some social centers activists retained their belief in participatory citizenship during the war, the vision of conformist citizenship clearly won out. The CPI emphasized the "unswerving loyalty" necessary for carrying out such a great military effort, and with legislation like the Espionage Act (1917) and the Sedition Act (1918)—acts that made almost any wartime dissent illegal—the federal government prized citizenship based on unquestioning faith in the nation and its political leaders. Participatory citizenship, on the other hand, stressed critical judgment, a value inimical to the conformist and conservative citizenship promoted during the war.[16]

The wartime stress on conformist citizenship even affected such a critical thinker as John Collier. Collier endorsed the community councils while retaining a suspicion of top-down organization. Nonetheless, when endorsing community councils, Collier emphasized the conservative and conformist visions they embodied. He argued that during wartime "the aroused emotions of the people need a local vehicle for their expression." The community center provided this place. Losing sight of democratic principles due to the war frenzy, Collier explained the type of citizenship community councils encouraged: "We are most deeply influenced by our own immediate group—by our neighbors and friends. When a neighborhood is organized toward a given end, the suggestion is for most men irresistible—they go with their neighborhood." Thus, the neighborhood forum was no longer a place for deliberation but for a conformist consensus.

Whereas Collier maintained a certain affinity for democracy, Samuel Wilson, another proponent of using social centers during the war, did not. Wilson drew out a wildly dualistic and conformist conception of citizenship he hoped community councils would take to heart: "There are only two classes of citizens—those who are Americans and those who should be interned." Localist progressives lost sight of their ideals of democratic and participatory citizenship during the war. Conformist unity displaced contentious democracy.[17]

While national unity and conformist citizenship dominated wartime culture, the war had a much more long-lasting impact on the social centers movement. The drive for national unity and conformist citizenship dried up, but the government's methods of manipulating the public—and the ideas informing this effort—had a devastating effect beyond the war. The hope for a democratic public died, and many of our contemporary, pessimistic ideas about democracy were born at this time. Instead of seeing the potential of building up a democratic public, intellectuals and activists during the 1920s questioned if such a potential existed. They no longer viewed the public as an active and deliberating body but, following the model of government propaganda during World War I, as a passive object to be manipulated by mass propaganda. A radical change occurred during World War I and into the 1920s: the concept of a democratic public, which was widespread during the Progressive Era, no longer constituted a key element in the American political imagination.

World War I and the Democratic Public

If the experience of war seriously challenged democracy and participatory citizenship, the idea that public opinion should make binding political judgments was nearly destroyed. The CPI worked on the premise that public opinion need not come from below but could be manipulated from above. The Community Councils of Defense had little deliberative power; rather, they accepted the proclamations of the federal government. Drawing from these experiences, intellectual leaders began to believe that public opinion could be manufactured and thus did not warrant the prized position it gained during the Progressive Era. Intellectuals started to argue that an effective democratic public could not be created from below. George Creel, the muckraker and head of the CPI who for some time after the war retained his faith in public opinion, stated in 1924, "The very *existence* of a forceful, effective public opinion is much to be doubted. There are gusts of anger, spasms of irritation, [and] moments of hysteria . . . but these excitements do not lend themselves to sustained decisions of moral judgments."[18]

The federal government, the CPI, and the community councils acted in the belief that the public could be manipulated, and intellectuals in the postwar period and into the 1920s further assaulted the hope in a democratic public. These intellectuals faced the same question social centers activists and intellectuals faced during the Progressive Era: How could democracy be made to work? Those who placed their hope in social centers knew "real democracy" was no easy task. It required large-scale institutional change and a serious rethinking of America's political values. Nonetheless, they believed a democratic public could develop. This type of political imagination atrophied during the 1920s. After the war intellectuals faced the same difficult question about how democracy could work, but their answers were simpler. For them democracy was a farce to be rejected flat out because of the major assumptions that underpinned democratic political faith. In rejecting democracy these thinkers codified many of our present-day views.

H. L. Mencken led the attack on democracy during the 1920s. Mencken was certainly one of America's most popular social critics, and his thought influenced significant currents in 1920s political thinking. After a crude reading of Friedrich Nietzsche's philosophy, Mencken embraced the role of the intellectual crank and argued that America suffered from democratic egalitarianism and from the lack of an aristocracy. His interpretation of democracy was simplistic and unimaginative. Mencken believed that "the average citizen of a democracy is a goose-stepping poltroon." The only conclusion he could draw about democracy was that he "enjoy[ed] democracy very much. It is incomparably idiotic, and hence incomparably amusing." Playing the role of the disenchanted, elite intellectual, Mencken condemned both regular citizens and any hope in democracy. Shunning the general public as philistine, puritanical, and hopelessly foolish, Mencken placed his faith in a "civilized minority." In the historian Steven Biel's words, Mencken seemed to "deny [social] criticism any public function." Mencken simply ridiculed the progressive faith in a democratic public.[19]

Mencken's lack of faith in democracy represented a broader tendency within post–World War I social thought. Intellectuals now questioned the average citizen's capacity for self-government. In political science, scientific naturalism (including Freudianism and other new patterns of thought that discovered the "irrationality" of regular citizens) and realism challenged the idea that human beings were capable of rational thought. As Edward Purcell explains: "By the end of the twenties many students of government had come to reject what they considered the romantic idea that all men should actively engage in governing the country, assuming the irrationality of most men and the practical impossibility of actual popular control." It was not only intellectual trends in political science that hampered a hope in democracy, it was also the lessons intellectuals drew from the CPI's experiments in propaganda and advertising. The wartime mobilization "for the American mind" provided a glaring example of how public opinion need not be organized democratically but rather from the top down and based on preordained outcomes. More important, this discovery had an impact on America long after the war.[20]

Edward Bernays's career and thought illustrate this clearly. Having worked with the CPI on its Committee in Latin America, Bernays went directly into mass advertising for corporations after the war. Bernays did not believe public opinion was entirely open to manipulation, but by focusing on the ability of large-scale organizations—be it government or big business—to shape public opinion, he thoroughly questioned the original faith in the power of democratic public opinion to direct politics in a meaningful way. Bernays studied what he called "public relations," a term coming into common use during the 1920s and one that conflicted with the social center activists' hope in democratic deliberation. In fact, Bernays was deeply influenced by one of Mary Parker Follett's intellectual foes—Gustave Le Bon. While Follett thought in terms of communication and interaction within small neighborhood groups, Bernays thought in terms of a massive crowd. His job was to direct this crowd. As he put it: "In this age . . . there must be a technique for the mass distribution of ideas. Public opinion can be moved, directed, and formed by such a technique." This was no theory of democratic deliberation, for what Bernays learned at the CPI taught him that citizens' ideas could be shaped from above in order to benefit the federal government. Instead of citizens shaping public opinion through deliberation and discussion, Bernays believed the public was a thing to be controlled by "public relations" experts. After the war, as the federal government became less important than private corporations, he pursued this lesson to benefit big business, honing his skills in the propaganda of commodities.[21]

Like Edward Bernays, Harold Laswell, a political sociologist, drew key lessons about democracy and public opinion from the activities of the CPI. Laswell pioneered in social science by studying propaganda technique used during World War I. He combined scientific naturalism and realism with empirical studies of agencies like the CPI. Drawing out the discovery of social science that public opinion could be manipulated from above, Laswell argued that democracy was futile. He explained: "This whole discussion about the ways and means of controlling public opinion testifies to the collapse of the traditional species of democratic romanticism and to the rise of a dictatorial habit of mind." As far as Laswell was concerned, "The democrats were deceiving themselves. The public has not reigned with benignity and restraint." Of course, what Laswell was referring to here—for when *did* the public truly "reign"?—was unclear. Nonetheless, Laswell believed that a faith in democracy should be replaced with a faith in the seemingly objective findings of social scientists. Social science's "business," Laswell argued, "is to discover and report, not to philosophize and reform." Accepting existing power dynamics, the social scientist would aid propagandists in their new quest for social control. The only thing necessary to give up was the "democratic romanticism" of the past.[22]

The tendencies captured so well in Bernays's and Laswell's thought culminated in the ideas of Walter Lippmann. A major progressive intellectual (although one with little faith in public opinion or social centers), Lippmann endorsed the war along with his fellow *New Republic* editors. Tiring of intellectual detachment and desiring action, Lippmann worked with the Inter-Allied Propaganda Board during the war. He wrote leaflets dropped behind German lines. The experience had an enormous impact on his political beliefs. After the war Lippmann began to reflect on this experience and developed the most damaging critique of public opinion and democracy yet written. His critique shaped intellectual thought about democracy for the rest of the twentieth century.[23]

In 1920 Lippmann explained to an editor that he was writing "a longish article around the general idea that freedom of thought and speech present themselves in a new light and raise new problems because of the discovery that opinion can be manufactured." The article turned into a book—*Public Opinion* (1922). The book was monumental in that it far transcended Lippmann's historical experiences. He had participated in propaganda experiments and witnessed the power of ideas coming from above during the war, and as his career entered the 1920s, he saw the growing power of the mass media and advertising (modern advertising skyrocketed during the twenties). But Lippmann went beyond these historical developments when he wrote *Public Opinion.* He made an abstract argument about fundamentals here—in this case about the *possibility* of a democratic public's becoming a reality. Due largely to its abstract and grand qualities, Lippmann's argument made a long-lasting impact on America's political imagination.[24]

In *Public Opinion* Lippmann started from an assumption that "what each man does is based not on direct and certain knowledge but on pictures made by himself or given to him." Stereotypes especially influenced people's thoughts. Since regular people had no sense of an objective reality and possessed only images in their minds, leaders could play upon these images to direct public opinion in ways they desired. Lippmann called this a "manufacture of consent." Based on this discovery, Lippmann pronounced democracy dead. Creating a false "democratic" opponent who blindly celebrated "the people," he stated his beliefs plainly: "It is no longer possible, for example, to believe in the original dogma of democracy; that the knowledge needed for the management of human affairs comes up spontaneously from the human heart." The only alternative to democracy, Lippmann believed, was turning the government over to political leaders. These leaders would be guided by experts who had a finer understanding of objective reality and could see beyond the limited horizons and stereotypes of average citizens. "In the absence of institutions and education by which the environment is so successfully reported that the realities of public life stand out sharply against self-centered opinion, the common interests very largely elude public opinion entirely, and can be managed only by a specialized class whose personal interests reach beyond the locality." Elites (who supposedly possessed knowledge of objective reality) were the answer, not democratic localities. The democratic public, Lippmann argued, was a myth.[25]

It is not surprising that John Dewey felt compelled to answer Lippmann's argument against a democratic public. Dewey responded to Lippmann's critique in a simple yet profound way. He agreed that Lippmann had discovered damaging evidence for a naive faith in democracy. But instead of agreeing with Lippmann's conclusions, Dewey refused to play the assigned role of the "romantic" democrat and instead rejuvenated the complex political imagination social centers activists and others had developed in the face of questions about democracy. He did not cave in to Lippmann's false argument that democrats merely glamorized "the people." Like social centers activists, Dewey realized democracy required fundamental institutional change and a reexamination of American political values. In the face of this difficult but utterly necessary challenge, Lippmann had thrown up his hands and renounced the task of political imagination. Dewey argued:

> The difficulty is so fundamental that it can be met . . . only by a solution more fundamental than [Lippmann] has dared to give. . . . Democracy demands a more thorough-going education than the education of officials, administrators, and directors of industry. Because this fundamental general education is at once so necessary and so difficult of achievement, the enterprise of democracy is so challenging. To sidetrack it to the task of enlightenment of administrators is to miss something of its range and challenge.

Dewey did not deny the hard work that Lippmann believed impossible. He simply argued that the ramifications of giving up on participatory democracy were too dangerous. Democracy required a "fundamental general education" that, as Dewey went on to argue in his later work *The Public and Its Problems* (1927), could come only from local communities forging a democratic public—the original vision he and others espoused for social centers.[26]

By 1922, when he had written his rebuttal of Lippmann's arguments, Dewey's argument seemed abstract. No doubt Dewey once had hope in the social centers movement as a way to facilitate communities forging a democratic public. But in the 1920s Dewey's argument seemed to be merely a hope void of any serious institutional alternative. Lippmann proposed experts advising politicians. What did Dewey propose instead but a vague hope in a community-based form of democratic education? During the second decade of the twentieth century Dewey could have pointed to the social centers movement as inspiration. In the 1920s he had nothing to offer. The social centers movement died with the war and with the general attacks made on democracy after the war. As we shall see by examining what happened to the social centers movement and its intellectual leaders during the 1920s, Dewey's hope was just that—a hope with little to no grounding in reality.[27]

The Death Throes of the Social Centers Movement

While intellectuals like Lippmann challenged the idea of a democratic public, the social centers movement was being thoroughly transformed. With Ward, Follett, and Collier gone, the movement gained the title of "community organization" and after the war threw all its weight into recreational issues, reflecting the general apolitical tone of the 1920s. By 1922 the *Survey* declared that "the recreational side of community organization has quite outstripped all other functions." As this occurred, social workers became more prominent in community center activities. In 1928 Seba Eldridge provided a broad interpretation of where the movement was going. In her first few words she mentioned an important development: "Most often . . . community organization means the organized efforts of professional social workers and their supporters for the community at large, or for certain 'underprivileged' elements thereof."

Whereas Ward and Follett criticized philanthropy, community organization activists embraced it. In his now classic book on the professionalization of social work, Roy Lubove has argued that although the original community center movement was democratic, by the 1920s it was taken over by professional social workers. Lubove argues that the movement's "intensive concern with the machinery and financing of social welfare diverted attention from cooperative democracy and the creative group life of the ordinary citizen to problems of agency administration service." Eleanor Touroff Glueck best summed up the trajectory of the social centers movement after World War I: "Considering the school center then from the point of view of the ideals set for it by Ward and others, who hoped that it would become the 'Citizens' Council Chamber' for the discovery of common interests, for the interchange of points of view, and for greater control of legislation by the people, we see how short it has fallen."[28]

Community organization during the 1920s was not only depoliticized but also transformed by academization and professionalization. In 1926 the *Survey* stated that "'community organization' has become an academic phrase." Academic writers who reflected upon the community organization movement drew very different conclusions about community and democracy than did Follett and Ward. During the 1920s academics ignored the critical and democratic potential behind terms like *community* and *neighborhood.* Instead, they incorporated the idea of community into the jargon of academic sociology. The section on community organization published regularly in the new academic sociology journal the *Journal of Social Forces* clearly represented this development. Here academic thinkers concerned with community organization questioned the faith in a democratic public and developed a consensus about the meaning of community that would dominate academic sociology for years to come. From this consensus grew many of our own contemporary ideas about community and democracy.[29]

Social theorists began to argue that local communities could not give birth to democracy but only to provincialism and reactionary traditions. In making this argument they simplified complicated issues and destroyed the hope for a democratic public. Localities were no longer starting grounds for participatory democracy. Instead, intellectual elites and an urban middle class rejected local communities for an emerging culture of consumption that promised more cosmopolitan experiences. Intellectuals during the 1920s pointed to social developments that created such a culture of consumption. Advertising was modernized: imagery was stressed over words and text, and social-psychological needs (popularity, feelings of belongingness, etc.) were created in the minds of consumers, which could be appealed to by advertisers. More important, the extension of the credit system during the 1920s allowed larger numbers of people to buy goods. These developments pointed to a new social constellation that had to be taken seriously by intellectuals and social analysts.[30]

Robert Park, the founding father of American academic sociology, took these developments very seriously indeed. Park acquired his background in "community organization," having participated in various conferences on the subject. With this background informing his intellectual vision, he helped change intellectuals' perception of community from being a source of democracy to a source of dread. Having written a devastating critique of the social centers movement for the *Community Center* in 1922 (the same year Lippmann's *Public Opinion* was published), Park put forth a more thorough analysis of community organization in the *Journal of Social Forces* in 1925. For Park, "professional people" were "indifferent to the interests of the particular geographical area in which they may happen to reside." Park here endorsed "social mobility"—a term coming into vogue among academic sociologists during the 1920s. Not only did professional people shun community but American political culture disregarded Aristotle's belief that humans found happiness in political participation. Aristotle's ideal, according to Park, "was more true of man then than it is today."

Park believed an emerging consumer culture replaced any popular concern for politics. Although he saw consumers' "restless search for excitement" as hopeless, Park nonetheless believed this frantic search marked the death of democratic participation growing out of communities and the birth of a new society based on mass culture and consumption. Americans were pursuing other interests as they shunned provincialism and democratic participation. Because community had no real impact on Americans' lives, Park argued that the only role left for community was as an object of social scientific study.[31]

Park's thoughts were echoed by others in the pages of the *Journal of Social Forces*, and a consensus among academic sociologists grew within its pages. Clarence Nickle, for example, drew out Park's ideas about provincialism. Arguing that local communities were not the sources of rigorous democratic participation but of reactionary "taboos," Nickle went on to claim, "Many taboos are so firmly imbedded in the tradition of leaders, and rational thinking has no opportunity even to smooth or grade, to say nothing of paving the way of progress. 'The people' have tried and failed." What the "way of progress" entailed, Nickle did not make clear. But he concluded his critique of provincialism and community life by declaring, "The masses will not rule." If localism was the equivalent of irrationality, then of course localistic democracy and any faith in a public emerging from below were completely absurd.[32]

According to W. S. Bittner, the new mass media of the 1920s was precisely what made localistic democracy absurd. Once a believer in social centers, Bittner now argued that the media appropriated the power communities once had to develop indigenous public opinion. Bittner cited Walter Lippmann when discussing the media and argued, "With the rapid expansion of communications, especially in our own time, . . . the local, geographical community and neighborhood bonds and compulsions are less significant than those which are operative from outside in accounting for typical expressions of public opinion." This argument provided the groundwork for a growing belief that America was becoming a rootless "mass society"—a society made up of nomadic consumers with no attachments to local communities. Americans now created public opinion not out of face-to-face dialogue with one another but rather out of reading large corporate newspapers and listening to the radio. With "professional people" shunning provincialism and with the power of the mass media growing, the hope for a democratic public developing out of local communities was dead.[33]

These ideas of Park, Nickle, and Bittner coalesced in the social thought of the most important thinker on community centers during the 1920s—Jesse Steiner. Steiner once supported social centers, as seen in his debate with Dwight Sanderson. In 1919 Sanderson argued that certain social forces destroyed local, urban communities. "The life of the city is dominated by the industrial process which brings together huge aggregates of humanity with little or nothing in common and held together by selective associations arising from the most frequent contacts and the strongest common interests." Due to this, Sanderson believed community centers created an artificial sense of community. Jesse Steiner responded to this argument in a thoughtful way. He believed Sanderson's arguments relied upon a conception of community that prized organicism and natural processes. Communities, Steiner argued, do not necessarily blossom naturally but are rather brought into being through conscious activities: "When the neighborhood association . . . brings the people of a given locality together on a common plane of interest, it is not stimulating the development of 'artificial units' but is bringing into the foreground the natural community life which is too buried amidst the strain and stress of city conditions." In

Steiner's eyes social centers helped bring into being a conscious sense of community—one that could have been buried by industrialism. This was an important and subtle point.[34]

It was a point Steiner later forgot. Only two years later he endorsed the professionalization of social work. In celebrating professionalism he attacked locally based democracy, arguing that there was "a point beyond which popular effort cannot go [in solving social problems] and maintain a high efficiency." At this point professional social workers entered the picture. With his newfound faith in professional social work and his argument against democracy, Steiner's political imagination ossified. In the mid-1920s Steiner, reversing his position of 1919, began to argue that the community center movement was doomed to failure. His thought grew out of the overall consensus developing among intellectuals during the 1920s.[35]

Steiner had some insight into the social centers movement, having studied it in depth. He claimed the movement concerned itself too much with achieving unity. Though there may have been some truth to this point, Steiner's conclusion was too dismissive. Instead of criticizing the movement's fascination with unity by bringing out those ideals within it that stressed the contingency found in political debate, Steiner argued that the whole premise of the local community as the source of democracy was outdated and reactionary. He wrote: "The limited opportunities of the neighborhood and the small community with the provincialism and conservatism that were the natural products of its restricted life make no appeal to the present generation." Like Clarence Nickle, Steiner believed that provincialism was a "hindrance . . . to progress." The only signs of "progress" Steiner pointed to, though, were not terribly appealing. He argued that social mobility, consumerism, and public indifference were transforming American society. Capitalist development and a mass culture destroyed local communities. These were the only social changes that Steiner alluded to in explaining what he meant by "progress."[36]

How did other thinkers on social centers respond to Steiner's arguments? Le Roy Bowman, the new secretary of the National Community Center Association during the 1920s, fully agreed. Bowman believed that social mobility ruined the local community, making social centers obsolete. Experts now worked on housing reform and city planning, and regular citizens had no role to play here. Bowman argued: "This [housing reform and city planning] is a far cry from the community religion of a few years ago when the drive was on to go out and get people into community organizations, democratic in the extreme and supposedly dominated by neighborly sentiments." Responding to this sort of sentiment, Clarence Perry argued, much as Park did, that the idea of a community mattered, but only for objective social scientists who studied it. These different positions staked out by Bowman and Perry marked the death of the social centers movement. While Bowman and Steiner argued that a new American mass culture destroyed the potential of community-based democracy, Park and Perry repudiated community-based democracy for supposedly objective social science.[37]

With the increased power of the federal government during World War I, the consolidation of a consumer culture in the 1920s, the intellectual attacks made on democracy after the war, and sociologists' dismissal of community throughout the 1920s, democratic experiments seemed completely outmoded. For many, democracy itself became a nostalgic dream. It was increasingly difficult to make any acceptable argument in its favor without sounding vague and over idealistic, since no vibrant institutions could provide the basis for such an argument. Any intellectual (and John Dewey seemed to be the only one) supporting the ideals of democracy spoke in a void. During the 1920s many Americans seemed to put any hope in a democratic public's directing its own affairs to rest.

Conclusion: America's Political Imagination and the Waning of Democratic Experimentation

During World War I and into the postwar society of the 1920s, the institutional and intellectual vision of the social centers movement died. Here was a vision of a new nation growing along democratic lines. Hoping to create a public capable of generating decisions through collective deliberation, activists eventually wanted this public to become the major locale of political power. No social movement of the entire twentieth century has articulated such a clear vision of participatory democracy and citizenship within the parameters of modernity. The general debate about democracy and the more specific debate about social centers that took place during the 1920s signified the death of democratic ideals and their institutional expression. It left Americans' democratic imagination severely impoverished.

Around this debate grew ideas about American democracy that have lasted until our own day and age. In the minds of many intellectuals writing during the 1920s, democracy had to give way to the pressures of a "mass society"—a society bulldozing any resistance in its way. Whereas community was the source of local democratic deliberation for social centers activists, for intellectuals in the 1920s "community" became a dying artifact—something swallowed up by large, bureaucratic institutions. Any sense of locality or place now seemed nostalgic to intellectuals, since urban, middle-class Americans embraced social mobility and neglected their local neighborhoods. Few citizens seemed concerned about a public or common good; rather, they seemed (during that so-called Jazz Age of the 1920s) obsessed with satisfying their private needs through the market of consumer goods and a culture of consumption. A democracy of equal citizens solving common problems gave way to a democracy of abundance, private goods, and passive consumption. Because of these new ideas and social forces, democracy seemed less of a hope and more of a farce to many intellectuals and activists.

Perhaps most damaging of all to Americans' democratic imagination, intellectuals during the 1920s attacked any hope in a democratic public as naive and foolhardy. A radical and paradigmatic shift took place here. A public was no longer to be created through the conscious efforts of citizens gathering to deliberate. Rather, the public was changed from being an active willing process—as Mary Parker Follett had envisioned it—to being a passive object manipulated by state propagandists and "public relations" agents who worked for big business. The public no longer willed its own decisions; it was manipulated by elites. It seemed impossible to many intellectuals and political leaders during the 1920s to imagine that a public could ever become the basis of a vital democracy.

Even worse, any effort to argue, in the face of mass society, that democracy could and should be supported as an ideal worth striving for was made to seem nostalgic, romantic, and unrealistic. Democratic realists like Lippmann and Steiner simply ridiculed any democratic argument as naively romanticizing "the people." A democratic straw man—a fictional opponent who mistakenly trusted the ignorant masses—was created in the minds of many writers during the 1920s. This imaginary enemy allowed Lippmann and others to ignore the complex efforts of social centers activists and democratic theorists. Writers like Lippmann and Steiner created simplistic arguments: either leaders realistically (and intelligently) accepted the rule of an elite or else naively had faith in letting the masses do whatever they wanted, proving over and over their errors at self-government. There seemed no middle ground between these two polar opposites. That is, the ideas of the social centers movement seemed to fade out of public discourse: no longer could one argue that perhaps the people were not to be romanticized or innocently trusted but should be allowed and actively encouraged to develop institutions where they educated themselves gradually into the processes of debate and decision making. This position now seemed indefensible, if even imaginable.

With the transition from the Progressive Era to World War I and the 1920s, a great historical opportunity was missed. During the Progressive Era public opinion was trusted and seen as the basis for a future democracy by many American political leaders. Based on this faith in public opinion, activists, who understood that a democratic public was needed before any other reform could take place, created institutions—adult education centers, forums, and social centers—in which democratic public opinion could actually form. Out of these experiments grew new democratic ideas. Intellectuals saw a rich connection between institutional practices found in social centers and more abstract arguments about citizenship and public life. In essence, democratic theory grew out of democratic practice. To the activists and intellectuals studied here, a "real democracy" seemed on the verge of blossoming during the Progressive Era.

But a democratic public could not grow within a nation preparing for war. Nor could it grow within an atmosphere hostile to democracy, the atmosphere of the 1920s. A serious opportunity for "real democracy" passed as the Progressive Era came to an end. Our present conceptions of democracy have been harmed by this missed opportunity. Today we have a hard time thinking about ways in which we could enliven American democracy. Like the defeated activists and intellectuals studied here, we often see a more vibrant democracy only as a nostalgic dream. But if we truly understand what these activists and intellectuals have to teach us, we will see democracy as an experiment that must be nurtured in our daily lives. That was the "great hope of democracy" for which these activists fought. It is a hope worth remembering and nurturing today.

CONCLUSION

The Future of American Democracy

The activists and intellectuals studied here had a distinct vision for American democracy that never came to fruition. Drawing from the general faith in public opinion during the Progressive Era, Charles Zueblin, Frederic Howe, Edward Ward, Mary Parker Follett, and others believed democracy must grow out of neighborhood-based publics that were forming in social centers and forums across America from the late 1890s until World War I. When they threw their support to the war, their hopes were dashed. Instead of a democratic nation growing out of the war, the opposite occurred. Not only did a stronger, more centralized government emerge, so too did a new conception of public opinion—one radically different from that espoused by social centers activists and other reformers during the Progressive Era. This new conception envisioned public opinion not as an active process willed by citizens in community arenas—Mary Parker Follett's conception—but as a passive object to be manipulated by political leaders and advertisers who had preordained objectives. The work carried out by the activists and intellectuals studied here represented a missed opportunity to transform American politics. One last question remains: What did this missed opportunity mean for American democracy?

In many ways it provided the backdrop for the development of modern American politics. Progressive Era activists succeeded in replacing a nineteenth-century system of government ruled by bosses and corrupt patronage with a more modern, efficient administration run by expert civil servants and democratically elected officials. Though corruption was not done away with, there can be no doubt that national and local bureaucratic administrations consolidated during the Progressive Era. But the other side of Progressive Era activists' hopes—the creation of a democratic public—never fully developed. Zueblin, Howe, and Ward hoped efficiency and democracy would go hand in hand. This never happened. But that is largely because their experiments were never allowed to develop; only one side of their vision was victorious. Due to this, modern American politics became marked by an increasingly weak democratic public alongside an increasingly strong administrative state.

Worse yet, the consumer culture and mass media that displaced social centers during the 1920s have become only that much stronger. Television and other forms of marketing and advertising make the culture of the 1920s seem passé. Social centers activists had feared that a commercially driven mass media would be incapable of developing a strong democratic public opinion. These fears have come true. With the television's growing power, a slicker consumer culture has transformed American politics. Many critics have argued rightfully that it is not consumerism per se that is so pernicious but its invasion into realms of life where it is inappropriate. As marketing and advertising encroached on the realm of politics, politics was transformed into consumption. Politicians today are turned into commodities to be packaged and sold to a passive television audience. Slogans and commercial advertisements—the techniques pioneered by marketing specialists—replace longer and more thoughtful political debates between candidates. When politicians express interest in learning about public opinion, they form "focus groups" where opinions are gleaned in order to help write the next round of election slogans. Politicians conceive of themselves and their aides as "spin doctors" who sell themselves (and their policies) to an increasingly passive audience.[1]

The recent growth of a souped-up consumer culture transformed not only the way politicians conceive of a public but also the public itself. Social centers activists believed that citizens had to be reconnected to public life in significant ways, but today there are fewer ways to find these connections. As citizens become redefined as consumers (a trend starting in the 1920s), their ability to make public judgments withers. Private and personal choice seems the only realm of judgment left to most citizens today.

Public discourse itself remains stunted at the level of personal discussion. In the first place, during the rare times when citizens are concerned with political choices—when they are electing a representative—the media often focuses on candidates' personal lives at the expense of their public positions. On a more regular basis, personal and private concerns litter public discourse. As "talk shows" (i.e., *Oprah, Geraldo,* etc.)—with their incessant broadcasting of private issues to a public audience—clutter the airwaves, public talk is increasingly shaped by private concerns. Many social critics have pointed out that our public talk seems framed by personal emotions and feelings—calling this phenomenon, among other things, "emotivism," "a culture of complaint," "a culture of narcissism," or "a therapeutic culture."

Perhaps the clearest indication of how citizens are limited to only personal and emotional ways of talking about issues is how people use the expression "I feel" instead of "I think" to preface their arguments. Citizens have a difficult time making the transition from personal feelings to public claims that go beyond their own private selves. Having witnessed the way citizens talk in the many public forums I have attended, it is clear that they find it difficult to engage in public talk, that is, talk which moves beyond personal feelings to concern for common issues. This poses a serious impediment to citizens engaging in democratic deliberation, and it represents a clear example of the crisis of democracy alluded to in the Introduction of this book.[2]

While it is important to understand that our democracy faces a crisis, it is also important to understand that the ideas espoused by the social centers activists are too ingrained in American history and traditions to have been forgotten after their historical demise. A major hope of this book is to establish the importance of the work done by the activists and intellectuals concerned with democracy during the Progressive Era. Throughout the twentieth century, citizens have continued to organize themselves within their local communities, often setting up forums to educate themselves about current political problems. For instance, the civil rights movement brought forth a renaissance of citizen activism that influenced American politics throughout the second half of the twentieth century. During the 1950s and 1960s Black citizens formed democratic publics within their churches to decide on what sort of collective action could be used to end racial segregation. The Black Baptist Church served as a place for citizens to gather and deliberate with their leaders about political action. Out of these forums came boycotts and civil disobedience in the name of social justice. The church, in essence, provided a budding ground for a democratic public. This sort of activism inspired students throughout America during the 1960s. As many of these young people participated in the civil rights movement and formed their own movement (what became known as the New Left), they criticized the passivity of a consumer culture and embraced the idea of participatory democracy developed by John Dewey in his *The Public and Its Problems*—a book that drew at least some of its inspiration from the activism studied here.[3]

These movements came to an end, but the belief in citizen participation and engagement in democratic public life did not. Although as early as the

1920s professional social work began to challenge the idea that regular citizens could solve their own community problems (see Chapter Six), democratic community organizing in America's cities emerged again under the leadership of Saul Alinsky, a famous activist who got his start in 1930s Chicago. His motto was "Never do for others what they can do for themselves." Critical of professional social workers, Alinsky inspired both a tradition of political work and an organization, the Industrial Areas Foundation (IAF), based on the idea that citizens could solve local community problems democratically. Today the IAF still trains organizers and is going strong. Edward Chambers, the executive director, argues that the IAF takes seriously the challenges of democratic public life and citizenship. The IAF sees citizens "having the right to act in, not gaze at, a public arena in which discourse is paramount and there is real negotiation, compromise, and reciprocity." Chambers lambastes definitions of democracy that envision the citizen as a consumer who ignores public issues. He argues: "An invitation to participate in our society must mean more than the ability to select from a panoply of consumer choices and to vote occasionally." Clearly, the idea of a democratic public informs the work of the IAF. Based on this connection, Harry Boyte has argued for a stronger conception of democracy that grows out of the efforts of these community organizers. Government officials in American cities have also learned from community organizers by incorporating neighborhood-based networks of participation into urban government. In certain ways participatory citizenship and democratic public life are alive and well.[4]

The hope for democracy captured in the work of community organizers and the IAF has recently inspired other activists to seek ways to re-create a democratic public. Over the last fifteen years citizens have set up forums that address public issues of great importance. Starting in 1981, different civic organizations, with the help of the Kettering Foundation, created the National Issues Forums (NIF) where citizens and political leaders gather to talk and educate one another about issues that have national political implications. As well, organizers of "study circles" gather citizens together in local, small groups to discuss problems like racism and public education, helping them to discover the principle of "public dialogue." In terms of this book the latter efforts are very important because, more than the efforts of Alinsky and the IAF, they directly capture the spirit of the social centers movement. Organizers of National Issues Forums and study circles understand public debate and deliberation as ends in themselves. They believe that unless we create spaces where citizens can engage in civic dialogue and mutual, collective education, democracy will become meaningless. Whether they are aware of it or not, organizers of National Issues Forums and study circles have inherited the hope of social centers activists to create a modern democratic public.[5]

Those who hope to create a democratic public today (and those people include more than just NIF and study-circles organizers) face new challenges, but they also confront problems similar to those faced by social centers activists. In the first place, when organizers argue that their work creates more democracy, they must be clear what they mean by this. It should be apparent from this work that democracy is a term too easily abused. Today, many citizens think democracy grows out of economic prosperity and the freedoms generated by a consumer society. This vision was first articulated in the 1920s, and it has grown ever stronger. Those who struggle for a democratic public need to show how a "real democracy" requires more than the freedoms of a consumer society. It requires the engagement of citizens in collective deliberation about public matters. In many ways the intellectual work of Edward Ward and Mary Parker Follett provides an important starting point for thinking and arguing more critically about what democracy requires in the modern world. However, we should not draw only from the conceptual thinking done by Ward and Follett but from the actual experimentation found in social centers. After all, the activists and intellectuals studied here understood that democratic theory must be informed by democratic practice.[6]

Contemporary organizers trying to create the institutional basis for a democratic public should pay special attention to certain lessons learned by social centers activists. First and foremost, trying to connect citizen deliberation to avenues of political power is no easy task. As shown in Chapter 3, when social centers activists crossed paths with political bosses intent on protecting privilege and power, they lost. Today, organizers of public forums should understand that open political discussion about pressing political matters can upset those who hold economic and political power. After all, citizens are not normally invited to participate in public debate for good reason, and if citizens are called to participate in public discussion that does not alter the way political decisions are made, they will become even more cynical about politics than they already are. Involving citizens in democratic deliberation is crucial, but this debate must lead to actual political decision making.

To create such a situation, though, takes time and patience—a second lesson to be learned from social centers activists. For when Follett and Ward supported World War I and tried to connect the public deliberation in social centers to the activities of the federal government, they acted too fast. The deliberative practices in social centers needed more time to be nourished and fully developed before they were attached to avenues of political power. A certain amount of independence from political choice and power is needed if open deliberation is going to evolve. Thus, a very difficult balance must be struck between making an impact on political power and retaining openness and freedom for deliberation—a balance that the social centers failed to make, resulting in their failure to transform American politics.

Finally, to ensure open and free discussion, organizers must make sure that citizens themselves institute the processes of deliberation. As social centers activists argued, only when citizens themselves help form the institutions necessary for democratic debate will they understand the importance of what they are doing. Due to this, organizers will have to make sure, as Frederic Howe failed to do at times, that while they provide leadership, their own goals and agendas cannot get in the way of open debate. These are large challenges for any organizer to face. Unless they are kept in mind, though, contemporary experiments to rejuvenate a democratic public will suffer from the problems social centers activists failed to solve.[7]

Admittedly, we live in a time very different from the Progressive Era. Today, democratic activists and intellectuals face new challenges: the suburbanization of America and the increasing loss of civic and public space, a much more powerful mass media, new computer technologies like the Internet that might facilitate more communication but are threatened by commercial pressures, and the increasing breakdown of communities in cities. Nonetheless, we have a lot to learn from the activists and intellectuals who struggled for a democratic public during the Progressive Era. For in the end we still have the same hope that the activists studied here had: the desire to stop political corruption and rejuvenate American democracy. From these activists we can learn a crucial lesson: without citizens creating the institutions necessary for facilitating the growth of public deliberation, democracy will be a meaningless term. Without political leaders articulating this idea and acting upon it, public life and citizenship will continue to stagnate.

The most important lesson of all to learn is that "real democracy" requires struggle. If we are serious about committing ourselves to this struggle, then we should understand that we can lose. A democratic public will never magically emerge. It takes time and effort to create the institutions that facilitate democratic debate and participatory citizenship. If the activists and intellectuals studied here teach us anything, it is that the "hope of democracy" will remain a hope until we commit ourselves to building institutions that make it a reality. With a growing concern about the state of American politics we are doing this again today, and only history will tell if we succeed. In the end the "hope of democracy" remains ours to discover and renew.

NOTES

Introduction: Creating a Democratic Public

1. John Dewey, *The Public and Its Problems* (Denver: Swallow Press, 1927), p. 208.

2. Harriet Lusk Childs, "The Rochester Social Centers," *American City*, July 1911, p. 19. For more on this experiment, see Chapter Three.

3. E. J. Dionne, *Why Americans Hate Politics* (New York: Simon and Schuster, 1991), p. 10. On the rise of imagery and commodification of politics, see Neil Postman, *Amusing Ourselves to Death: Public Discourse in the Age of Show Business* (New York: Penguin Books, 1985), and the more historical work of Robert Westbrook, "Politics as Consumption: Managing the Modern Election," in *The Culture of Consumption: Critical Essays in American History, 1880–1980*, ed. Richard Wightman Fox and T. J. Jackson Lears (New York: Pantheon, 1983). The best essay on consumer society and its dynamics is still Theodor Adorno and Max Horkheimer, "The Culture Industry: Enlightenment as Mass Deception," in *The Dialectic of Enlightenment* (New York: Continuum, 1972).

4. Robert Dahl, *Democracy and Its Critics* (New Haven: Yale University Press, 1989), p. 2. On the Kitchen Debate, see Stephen Whitfield, *The Culture of the Cold War* (Baltimore: The Johns Hopkins University Press, 1991), pp. 73–75.

5. For Joseph Schumpeter's interpretation of democracy, see his *Capitalism, Socialism, and Democracy* (1942; reprint, New York: Harper and Row, 1976). See especially p. 263 where Schumpeter discusses how the "ways in which issues and the popular will on any issue are being manufactured is exactly analogous to the ways of commercial advertising." On these points, see also Michael Sandel's analysis in his *Democracy's Discontent: America in Search of a Public Philosophy* (Cambridge, Mass.: Harvard University Press, 1996).

6. See here Robert Putnam, "Tuning in, Tuning Out: The Strange Disappearance of Social Capital in America," *PS: Political Science and Politics*, December 1995, pp. 664–83; "Bowling Alone: America's Declining Social Capital," *Journal of Democracy*, January 1995, pp. 65–78; and the debates on Putnam's work in the *American Prospect*, March–April 1996, pp. 17–28. See also Alan Wolfe, *Whose Keeper? Social Science and Moral Obligation* (Berkeley and Los Angeles: University of California Press, 1989), and Jean Bethke Elshtain, *Democracy on Trial* (New York: Basic Books, 1995), pp. 5–21.

7. Thomas Jefferson in a letter to Joseph Cabell (2 February 1816), *Writings* (New York: Library of America, 1984), p. 1380.

8. C. Wright Mills, "On Knowledge and Power," in *Power, Politics, and People: The Collected Essays of C. Wright Mills*, ed. Irving Louis Horowitz (New York: Oxford University Press, 1967), p. 613; Dewey, *The Public and Its Problems*, p. 216; Benjamin Barber, *The Conquest of Politics: Liberal Philosophy in Democratic Times* (Princeton: Princeton University Press, 1988), p. 200. For two examples of more contemporary theories of participatory democracy, see Carole Pateman, *Participation and Democratic Theory* (Cambridge: Cambridge University Press, 1970), and Hanna Fenichel Pitkin and Sara Shumer, "On Participation," *democracy*, Fall 1982, pp. 43–54.

9. The expression "democratic public" is my term. The activists and intellectuals studied in this book used the words "real democracy" and "true democracy" but not "democratic public." I believe that the term "democratic public" best describes what these activists and intellectuals worked and struggled for, as I will show throughout this work.

10. James Harvey Robinson, *The New History* (1912; reprint, New York: The Free Press, 1965), p. 17. To look ahead, it is interesting to note that James Harvey Robinson connected a new form of history to the development of a democratic public through the type of university extension studied here in Chapter One. See his "Suggestions for the Study of History," *University Extension*, February 1893, pp. 225–29. For a good treatment of how Charles Beard saw history as connected to public issues, see Thomas Bender, "The New History: Then and Now," *Reviews in American History* 12 (1984): 612–22 and his *Intellect and Public Life: Essays on the Social History of Academic Intellectuals in the United States* (Baltimore: The Johns Hopkins University Press, 1993), pp. 75, 93.

11. I am well aware that my idea about history's relation to social criticism is not accepted by many professional historians who are enamored with the idea of "objectivity" in historical analysis. On this point, see Peter Novick, *That Noble Dream: The "Objectivity Question" and the American Historical Profession* (Cambridge: Cambridge University Press, 1988), and Thomas Haskell's perceptive review of Novick's work, "Objectivity Is Not Neutrality: Rhetoric Versus Practice in Peter Novick's *That Noble Dream*," *History and Theory* 29 (1990): 129–57.

12. There are many sources on how the Progressive Era relates to the development of the modern American nation. See, for instance, John Milton Cooper, *Pivotal Decades: The United States, 1900–1920* (New York: Norton, 1990); Arthur Link and Richard McCormick, *Progressivism* (Arlington Heights: Harlan Davidson, 1983); and Robert Wiebe, *The Search for Order, 1877–1920* (New York: Hill and Wang, 1967). For more specific works, see: on modern economics, Martin Sklar, *The Corporate Reconstruction of American Capitalism, 1890–1916* (Cambridge: Cambridge University Press, 1988); on modern state development, Stephen Skorownek, *Building a New State: The Expansion of National Administrative Capacities, 1877–1920* (Cambridge: Cambridge University Press, 1982); on modern culture, Henry May, *The End of American Innocence: A Study of the First Years of Our Own Time, 1912–1917* (New York: Knopf, 1959).

13. The expression "age of reform" comes from Richard Hofstadter's classic work *The Age of Reform* (New York: Vintage, 1955). On the various movements cited here, see James Weinstein, *The Decline of Socialism in America, 1912–1925* (New York: Monthly Review Press, 1967); August Meier, *Negro Thought in America, 1880–1915: Racial Ideologies in the Age of Booker T. Washington* (Ann Arbor: University of Michigan Press, 1963); and Nancy Cott, *The Grounding of Modern Feminism* (New Haven: Yale University Press, 1987). For how intellectuals committed themselves to a critical examination of the inherited forms of political and social thought during this period, see James Kloppenberg, *Uncertain Victory: Social Democracy and Progressivism in European and American Thought, 1870–1920* (New York: Oxford University Press, 1986).

14. Herbert Croly, *Progressive Democracy* (New York: Macmillan Co., 1914), p. 145. It should be noted that Croly changed many of his earlier ideas found in *The Promise of American Life* (New York: Macmillan Co., 1909), a book that was quite antidemocratic. For more on Croly's development as a thinker, see David Levy, *Herbert Croly of "The New Republic"* (Princeton: Princeton University Press, 1985). For an entertaining treatment of political corruption prior to and during the Progressive Era, see Matthew Josephson's *The Robber Barons* (New York: Harcourt, Brace and Co., 1934). For an analysis of the rise of the boss system in the American city, see Amy Bridges, *A City in the Republic: Antebellum New York and the Origins of Machine Politics* (Cambridge: Cambridge University Press, 1984). Richard McCormick has shown how the Progressive Era was framed by the belief that business had corrupted politics and that a "public" could do something about it. See his "The Discovery That Business Corrupts Politics: A Reappraisal of the Origins of Progressivism," *American Historical Review* 86 (1981):

247–74. On muckrakers and their ideas about public opinion, see David Mark Chalmers, *The Social and Political Ideas of the Muckrakers* (New York: Books for Libraries Press, 1964). On direct democracy initiatives during the Progressive Era, see Thomas Cronin, *Direct Democracy: The Politics of Initiative, Referendum, and Recall* (Cambridge, Mass.: Harvard University Press, 1989), pp. 50–59. For a recent work of political criticism that discusses parallels between the Progressive Era and our own time, see E. J. Dionne, *They Only **Look** Dead: Why Progressives Will Dominate the Next Political Era* (New York: Simon and Schuster, 1996).

15. William Sullivan, *Reconstructing Public Philosophy* (Berkeley and Los Angeles: University of California Press, 1982), p. 7.

16. Thomas Bender, "Metropolitan Life and the Making of Public Culture," in *Power, Culture, and Place,* ed. John Mollenkompf (New York: Russell Sage Foundation, 1988), p. 262.

17. It should be noted that I do not study any of the people in this book from an overall biographical perspective. I study those elements of their lives that relate to the larger historical developments I am tracing.

18. Samuel Haber, *Efficiency and Uplift: Scientific Management in the Progressive Era, 1890–1920* (Chicago: University of Chicago Press, 1964), p. ix. Christopher Lasch, *The Revolt of the Elites and the Betrayal of American Democracy* (New York: Norton, 1995), p. 171. For a contemporary argument that links democracy and efficiency, see Philip Slater's sloppy *A Dream Deferred: America's Discontent and the Search for a New Democratic Ideal* (Boston: Beacon Press, 1991). It should be noted here that historians have also misunderstood the use of the word "science" during the Progressive Era. This term also has been associated with technocracy and expertise, but David Hollinger has shown otherwise in an interpretation of Walter Lippmann's early work in which science was seen not as efficiency but as rational intersubjectivity. See David Hollinger, *In the American Province: Studies in the History and Historiography of Ideas* (Baltimore: The Johns Hopkins University Press, 1989), especially pp. 48–49.

19. For an eloquent treatment of social control, see Christopher Lasch, *The New Radicalism in America, 1889–1963* (New York: Norton, 1965), especially chap. 5; see also Paul Boyer, *Urban Masses and Moral Order in America, 1820–1920* (Cambridge, Mass.: Harvard University Press, 1978). For good criticisms of the social control thesis, see William Muraskin, "The Social Control Theory," *Journal of Social History* 9 (1976): 559–69, and Robert Westbrook, *John Dewey and American Democracy* (Ithaca: Cornell University Press, 1991), p. 172, n. 22. For a rich treatment of middle-class activism from a contemporary viewpoint that provides a balanced account, see Robert Coles, *The Call of Service: A Witness to Idealism* (Boston: Houghton Mifflin Co., 1993).

20. For an excellent historical treatment of how the death of partisanship entailed the death of popular politics, see Michael McGerr, *The Decline of Popular Politics: The American North, 1865–1928* (New York: Oxford University Press, 1986). On pp. 151–52 McGerr deals with progressives.

21. For more on the growing reality of the modern state during the Progressive Era, see Skorownek, *Building a New State.*

Chapter 1: Searching for a Public

1. Charles Zueblin, *A Decade of Civic Development* (Chicago: University of Chicago Press, 1905), p. 22.

2. The historian Peter Filene has called for an "obituary for the Progressive Era," believing that there were only disparate movements with no unifying theme. See his "An Obituary for the Progressive Movement," *American Quarterly* 22 (1970): 20–34. See also Daniel Rodgers,

"In Search of Progressivism," *Reviews in American History* 10 (1982): 113–32. My argument that public opinion was seen as the solution for political corruption during the Progressive Era draws from Richard McCormick's "The Discovery That Business Corrupts Politics: A Reappraisal of the Origins of Progressivism," *American Historical Review* 86 (1981): 247–74.

3. For an overdismissive treatment of how the small-town ideal lived on during the Progressive Era, see Jean Quandt, *From the Small Town to the Great Community: The Social Thought of Progressive Intellectuals* (New Brunswick: Rutgers University Press, 1970). On the transition to the city, see the overview provided by Raymond Mohl, *The New City: Urban America in the Industrial Age, 1860–1920* (Arlington Heights: Harlan Davidson, 1985).

4. David Mark Chalmers, *The Social and Political Ideas of the Muckrakers* (New York: Books for Libraries Press, 1964), p. 105. Chalmers traces out the muckrakers' faith in public opinion on pages 46–49. On the rise of the political boss, see Amy Bridges, *A City in the Republic: Antebellum New York and the Origins of Machine Politics* (Cambridge: Cambridge University Press, 1984). For a wonderful example of the best of muckraker-writing on cities, see Lincoln Steffens, *The Shame of the Cities* (1902; reprint, New York: Hill and Wang, 1963), and his *The Autobiography of Lincoln Steffens* (New York: Harcourt, Brace and Co., 1931). My analysis of the weakness of muckrakers draws from Stanley Schultz, "The Morality of Politics: The Muckrakers' Vision of Democracy," *Journal of American History* 52 (1965): 527–47; Chalmers's work; and McCormick's "The Discovery That Business Corrupts Politics."

5. Thomas Bender, "Metropolitan Life and the Making of Public Culture," in *Power, Culture, and Place*, ed. John Mollenkompf (New York: Russell Sage Foundation, 1988), p. 262. The best sources for understanding the modern sense of urban life as an overwhelming and chaotic social formation come from literature and social theory. See, for example, Theodore Dreiser's description of Chicago in *Sister Carrie* (1900; reprint, Indianapolis: Bobbs-Merrill, 1970), pp. 22–24. See also Henry James's comments about New York City in his *The American Scene* (New York: Harper and Brothers, 1907). For a social theorist's treatment of the anonymity of modern city life, see Georg Simmel's turn-of-the-century essay "The Metropolis and Mental Life," in *The Sociology of Georg Simmel*, ed. Kurt Wolff (New York: The Free Press, 1950). For historical treatments of the city's creation of an overwhelmed and passive public, see Marshall Berman, *All That Is Solid Melts into Air: The Experience of Modernity* (New York: Simon and Schuster, 1982), and Alan Trachtenberg, *The Incorporation of America: Culture and Society in the Gilded Age* (New York: Hill and Wang, 1982).

6. William Wilson, "J. Horace McFarland and the City Beautiful Movement," *Journal of Urban History* 7 (1981): 315. For two examples of citizens' efforts, see Joseph Dannenberg, "The Advance of Civic Art in Baltimore," *Craftsman* 9 (1905): 202–3, and Mary Rankin Cranston, "The Garden as a Civic Asset," *Craftsman* 16 (1909): 205–10. On the billboard campaign, see William Wilson, "The Billboard: Bane of the City Beautiful," *Journal of Urban History* 13 (1987): 394–425. Many other works cited throughout this chapter list local efforts. For more on the national organizations and the movement as a whole, see Jon Peterson, "The City Beautiful Movement: Forgotten Origins and Lost Meanings," *Journal of Urban History* 2 (1976): 415–34; William Wilson, *The City Beautiful Movement* (Baltimore: The Johns Hopkins University Press, 1989).

7. *First Report of the Park and Outdoor Art Association* (Louisville, Kentucky: APOAA, 1897), p. 21. On antiurbanism as a tradition, see Morton and Lucia White, *The Intellectual Versus the City* (Cambridge, Mass.: Harvard University Press, 1962).

8. Joseph Wheelock in *The Second Report of the American Park and Outdoor Art Association* (Boston: Rockwell and Churchill Press, 1898), p. 52.

9. Woodruff's speech is in the American Park and Outdoor Art Association's *Year Book and Record of the Seventh Annual Meeting* (Rochester: Democrat and Chronicle, 1903), p. 78.

10. Barr Ferree, "The Lesson of Sculpture," *Craftsman* 7 (1904–5): 117; Karl Bitter, "Mu-

nicipal Sculpture," *Municipal Affairs* 2 (1898): 74; Charles Shean, "Mural Painting," *Craftsman* 7 (1904): 18, 26. For the argument about artists as citizens, see Frederick S. Lamb, "Municipal Art," *Municipal Affairs* 1 (1897): 684. Charles Mulford Robinson, one of the most influential city beautiful activists, spoke of "the public spirit" found in city beautiful activities. See his *The Improvement of Towns and Cities or The Practical Basis of Civic Aesthetics* (New York: G. P. Putnam and Sons, 1901), pp. 198, 214. For a thoroughly democratic vision of public art, see "Mural Painting—An Art for the People and a Record of the Nation's Development," *Craftsman* 10 (1906): 60.

11. Theodore Burton, "Civic Betterment," *American City*, September 1909, p. 14; H. K. Bush-Brown, "Parks," *Craftsman* 6 (1904): 121; J. Horace McFarland, "The Great Civic Awakening," *Outlook*, 18 April 1903, p. 919. Once again Robinson spoke of citizen loyalty to the city: see his *Improvement of Towns and Cities*, p. 219, and his "Improvement in City Life: Part III, Aesthetic Progress," *Atlantic Monthly*, June 1899, p. 785. Here Robinson wrote, "The happier people of the rising City Beautiful will grow in love for it, in pride in it. They will be better citizens, because better instructed, more artistic, and filled with civic pride."

12. J. G. Phelps-Stokes quoted in Frederick C. Ford, comp., *The Grouping of Public Buildings* (Hartford: The Municipal Art Society, 1904), p. 22; John De Witt Warner, "Civic Centers," *Municipal Affairs* 6 (1902): 5; Frederick S. Lamb, "The Beautifying of Our Cities," *Craftsman* 2 (1902): 175.

13. Michele Bogart, *Public Sculpture and the Civic Ideal in New York City, 1890–1930* (Chicago: University of Chicago Press, 1989), pp. 27–28; John De Witt Warner, "Matters That Suggest Themselves," *Municipal Affairs* 2 (1898): 124, 125. Bogart draws upon Howard Mumford Jones, "The Renaissance and American Origins," in his *Ideas in America* (Cambridge, Mass.: Harvard University Press, 1944). For a shorter treatment of New York City's elitist city beautiful movement, see Harvey Kantor, "The City Beautiful in New York," *New York Historical Society Quarterly* 57 (1973): 149–71.

14. Arnold Brunner, "City and Town Planning Suggesting Beauty Based on Business Conditions," *Craftsman* 17 (1909–10): 657; Edwin Howland Bashfield, "Mural Painting," *Municipal Affairs* 2 (1898): 100–101, and "A Word for Municipal Art," *Municipal Affairs* 3 (1899): 582–83; George Kriehn, "The City Beautiful," *Municipal Affairs* 3 (1899): 598, 599. There are other examples of these views. See for instance "Public Art in American Cities," *Municipal Affairs* 2 (1898): 1–13.

15. On Irene Sargent, see Eileen Boris, *Art and Labor: Ruskin, Morris, and the Craftsman Ideal* (Philadelphia: Temple University Press, 1986), p. 74. The connections between the city beautiful movement and the arts and crafts movement were many. For instance, see Charles Mulford Robinson, "Handicraft Workers and Civic Beauty," *Craftsman* 5 (1903): 235–39; American Park and Outdoor Art Association, *Bulletin* 5 (1902): 10; "Survey of Civic Betterment," *Chautauquan*, September 1903, p. 69. City beautiful activists were often influenced by the more democratic side of the arts and crafts movement.

16. Irene Sargent, "Private Simplicity as a Promoter of Public Art," *Craftsman* 2 (1902): 211; and Sargent "Municipal Art: A Lesson from Foreign Towns," *Craftsman* 6 (1904): 322. It should be noted that Sargent criticized German municipal art for turning the public into a pawn of power. See her "A Second Lesson of Sculpture," *Craftsman* 7 (1904–5): 126–27.

17. Sargent, "Private Simplicity as a Promoter of Public Art," p. 213. For her point that people could not go back to the past, see p. 214.

18. For more on the settlement house as it relates to progressive democracy, see Chapter Three in this book. On how progressives were tied to an older culture of religion and the ministry, see Robert Crunden, *Ministers of Reform: The Progressives' Achievement in American Civilization, 1889–1920* (New York: Basic Books, 1982).

19. For Zueblin's biography the best source is the University of Chicago's Presidential Pa-

pers, 1889–1925, University of Chicago Library. Here there is a eulogy for Zueblin, probably from the fall of 1923. See the Presidential Papers, 1899–1925, Box 11, Folder 13. See also Peterson, "The City Beautiful Movement," p. 421.

20. Charles Zueblin, "The Return to Nature," *Chautauquan,* May 1904, p. 257. For his celebration of the city's diversity, see Charles Zueblin, *American Municipal Progress* (New York: Macmillan Co., 1916), p. 6. For Zueblin's hope for urban activism, see his "The New Civic Spirit," *Chautauquan,* September 1903, pp. 55–59.

21. Charles Zueblin, "The Making of the City," *Chautauquan,* November 1903, p. 275; Zueblin, "The Training of the Citizen," *Chautauquan,* October 1903, p. 165.

22. Zueblin, *American Municipal Progress,* pp. 395, 2, 400, 387, respectively. For how some progressives endorsed *commission* government for its support of the initiative and referendum, see Bradley Rice, *Progressive Cities: The Commission Government Movement in America, 1901–1920* (Austin: University of Texas Press, 1977), pp. 72–75.

23. Zueblin, *American Municipal Progress,* p. 397; "The Training of the Citizen," p. 166; Zueblin "Greater New York," *Chautauquan,* February 1904, p. 574. I deal with the People's Institute in the next chapter.

24. Harper quoted in Richard Storr, *Harper's University: The Beginnings* (Chicago: University of Chicago Press, 1966), p. 197. On Chautauqua, see Theodore Morrison, *Chautauqua: A Center for Education, Religion, and the Arts in America* (Chicago: University of Chicago Press, 1974), and James McBath, "The Emergence of Chautauqua as a Religious and Educational Institution, 1874–1900," *Methodist History* 20 (1981), pp. 3–12. It should be made clear that the university extension of the 1890s was distinct from the later "Wisconsin Idea" of using the university as a servant to state government. The university in the 1890s was a servant to the public, not the state. George Woytanowitz argues that the University of Wisconsin's later ideal was one where the university was the "solver of specific social problems." He goes on to say, "The extension ideology of the 1890s, on the contrary, viewed the university as an informative influence on citizens, enabling them to cast their ballots more wisely." George Woytanowitz, *University Extension: The Early Years in America, 1885–1915* (Iowa City: National University Extension Association, 1974), pp. 106–7.

25. Allen Davis, "Continuing Education," *History of Education Quarterly* 20 (1980): 224, 225; Woytanowitz, *University Extension,* p. ix. "University Extension Circular," found in the Presidential Papers, 1889–1925, University of Chicago Library, Box 20, Folder 9.

26. For his lecture titles, see the Presidential Papers, 1889–1925, University of Chicago Library, Box 20, Folder 10. The eulogy is found in Box 11, Folder 13. On Zueblin's early activities, see Charles Zueblin, "The Chicago Society for University Extension," *University Extension,* March 1892, pp. 273–75.

27. Charles Zueblin, "Results and Prospects of University Extension," *Dial,* 1 April 1897, p. 208. For his belief that university extension would help create a new form of citizenship, see Zueblin's presidential address in *Nation-Wide Civic Betterment: A Report on the Third Annual Convention of the American League for Civic Improvement* (Chicago: American League for Civic Improvement, 1903), p. 14.

28. Charles Zueblin, "The Lecturer and the Laborer," *University Extension,* January 1894, p. 214; Zueblin, "Results and Prospects of University Extension," p. 208. On the commercial corruption of the nineteenth-century lyceum, see James Pond, "The Lyceum," *Cosmopolitan,* April 1896, p. 599; Carl Bode, *The American Lyceum: Town Meeting of the Mind* (New York: Oxford University Press, 1956), p. 200; and David Mead, *Yankee Eloquence in the Middle West: The Ohio Lyceum, 1850–1870* (East Lansing: Michigan State College Press, 1951), p. 231.

29. Zueblin, "The Lecturer and the Laborer," pp. 213, 216, 215, respectively. For more on how intellectuals can be connected to their public, see Michael Walzer, *The Company of Critics: Social Criticism and Political Commitment in the Twentieth Century* (New York: Basic Books, 1988).

30. For Zueblin's money conflicts, see the Presidential Papers, 1889–1925, University of Chicago Library, Box 11, Folder 13. For Judson's lack of support for university extension, see Storr, *Harper's University*, p. 370, and Steven Diner, *A City and Its Universities, Public Policy in Chicago, 1892–1919* (Chapel Hill: University of North Carolina Press, 1980), p. 47. For more on the growth of the modern university, see Laurence Veysey, *The Emergence of the American University* (Chicago: University of Chicago Press, 1965). It is interesting to note that Zueblin's books were received with hesitation by some academics due to the popular mode in which they were written. See for instance how J.A.F. in the *American Political Science Review* complains that Zueblin's *Decade of Civic Development* was "written for a popular audience" and lacks "scientific" qualities and "critical discussion." *American Political Science Review* 1 (1907): 666. See also *American Journal of Sociology* 9 (1904): 844, where *American Municipal Progress* is reviewed.

31. The quotes from Judson are from two letters written to Zueblin. The first is dated 7 March 1908, and the second is dated 27 November 1907. They are found in the Presidential Papers, 1889–1925, University of Chicago Library, Box 11, Folder 13. The Edward Bemis case is a famous case of academic freedom. See Veysey, *The Emergence of the American University*, p. 368, and Harold Bergquist, "The Edward Bemis Case at the University of Chicago," *American Association of University Professors Bulletin* 58 (1972): 383–93. On the general problem of the academy and political controversy, see Mary Furner, *Advocacy and Objectivity: A Crisis in the Professionalization of American Social Science, 1865–1905* (Lexington: University Press of Kentucky, 1975); Dorothy Ross, "Socialism and American Liberalism: Academic Social Thought in the 1890s," *Perspectives in American History* 11 (1977–78): 1–79; and Ross, *The Origins of American Social Science* (Cambridge: Cambridge University Press, 1991). Another case occurred after Bemis's and before Zueblin's. Jerome Raymond, a public lecturer and associate professor of sociology (the exact same position as Zueblin's), quit because of complaints about the political content of his talks. See his letter to Harper announcing his resignation in which he complains that he cannot be "cautious" in his lectures. See the Presidential Papers, 1889–1925, University of Chicago Library, Box 21, Folder 3. The letter is dated 15 December 1903.

32. In a letter to Judson from Jerome Raymond dated 13 May 1913, Raymond states that a new University Extension Society had started outside of the University of Chicago and that Zueblin was involved. See the Presidential Papers, 1889–1925, University of Chicago Library, Box 21, Folder 3. On Zueblin's involvement in the Ford Hall Forum, see George Coleman, ed., *Democracy in the Making: Ford Hall and the Open Forum Movement* (Boston: Little, Brown and Co., 1915), p. 38 (on Zueblin's speaking engagements) and p. 129, for Zueblin's written praise for Ford Hall's forums. For more on Ford Hall, see the next chapter.

33. For more on how the university has looked down upon popular and political education, see Thomas Bender's concluding essay in his *Intellect and Public Life: Essays on the Social History of Academic Intellectuals in the United States* (Baltimore: The Johns Hopkins University Press, 1993).

Chapter 2: From Tent Meetings to the Forum Movement

1. Frederic Howe, *The British City: The Beginnings of Democracy* (New York: Charles Scribner's Sons, 1907), p. 360.

2. This chapter is not a straightforward biography but is rather theme oriented. I am not studying Howe's entire life here but rather how he related to certain institutions. This chapter will be as much about those institutions as about Howe's career. Howe's autobiography is *The Confessions of a Reformer* (1925; reprint, New York: Quadrangle Books, 1967).

3. Frederic Howe, "Cleveland's Group Plan," *Charities*, 1 February 1903, p. 1548; *The Confessions of a Reformer*, p. 115. For Howe's invoking of Pericles in his discussion of Cleveland's civic center, see his "Plans for a City Beautiful," *Harper's Weekly*, 23 April 1904, p. 624. See also here Howe's "Cleveland—A City 'Finding Itself,' " *World's Work*, October 1903, pp. 3988–99. On Cleveland's civic center, see Daniel Burnham et al., "The Grouping of Public Buildings at Cleveland," *Inland Architect and News Record* 42 (1903): 13–15. For Howe's training in professional political science, see his *Confessions of a Reformer*, p. 27 and chap. 4 (on Woodrow Wilson at Johns Hopkins). See also Howe's *Taxation and Taxes in the United States Under the Internal Revenue System, 1791–1895* (New York: Thomas Crowell and Co., 1896).

4. Frederic Howe, "Tom Johnson and the City of Cleveland," *Reader Magazine*, October 1907, p. 503. For Johnson's reference to an "ideal city," see Tom Johnson, "The Ideal City," *Saturday Evening Post*, 9 November 1901, pp. 1–2. See Brand Whitlock's discussion of Johnson's belief that Cleveland was a "city on the hill" in his *Forty Years of It* (New York: D. Appleton, 1914), p. 172. Howe explained his whole life in his *Confessions of a Reformer* as an "unlearning" of his past—his small-town background, his Methodist upbringing, and his faith in Republicans and "good men." Johnson played a large role in this "unlearning." See *Confessions*, pp. 92–99.

5. William Suit, "Tom Loftin Johnson, Businessman Reformer," Ph.D. diss., Kent State University, 1988, p. 101. Suit's dissertation is a fine source on Johnson's life. See also Tom Johnson's autobiography, *My Story* (New York: B. W. Huebsch, 1913). Eugene Murdock's articles are also helpful: "Cleveland's Johnson: Elected Mayor," *Ohio Historical Quarterly* 65 (1956): 28–43; "Cleveland's Johnson: At Home," *Ohio Historical Quarterly* 63 (1954): 319–35.

6. This information is culled from the sources cited in the last footnote. On George's political and economic philosophy I rely on his classic *Progress and Poverty* (1877; reprint, New York: Robert Schalkenbach Foundation, 1955). For George's urban vision, see John Thomas, *Alternative America: Henry George, Edward Bellamy, Henry Demarest Lloyd, and the Adversary Tradition* (Cambridge, Mass.: The Belknap Press of Harvard University Press, 1983), p. 124. It is interesting to note how Johnson's self-questioning and "conversion" came at a time (the late nineteenth century) when many upper-middle-class people suffered from breakdowns and nervous disorders (i.e., William James, Jane Addams, Henry Adams, etc.). Though Johnson's experience was not psychological, its similarity to these other breakdowns is interesting. The late nineteenth century was clearly a time of general psychic breakdown and a building up of new ideas. It should also be noted that Johnson's alliance with Populists illustrates a direct connection between populism and progressivism.

7. George Sikes, "Tom L. Johnson, Mayor of Cleveland," *World Today*, July 1906, p. 698; Lincoln Steffens, *The Struggle for Self-Government* (New York: McClure, Phillips, and Co., 1906), p. 183. On Johnson's accomplishments, see Edward Bemis (the same Edward Bemis fired from the University of Chicago before Zueblin), "Tom L. Johnson's Achievements as Mayor of Cleveland," *Review of Reviews*, May 1911, pp. 558–60; Eugene Murdock, "Cleveland's Johnson: First Term," *Ohio Historical Quarterly* 67 (1958): 35–49; William Norton, "Chief Kohler of Cleveland and His Golden Rule Policy," *Outlook*, 6 November 1909, pp. 537–42; and Suit's "Tom Loftin Johnson."

8. For this story of Johnson's struggle, I rely on Johnson's *My Story*; "Mayor Johnson and the Traction Companies," *Outlook*, 4 August 1906, pp. 777–78; Edward Bemis, "The Cleveland Street Railway Settlement," *Quarterly Journal of Economics* 24 (1910): 550–60; Suit, "Tom Loftin Johnson"; Eugene Murdock, "Cleveland's Johnson," *Ohio Archaeological and Historical Quarterly* 62 (1953): 323–33; Robert Bremner, "The Street Railway Controversy in Cleveland," *American Journal of Economics and Sociology* 9 (1950): 185–206; Robert Briggs, "The Progressive Era in Cleveland, Ohio: Tom L. Johnson's Administration, 1901–1909," Ph.D. diss., University of Chicago, 1962.

9. For Howe's state senator term, see his *Confessions of a Reformer*, pp. 160–66. The city as the "hope of democracy" comes from Howe's most famous book during this period of time, *The City: The Hope of Democracy* (New York: Charles Scribner's Sons, 1905).

10. Johnson, *My Story*, pp. 148–49; Tom Johnson, "Our Leaders in Reform Are the Cities," *Smith's Magazine*, July 1906, unpaginated.

11. Joseph Miller, "Home Rule: A Plea for Free Cities," *American Journal of Politics* 4 (1894): 39, 44. See also Ellis Oberholtzer, "Home Rule for Our American Cities," *Annals of the American Academy of Political and Social Sciences* 3 (1892): 736–63; Simon Patten, "The Decay of Local Government in America," *Annals of the American Academy of Political and Social Science* 1 (1890): 26–42; William Ivins, "Municipal Government," *Political Science Quarterly* 2 (1887): 291–312. Samuel "Golden Rule" Jones, the mayor of Toledo, also believed home rule could make cities more democratic. He argued that city government was "better than state and national government, because at least city government was closer to the people and more democratically responsive." Quoted in Howard Weiner, "The Response to the American City (1885–1915) as Reflected in Writings Dealing with the City in Scholarly and Professional Serial Publications," Ph.D. diss., New York University, 1972, p. 37. This democratic thought on city life is connected to the "vogue" of celebrating Switzerland, with its local and participatory cantonal government system, which also swept American political thought in the 1890s.

12. Howe, *The City: The Hope of Democracy*, pp. 101, 308; Howe, *The British City*, p. 56. *The City: The Hope of Democracy*, pp. 164–65.

13. Howe, *The City: The Hope of Democracy*, p. 123; Howe, *The British City*, p. 183. Frederic Howe, "The Case for Municipal Ownership," *Publications of the American Economics Association* 7 (1906): 114. On the democratic origins of British municipal socialism, see James Kloppenberg, *Uncertain Victory: Social Democracy and Progressivism in European and American Thought, 1870–1920* (New York: Oxford University Press, 1986), pp. 267–68. It was precisely the localism of municipal socialism that made it more democratic than later movements in British socialism. The original exponents of this political faith, Beatrice and Sidney Webb, both became technocrats by 1902. See Kloppenberg's analysis on pp. 272–73.

14. Johnson, "The Ideal City," p. 1.

15. "The Week," *Nation*, 13 April 1911, p. 357.

16. For examples of Johnson's invoking the idea of the "public" and the "people," see his "Nine Years' War with Privilege," *Hampton's Magazine*, July 1911, pp. 4, 6. For more on the muckrakers and their failure, see the Introduction and Chapter One in this book.

17. Johnson, *My Story*, pp. 82, 83. For the populists' attempts to create a public through political education, see Lawrence Goodwyn, *The Populist Moment: A Short History of the Agrarian Revolt in America* (New York: Oxford University Press, 1978), pp. 34, 45, 154–56.

18. Thomas Campbell, "Mounting Crisis and Reform: Cleveland's Political Development," in *The Birth of Modern Cleveland, 1865–1930*, ed. Thomas Campbell and Edward Miggins (London: Associated University Presses, 1988), p. 308. For how Johnson ensured his opposition to free speech, see Carl Lorenz, *Tom L. Johnson: Mayor of Cleveland* (New York: A. S. Barnes Co., 1911), p. 101, and "Mayor Johnson's Latest Victory for Good Government," *Arena*, August 1903, p. 209. On how there were always question-answer periods, see Robert Bremner, "Tom L. Johnson," *Ohio Archaeological and Historical Quarterly* 59 (1950): 9. On how Johnson made sure meetings did not degenerate into mere entertainment, see Briggs, "The Progressive Era in Cleveland, Ohio," p. 106, and Lorenz, *Tom L. Johnson: Mayor of Cleveland*, p. 99. For the liveliness of tent meetings, see Whitlock, *Forty Years of It*, pp. 169–70. For more on Johnson's support among working-class ethnics, see Briggs, "The Progressive Era in Cleveland, Ohio," p. 142; Howe, *The Confessions of a Reformer*, pp. 109–10; "Municipal Tendencies," *Review of Reviews*, May 1903, p. 533.

19. Tom Johnson, "My Fight Against a Three-Cent Fare," *Hampton's Magazine*, September 1911, p. 373.

20. Johnson, *My Story*, p. 283. On Johnson's willingness to debate opponents, see Briggs, "The Progressive Era in Cleveland, Ohio," p. 103; on allowing Emma Goldman to speak, see Howe, *The Confessions of a Reformer*, p. 138.

21. Lorenz, *Tom L. Johnson: Mayor of Cleveland*, p. 139. Tom Johnson, "The Three-Cent Fare Fight in Cleveland," *Hampton's Magazine*, October 1911, p. 498. See also "The Failure of Tom Johnson," *World's Work*, January 1909, p. 11085; Bremner, "Tom L. Johnson," p. 3. On Johnson's legal battle, see "A Review of the World," *Current Literature*, November 1907, p. 477. On Johnson's attempt to block the referendum, see Lorenz, *Tom L. Johnson*, p. 197. It should be noted here that Tom Johnson never made tent meetings a part of the permanent municipal governing apparatus. He should have thought more about making public meetings a prerequisite for passing legislation.

22. Howe, *The Confessions of a Reformer*, p. 181. Howe quoted in "People's Institute Defining a Better New York," *Survey*, 22 November 1913, p. 198. Frederic Howe, *The Modern City and Its Problems* (New York: Charles Scribner's Sons, 1915), p. 117. Frederic Howe, "The Constitution and Public Opinion," *Proceedings of the Academy of Political Science* 5 (1914): 18.

23. Frederic Howe, *European Cities at Work* (New York: Charles Scribner's Sons, 1913), pp. 348–49. For how experts would become servants of a public, see Howe, *The Modern City and Its Problems*, pp. 97–98. On Wisconsin, see Frederic Howe, *Wisconsin: An Experiment in Democracy* (New York: Charles Scribner's Sons, 1912), especially pp. 39–42, 43, 59, 156–60. For more information on Wisconsin, see David Thelen, *Robert M. La Follette and the Insurgent Spirit* (Boston: Little, Brown and Co., 1976). Interestingly enough, Howe spoke in his book on Wisconsin as if the initiative and referendum were in place there. They were not, and this seriously harmed his understanding of the amount of democracy available in Wisconsin. For a good critique of Howe's faith in expertise and democracy, see Frank Watson's review of Howe's *Socialized Germany* in *Annals of the American Academy of Political and Social Science* 64 (1916): 236.

24. Charles Sprague Smith, *Working with the People* (New York: A. Wessels Co., 1904), p. 24.

25. People's Institute Constitution, found in the People's Institute Records, New York Public Library, Box 1. Charles Sprague Smith, "The People's Institute of New York and Its Work for the Development of Citizenship Along Democratic Lines," *Arena*, July 1907, p. 50. For an example of Smith sending a resolution to a politician, see the People's Institute Records, New York Public Library, Box 10, Folder Entitled "Adult Education—Cooper Union—Lectures, Meetings, and Classes—Printed Fliers." The best secondary source on the People's Institute is Robert Fisher's excellent dissertation "The People's Institute of New York City, 1897–1934: Culture, Progressive Democracy, and the People," Ph.D. diss., New York University, 1974.

26. Jacob Riis, "The People's Institute of New York," *Century Magazine*, April 1910, p. 858. On one lively floor dynamic, see People's Institute Records, New York Public Library, Box 37, Folder on the year 1907 where a banker who reported on socialism gets booed. See also an article on "Pinchot Heckled at Cooper Union (Box 39)." Robert Fisher explains the makeup of the People's Institute's public: "The typical person who participated in the activities of the Institute at Cooper Union was a foreign-born working-class male, above the age of eighteen, who lived in a Lower East Side tenement." Robert Fisher, "The People's Institute of New York," p. 81. On the issues discussed at the People's Institute, see Fisher, pp. 126–51. On the vote against intervention in the Philippines, see the People's Institute Records, Box 37, Folder on 1900.

27. John Collier, "The People's Institute," *Independent*, 30 May 1912, p. 1148. Howe in the *People's Institute Seventeenth Annual Report*, found in the People's Institute Records, New York Public Library, Box 36 (Printed Matter). For what was lectured on during Howe's directorship, see People's Institute Records, Box 10, Folder entitled "Adult Education—Cooper Union—Lectures, Meetings, and Classes." Howe in a letter to Ellery Stowell, 5 April 1915, found in People's Institute Records, Box 8. Howe in the *Eighteenth Annual Report*, found in Box 36 of the People's Institute Records.

28. Zueblin quoted in *Democracy in the Making: Ford Hall and the Open Forum Movement,* ed. George Coleman (Boston: Little, Brown and Co., 1915), p. 129. This book is an excellent source on Ford Hall. See also Reuben Lurie, *The Challenge of the Forum: The Story of Ford Hall and the Open Forum Movement* (Boston: Richard Badger, 1930). On Boston's wider public culture, including further analysis of the institutions Zueblin referred to, see Martin Green, *The Problem of Boston* (New York: Norton, 1966). For Zueblin's endorsement of the People's Institute, see his "Greater New York," *Chautauquan,* February 1904, p. 574, and the first chapter of this work. It is important to note that Zueblin saw the forum going beyond the older nineteenth-century forms of public culture in Boston, which were tied to an urban gentry. In many ways he was arguing for a new form of public culture appropriate for the new members of the American city—working-class immigrants.

29. For the report on one hundred forums in 1916, see the *Christian Science Monitor,* 12 September 1916. I found this article in a People's Institute scrapbook: see the People's Institute Records, New York Public Library, Box 40. On the spread of the forum movement, see Lurie, *The Challenge of the Forum,* especially pp. 140–44. I also consulted the magazine put out by Ford Hall called the *Community Forum,* 1916–1921 (copies found at the New York Public Library, general collection, and some in the People's Institute Records, Box 36, Printed Matter). See the advertisements for the Open Forum Bureau in this magazine. Here the famous speakers are often listed.

30. Stanton Coit quoted in *Democracy in the Making,* ed. Coleman, p. 135. Glenn Frank, "The Parliament of the People," *Century,* July 1919, p. 415. For more on how intellectuals at the People's Institute envisioned their audience, see the People's Institute Records, New York Public Library, Box 10, Folder entitled "Adult Education—Cooper Union—Lectures, Meetings, and Classes, Misc. Printed Matter."

31. Percy Stickney Grant, "The Open Forum Movement," *North American Review,* January 1916, p. 90. Frank, "The Parliament of the People," p. 403. Joseph Walker, "The Initiative, Referendum, and the Open Forum," *Community Forum,* November 1917, p. 12. For a contemporary distinction between an audience and a public, see Thomas Bender, "Wholes and Parts: Continuing the Conversation," *Journal of American History* 73 (1986): 129. For other examples of writers who argued for the connection between forums and direct legislation, see George Coleman, "Legislators Learn About Forums," *Community Forum,* March 1918, p. 11.

32. Howe quoted in Robert Arthur Huff, "Frederic C. Howe, Progressive," Ph.D. diss., University of Rochester, 1966, p. 140. Howe, *The Confessions of a Reformer,* p. 245. For Smith's control over the People's Institute, see Fisher, "The People's Institute of New York," p. 114; for Coleman's control over Ford Hall, see Lurie, *The Challenge of the Forum,* p. 85. I am not arguing here that citizens at the People's Institute meeting on subway contracts did not deliberate and agree with Howe's views. What I want to make clear is that Howe's description betrays his limited sense of what role a democratic public should play in political decision making.

33. See here Frederic Howe, "Discovering the Schoolhouse," *Saturday Evening Post,* 1 June 1912, pp. 14–15, 54–56. Before school centers formed, the People's Institute also experimented with "People's Clubs" based in schools. These too were predecessors to social centers. For reference to the "People's Clubs," see the People's Institute Records. For Howe's earliest references to using schools as centers for public life, see *The City: The Hope of Democracy,* p. 286; *The British City,* p. 342. Though these references to using schools after hours were quite early, while at Cleveland Howe did not try to form social centers. He began these efforts much later while at the People's Institute.

Chapter 3: "Buttressing the Foundations of Democracy"

1. Quoted in Edward Ward, *The Social Center* (New York: D. Appleton and Co., 1913), p. 175.

2. Charles Eliot, "The Full Utilization of a Public School Plant," *Journal of Proceedings and Addresses of the 42nd Annual Meeting of the National Education Association* (Winona, Minn.: NEA, 1903), pp. 246, 247. In 1905 Ruric Nevel Roark, the dean of the Department of Pedagogy at Kentucky State College, argued: "Practically everywhere, except in a few large cities, schoolhouses stand unused from three to five months out of every year, and during that time they are in service, are used only for the teaching of children. . . . Educational economy calls loudly for the prevention of waste resulting from this condition. Every schoolhouse should be used as a *community center of education.*" *Economy in Education* (New York: American Book Co., 1905), p. 238. See also William Maxwell, "The Economical Use of School Buildings," *Journal of Proceedings and Addresses of the 48th Annual Meeting of the National Education Association* (Winona, Minn.: NEA, 1910). Benjamin Marsh argued that "it does not pay the city to carry investment in buildings which serve only as an ornament to a district." See "The Unused Aspects of Our Public Recreation Facilities," *Annals of the American Academy of Political and Social Science* 35 (1910): 383. For the general use of the principle of efficiency during the Progressive Era, see Samuel Haber, *Efficiency and Uplift: Scientific Management in the Progressive Era, 1890–1920* (Chicago: University of Chicago Press, 1964).

3. The quote on "old town sentiment" comes from "Schools as Social Centers," *Independent,* 14 July 1904, p. 111. Eleanor Touroff Glueck, *The Community Use of Schools* (Baltimore: Williams and Wilkins Co., 1927), p. xi. For another example of trying to create small-town unity through social centers, see J. K. Paulding, "The Public School as a Center of Community Life," *Educational Review* 15 (1898): 150. For the argument that people had rights to use their schools, see Osian Lang, "The Common School Community," *Journal of Proceedings and Addresses of the National Education Association* (Chicago: NEA, 1902); for making the school utilitarian, see Carl Neligh, "The School: A Social and Industrial Center," *Southern Workman* 36 (1907): 604–12. Due to these arguments it is not surprising to find the National Education Association supporting the movement, hoping that it would legitimate the school in the eyes of many communities. See "Some Social Aspects of the School," *Charities,* 18 July 1903, pp. 61–63. On the expansion of the public high school system, see Edward Krug, *The Shaping of the American High School,* 2 vols. (New York: Harper and Row, 1964). For a classic endorsement of progressive education which argued that by widening the use of the school the school gained legitimacy, see Randolph Bourne, *The Gary Schools* (1916; reprint, Cambridge: MIT Press, 1970), pp. 38–39, 60.

4. Louise Montgomery, "Social Work in the Hamline School," *The Elementary School Teacher,* November 1907, p. 115. Mary Van Grice, *Home and School United in Widening Circles of Inspiration and Service* (Philadelphia: Christopher Sower Co., 1909). For a standard statement on parent-teacher associations, see William Bulkley, "The School as a Social Center," *Charities and the Commons,* 7 October 1905, pp. 76–78. On the call for "intelligent citizenship" through parent-teacher associations, see Robert Burns, "Schools as Community Centers," *Pennsylvania School Journal* 57 (1909): 496–97. For a good history of community control of schools during the Progressive Era, see William J. Reese, *Power and the Promise of School Reform: Grassroots Movements During the Progressive Era* (Boston: RKP, 1986).

5. John Dewey, "The School as a Social Centre" (1902), in *John Dewey: The Middle Works, 1899–1924,* ed. Jo Ann Boydston (Carbondale: Southern Illinois University Press, 1976), pp. 81–82, 83, 92, 93. For more on Dewey and his philosophical development, see Robert Westbrook, *John Dewey and American Democracy* (Ithaca: Cornell University Press, 1991). For more on Jane Addams and the settlement house movement, see Jane Addams, "The Objective Value of a Social Settlement" (1892), in *The Social Thought of Jane Addams,* ed. Christopher Lasch (Indianapolis: Bobbs-Merrill, 1965), and *Twenty Years at Hull-House* (1910; reprint, New York: Signet Classics, 1960). Most historians criticize the settlement house movement as a means of social control. See for instance Paul Boyer, *Urban Masses and Moral Order in America, 1820–1920* (Cambridge, Mass.: Harvard University Press, 1978), p. 157; Christopher Lasch, *The New Radicalism in America, 1889–1963* (New York: Norton, 1965), chaps. 1 and 5; Judith

Ann Trolander, "Hull House and the Settlement House Movement," *Journal of Urban History* 17 (1991): especially p. 415. I disagree with these approaches, for I think Addams wanted Hull House to generate open meetings and discussions on local affairs, thus making Hull House a project of collective self-education of the people. I do agree that Addams's philanthropic support and class background often injured her own good intentions.

6. On the use of schools as social centers in 1906, see Thomas Riley, "Increased Use of Public School Property," *American Journal of Sociology* 11 (1906): 655–62.

7. On light industry, see Ray Stannard Baker, "Do It for Rochester," *American Magazine*, September 1910, p. 684; on freestanding homes, see Blake McKelvey, *Rochester: The Quest for Quality, 1890–1925* (Cambridge, Mass.: Harvard University Press, 1956), p. 3. McKelvey's history is an excellent source on Rochester's history during the Progressive Era and can be consulted for the general developments of modernization. On immigration, see McKelvey's article, "Rochester's Ethnic Transformations," *Rochester History* 25 (1963): especially p. 6. On the city beautiful movement in Rochester as one example of progressive reform, see McKelvey, "A History of City Planning in Rochester," *Rochester History* 6 (1944): 1–24. For a general history of urban modernization, see Raymond Mohl, *The New City: Urban America in the Industrial Age, 1860–1920* (Arlington Heights: Harlan Davidson, 1985).

8. For the University of Rochester extension program, see McKelvey, *Rochester: The Quest for Quality*, p. 235. On the YMCA debates, see the report on the debate over socialism in *Democrat and Chronicle*, 3 May 1907, p. 18. (From hereon in the *Democrat and Chronicle* will be abbreviated *D&C*.) On the Political Equality Club, see *D&C*, 24 October 1907, p. 11. On the Women's Educational and Industrial Union, see their promotion of Charles Zueblin as an outside speaker: *D&C*, 13 June 1908, p. 19. On the "Labor Lyceum," see John Dutko, "Socialism in Rochester, 1900–1917," Master's thesis, University of Rochester, 1953, p. 24, for how this forum was open to various points of view and was widely attended. Also see issues of *Rochester Socialist*, where debates are reported on regularly (to be found in Local History Department of the Rochester Public Library). On the People's Sunday Evenings, see *D&C*, 31 October 1908, p. 14. On Walter Rauschenbusch, see how Paul Minus shows that "Rauschenbusch repeatedly involved himself in the public life of the city." Paul Minus, *Walter Rauschenbusch: American Reformer* (New York: Macmillan Co., 1988), p. 119. Minus's book is an excellent source on Rauschenbusch's relation to Rochester's public life. For his relation to the People's Sunday Evenings, see p. 129. On Rauschenbusch's relation to the Labor Lyceum, see Blake McKelvey, "Walter Rauschenbusch's Rochester," *Rochester History* 14 (1952): 6–7. It should also be noted that Charles M. Robinson, a key leader of the city beautiful movement, lived in Rochester and led the movement there.

9. *D&C*, 14 October 1909, p. 19. See also Edward Ward's contrasting of New York City's public lecture system to Rochester's social centers in his *The Social Center*, pp. 178–79.

10. On the groups who fought for social centers originally, see Harriet Lusk Childs, "The Rochester Social Centers," *American City*, July 1911, p. 18, and *D&C*, 15 February 1907, p. 15. *Proceedings of the Board of Education of the City of Rochester* (1908), p. 51; *Proceedings of the Board of Education of the City of Rochester* (1909), p. 64. These proceedings are found in the Local History Department at the Rochester Public Library. For the Board of Education's independence from Boss Aldridge, see McKelvey, *Rochester: The Quest for Quality*, p. 83. For classic statements on how the social center movement was based on free discussion and self-government, see John Collier, "The Keystone of the Arch," *Survey*, 18 November 1911, p. 1200.

11. For the quote, see *D&C*, 8 May 1909, p. 15. For the attendance rule, see *Proceedings of the Board of Education of the City of Rochester* (1909), p. 55; *D&C*, 10 December 1909, p. 21.

12. F. D. Tyson, review of *The Social Center* by Edward Ward, *Annals of the American Academy of Political and Social Science* 48 (1913): 291. On how many progressives were tied to a disillusionment with religion, see Robert Crunden, *Ministers of Reform: The Progressives' Achievement in*

American Civilization, 1889–1920 (New York: Basic Books, 1982). For Ward's biography I draw on Ward's entrance in *Who Was Who in America*, 2 vols. (Chicago: A. N. Marquis Co., 1950), 2: 556, as well as the biography given in *D&C*, 23 June 1910, p. 12.

13. George Forbes quoted in *D&C*, 7 January 1908, p. 13. Ray Stannard Baker, "Do It for Rochester," *American Magazine*, September 1910, p. 686. On Ward's statement against charity, see *D&C*, 27 September 1907, p. 18. Edward Ward, "The Rochester Movement," *Independent*, 14 October 1909, p. 860. Allen Davis points out that Ward directly discussed his plans with Jane Addams. See his *Spearheads for Reform: The Social Settlements and the Progressive Movement* (New York: Oxford University Press, 1967), p. 80. For the influence of Dewey, see Ward's bibliography in his *The Social Center*, p. 346. Where Addams most clearly argued against philanthropy was in her belief that the poor had something to teach the middle-class activists in settlement houses. She never strayed from this position during her early years at Hull House. Historians often ignore this critique of philanthropy when they discuss the efforts at "social control" by progressive reformers. It is important to understand that a distinct language of democracy, which was tied to a critique of philanthropy, developed during the Progressive Era. For another example of this critique of philanthropy from a democratic outlook, see Josiah Royce, *The Philosophy of Loyalty* (New York: Macmillan Co., 1908), pp. 216–17.

14. First constitutional preamble is quoted in "The Effect of a Social Center on a Community," *Settlement Bulletin* (Rochester) 2 (1908): 5. The second is quoted in Herbert S. Weet, "Citizenship and the Evening Use of School Buildings, II," *Common Good*, February 1911, p. 8. Livy Richard, "School Centers as 'Melting Pots,' " *New Boston*, April 1911, p. 530. For "democratic eloquence," see Kenneth Cmiel, *Democratic Eloquence: The Fight over Public Speech in 19th Century America* (Berkeley and Los Angeles: University of California Press, 1990). The quote on "fundamental element" comes from the *Common Ground* (April 1910, p. 4), a short-lived magazine published by Rochester's social centers activists. Copies of it can be found in the Local History Department of the Rochester Public Library. For a newspaper account of civic clubs, see *D&C*, 27 September 1908, p. 18. It should be noted that there were often separate civic clubs for men and women. This not only followed the social mores of the day, it also reflected these activists' sympathy for "social feminism"—the belief that women *did* have important public concerns (and that they should be allowed to vote and deliberate) but that these concerns predominantly grew out of distinct domestic issues.

15. Ward quoted in *D&C*, 4 January 1910, p. 15. On the first season, see Edward Ward, *The Social Center*, p. 186. For the Board of Education policy, see *Proceedings of the Board of Education of the City of Rochester* (1909), p. 55. For the 1909 figures, see *Rochester Social Centers and Civic Clubs* (Rochester: League of Civic Clubs, 1909), pp. 116–17. The general growth during 1910 and the 25 percent immigrant fact are reported in *D&C*, 9 November 1910, p. 14. On the report of people being turned away, see *D&C*, 15 January 1910, p. 17. Another point to be made here is that although the social centers would close during summer, civic clubs would maintain themselves; see *D&C*, 11 April 1909, p. 24.

16. *Rochester Social Centers and Civic Clubs*, p. 13; *D&C*, 20 March 1910, p. 31.

17. For the first quite controversial debate on immigration, see *D&C*, 31 January 1908, p. 15. Many of the debates and topics are found in *Rochester Social Centers and Civic Clubs*, pp. 36, 43, 76, and 108. But here I rely on the reports in *D&C* (unless otherwise noted): on streetcar development, see 22 January 1909, p. 17; on local housing conditions, see 7 November 1909, p. 27; on municipal ownership of the telephone company, see *Rochester Socialist*, 10 January 1908, p. 3; for city planning, which turned into an interesting discussion of the Chamber of Commerce, see 28 January 1910, p. 21; for the public library, see 22 January 1911, p. 22. On the Board of Education's budget, see 1 March 1909, p. 11; on free textbooks, see 20 December 1908, p. 19; on vocational training, see 27 December 1907, p. 11. See also 27 February 1910, p. 27. On direct primaries and race relations, see 1 March 1909, p. 11; on "ways and means

of reform" and "the new nationalism," see 27 November 1910, p. 25; on women's suffrage, see 2 December 1908, p. 14; on "public health as a political issue," see 14 November 1909, p. 26; on labor unions see 9 October 1907, p. 13; on the Philippines see Perry, *Wider Use of the School Plant* (New York: Russell Sage Foundation, 1910), p. 253.

18. *D&C*, 10 October 1909, p. 25. On immigration and three different viewpoints, see *D&C*, 27 February 1910, p. 27. On Democrats, Republicans, Socialists, and Prohibitionists, see *D&C*, 19 April 1908, p. 15. The alderman is quoted in Ward, *The Social Center*, p. 51.

19. The textbook discussion is reported in *D&C*, 20 December 1908, p. 19; 22 December 1908, p. 15; and 29 December 1908, p. 10. For the debate on capital punishment, see 19 April 1908, p. 15; on prohibition, see 28 March 1909, p. 26; on the exclusion of the Japanese, see 28 January 1909, p. 11. On the journalist joining in a debate, see Ward, "The Rochester Movement," p. 861.

20. Ward, *The Social Center*, pp. 63–64.

21. *Rochester Social Centers and Civic Clubs*, p. 70.

22. Childs, "The Rochester Social Centers," p. 19; *D&C*, 10 April 1908, p. 17. In some ways the goal of progressive education and progressive democracy were the same. In the mind of John Dewey and others progressive education intended to create independent and creative citizens, and so did progressive democracy—as found in social centers. Progressive educators allowed students to learn by problem solving, and progressive democrats allowed citizens to learn by debating in preparation for problem solving.

23. All information is from *D&C* unless otherwise stated: the speaker on the civic ideal is quoted in 10 January 1909, p. 20. On playgrounds, see 11 September 1908, p. 15; on the sewage system, see 2 April 1910, p. 17; on the dam, see 11 December 1910, p. 28; on the public library, see 22 January 1911, p. 22; on plays, see 19 April 1908, p. 15; on improving schools, see 19 November 1910, p. 18; on curbing real estate speculation, see *Rochester Social Centers and Civic Clubs*, p. 90; on railroad regulation and cooperative marketing, see Ward, *The Social Center*, p. 202, and *Common Ground*, April 1910, p. 21. On art exhibits, see *Common Ground*, April 1910, p. 10, and *D&C*, 13 February 1910, p. 32.

24. For a general report on Hughes's visit, see the *Rochester Herald*, 9 April 1909, pp. 6, 12, 13. Both the quotes come from *D&C*, 9 April 1909, pp. 17, 19. On Hughes's career and his connection to the Progressive movement, especially within the Republican Party, see Robert Wesser, *Charles Evan Hughes: Politics and Reform in New York, 1905–1910* (Ithaca: Cornell University Press, 1967).

25. See Ward's defense, *D&C*, 10 March 1909, p. 12. The accusation of "anarchy" by city churches is reported in *D&C*, 22 November 1909, p. 11. On the Catholic attack and social center defense, see *D&C*, 30 November 1909, p. 6.

26. Editorial in the *Post-Express*, 7 February 1911, p. 4. For Baker's conspiracy theory, see Baker, "Do It for Rochester," pp. 693–95. On how Edgerton was Aldridge's pawn, see McKelvey, *Rochester: The Quest for Quality*, pp. 104–5.

27. The "extremely popular" quote comes from *D&C*, 28 September 1908, p. 10. The speech is found in *D&C*, 7 February 1911, p. 6. The attack made by the Sons of the American Revolution is found in *D&C*, 8 February 1911, p. 14. For the Catholic attack, see *D&C*, 15 February 1911, p. 16. On what happened to Shedd, see Dutko, "Socialism in Rochester," pp. 168–78. For the declaration of the social centers' end and the protest against the move, see *D&C*, 18 February 1911, p. 17.

28. Reverend quoted in *D&C*, 29 December 1908, p. 10. *Rochester Social Centers and Civic Clubs*, p. 123.

29. Forbes quoted from *D&C*, 16 December 1911, p. 14. For Forbes's defense, see *Rochester Herald*, 16 December 1911, p. 13. For the Jewish community's and women's clubs calls to reopen the social centers, see *D&C*, 29 November 1911, p. 12, and 4 December 1911, p. 14.

The Political Equality Club supported the reopening of social centers; see *D&C*, 16 December 1911, p. 14. For the failure of the Board of Education to get funds for social centers, see *Proceedings of the Board of Education of the City of Rochester* (1912), p. 54.

30. For the experience of the women's civic club locked in the school building, see *D&C*, 28 March 1911, p. 8. For a pessimistic report about how funding cuts (among other things) would make the movement impossible, see Edwin Rumball, "Are We Wrong in Using the School Buildings as Social Centers?" *Common Good*, February 1914, pp. 74–75.

31. On Cutler and his approval of the movement, see McKelvey, *Rochester: The Quest for Quality*, pp. 94–95. Cutler also expanded Rochester's park system. Ward's point is made in *The Social Center*, pp. 188, 197.

32. George Edwards, *The School as a Social Center* (Bulletin of the University of South Carolina, 1913), p. 12. George Forbes, "Buttressing the Foundations of Democracy," *Common Good*, January 1912, p. 12. For the increase in numbers during 1910, see n. 15. For an example of how political the movement was during 1910, see the reports about what was to be discussed in just one week: "Ways and Means of Reform," "The New Nationalism," and "Local Improvements" (*D&C*, 27 November 1910, p. 25). Other examples can be found in *D&C*.

33. On Weet's call to regulate social centers from above, see *D&C*, 17 February 1911, p. 15.

34. *D&C*, 5 September 1909, p. 18. James Downey, "Educational Progress in 1909," *School Review* 18 (1910): 423. On visitors from New York, Chicago, and Toronto, see *D&C*, 14 September 1908, p. 8. For Zueblin's visit and remark, see *D&C*, 11 December 1908, p. 20. On Steffens's visit, see *Rochester Herald*, 5 November 1909, p. 8.

35. Lee Hanmer, "The Schoolhouse Evening Center—What It Is, What It Costs, and What It Pays," *Journal of Proceedings and Addresses of the National Education Association* (Ann Arbor: NEA, 1913), p. 61. On Oklahoma, see A. Grant Evans, "Social Center Movement in Oklahoma," *Survey*, 18 May 1912, p. 297; on Ohio, see Charles Hebble and Frank Goodwin, eds., *The Citizens' Book* (Cincinnati: Stewart and Kidd Co., 1916), p. 125; on Columbus, Ohio, see "Social Centers in Columbus Schools," *Survey*, 12 February 1910, pp. 696–97; on Minneapolis, see *American City*, September 1912, p. 203; on Indiana, see *American City*, March 1913, p. 321; on the Southwest in general, see Charles Holman, "Focusing Social Forces in the Southwest," *Survey*, 23 September 1911, pp. 866–68. On the general spread westward, see Ward, *The Social Center*, p. 203. On the 1917 figure, see *Survey*, 24 February 1917, p. 607.

36. Livy Richard, "The Public Schools as Social Centers: Edward J. Ward's Work in Rochester, NY," *La Follette's Weekly Magazine*, 9 July 1910, p. 2. For information on Ward's biography, see note 12 above. For his move to Wisconsin see *D&C*, 26 June 1910, p. 20, and *American City*, August 1910, p. 101. For his move to the Bureau of Education, see *Survey*, 20 November 1915, p. 195.

37. Glueck, *The Community Use of Schools*, p. 137. La Follette quoted in Edward Ward, "The First Social Center Conference," *Survey*, 18 March 1911, p. 1003. Woodrow Wilson, "An Address in Madison, Wisconsin, on Community Centers," in *The Papers of Woodrow Wilson*, ed. Arthur Link, 60 vols. (Princeton: Princeton University Press, 1977), 23: 487. Theodore Roosevelt quoted in "The Political Use of School Buildings," *Outlook*, 14 September 1912, p. 52. For the law of 1911, see Glueck, *The Community Use of the Schools*, p. 27. On the law, see also "The Political Use of School Buildings," p. 51. For Milwaukee, see "Funds for Social Center Extension," *Survey*, 25 May 1912, p. 328; "Milwaukee's Recreation Movement," *Survey*, 18 February 1911, pp. 832–33. For Ward's efforts in Madison, though from a fairly dismissive perspective, see Victor Jew, "Social Centers in Wisconsin, 1911–1915," *UCLA Historical Journal* 8 (1987): 97–113. For David Thelen's analysis, see his *The New Citizenship: Origins of Progressivism in Wisconsin, 1885–1900* (Columbia: University of Missouri Press, 1972), and his *Robert M. La Follette and the Insurgent Spirit* (Boston: Little, Brown and Co., 1976), where he too dismisses

the social centers movement in Wisconsin (pp. 108–9). Though certain of these criticisms of Thelen and Jew are right, there were also successes in Wisconsin that are too easily overlooked.

38. The information about Ward losing sight of the local level at times comes from the Charles Van Hise Papers, University of Wisconsin–Madison Library, Box 39, Folder 616, May 1914–June 1914.

39. George Ford, "Madison Conference on Social Centers," *Survey*, 18 November 1911, p. 1229. On the Madison conference in general, see "Social Centers," *American City*, November 1911, p. 312. On working with various other organizations, see Edward Ward, "A Point of Agreement," *American City*, October 1912, pp. 326–27.

Chapter 4: Envisioning Democracy

1. "Civic Nerve Centers," *New Boston*, May 1910, pp. 35–36.

2. Robert Fisher, "Grass Roots Organizing in the Community Center Movement, 1907–1930," in *The Roots of Community Organizing, 1917–1939*, ed. Neil Betten and Michael Austin (Philadelphia: Temple University Press, 1990), p. 84; Victor Jew, "Social Centers in Wisconsin, 1911–1915," *UCLA Historical Journal* 8 (1987): 109; Edward Stevens, "Social Centers, Politics, and Social Efficiency in the Progressive Era," *History of Education Quarterly* 12 (1972): 18, 28, 29–30; Jean Quandt, *From the Small Town to the Great Community: The Social Thought of Progressive Intellectuals* (New Brunswick: Rutgers University Press, 1970), p. 157.

3. Other historians have recognized a radical democratic tendency during the Progressive Era in general. See, for instance, David Thelen, *The New Citizenship: Origins of Progressivism in Wisconsin, 1885–1900* (Columbia: University of Missouri Press, 1972); William J. Reese, *Power and the Promise of School Reform: Grassroots Movements During the Progressive Era* (Boston: RKP, 1986); David Price, "Community and Control: Critical Democratic Theory in the Progressive Period," *American Political Science Review* 68 (1974): 1663–78; Robert Westbrook, *John Dewey and American Democracy* (Ithaca: Cornell University Press, 1991), especially p. 189.

4. Edward Ward, *The Social Center* (New York: D. Appleton and Co., 1913), p. 69.

5. Charles Gilbert, *The School and Its Life* (New York: Silver, Burdett, and Co., 1906), pp. 229–30; Clarence Perry, *Ten Years of the Community Center Movement* (New York: Russell Sage Foundation, 1921), p. 4; C. J. Bushnell, "The Community Center Movement as a Moral Force," *International Journal of Ethics* 30 (1920): 335. For Ward, see, for instance, his *The Social Center*, pp. 100–102, and "The Little Red Schoolhouse," *Charities and the Commons*, 7 August 1909, pp. 640–49.

6. M. Clyde Kelly, *The Community Capitol: A Program for American Unity* (Pittsburgh: Mayflower Press, 1921), p. 41.

7. Anna Pendleton Schenck, "The Need for Neighborhood Centers in American Cities," *American City*, April 1915, p. 337; "Social Centers," *American City*, February 1910, p. 83.

8. Ward, *The Social Center*, pp. 109–10. On the same pages Ward provides a strong attack on the city beautiful movement for being too superficial and not democratic enough.

9. Ibid., pp. 76–77; *Common Ground*, April 1910, p. 1. On the concept of public judgment within contemporary political theory, see Michael Walzer, "Political Decision-Making and Political Education," in *Political Theory and Political Education*, ed. Melvin Richter (Princeton: Princeton University Press, 1980), and John Dunn, *Interpreting Political Responsibility* (Princeton: Princeton University Press, 1990), pp. 210–14. Benjamin Barber equates public judgment with "political judgment," which is "a function of commonality that can be exercised only by citizens interacting with one another in the context of mutual deliberation and

decision." See his *The Conquest of Politics: Liberal Philosophy in Democratic Times* (Princeton: Princeton University Press, 1988), p. 200.

10. Kelly, *The Community Capitol,* p. 55; Edward Ward, "Where Suffragists and Anti's Unite," *American City,* June 1914, p. 523.

11. Irving King, "Comment on the School as a Social Center," in *Social Aspects of Education: A Book of Sources and Original Discussions,* ed. Irving King (New York: Macmillan Co., 1913), p. 95. Forbes quoted in "Echoes from the First National Conference on Social Centers," *Common Good,* December 1911, p. 24. George Forbes, "Buttressing the Foundations of Democracy," *Common Good,* January 1912, p. 8. Professor Elliot quoted in Ward, *The Social Center,* p. 329. All of these ideas made social centers activists sensitive to what later democratic theorists have termed the concept of "developmental democracy." David Held writes: "With the decline in the efficacy of old political and religious traditions, the nature and consequences of citizens' involvement in government became a special concern. . . . In this context, the idea of 'developmental democracy,' which emphasized the indispensability of an active, involved citizenry, [grew]. . . ." David Held, *Models of Democracy* (Stanford: Stanford University Press, 1987), p. 72. See also here Carole Pateman, *Participation and Democratic Theory* (Cambridge: Cambridge University Press, 1970), pp. 42–43.

12. Hughes quoted in *Democrat and Chronicle,* 9 April 1909, p. 17. Charles Ferguson, *The University Militant* (New York: Mitchell Kennerley, 1911), p. 19. The skills quote comes from a constitution of a social center reprinted in Herbert S. Weet, "Citizenship and the Evening Use of School Buildings, II," *Common Good,* February 1911, p. 8. Ward cites Charles Ferguson in *The Social Center,* p. 346. Although I think his idea of deliberation is a bit too limited, see the important connection James Fishkin draws between deliberation and political equality in *Democracy and Deliberation* (New Haven: Yale University Press, 1991), pp. 31–36. Notice also the recent emphasis liberals have placed on civic equality (versus money equality): see, for instance, Mickey Kaus, *The End of Equality* (New York: Basic Books, 1992).

13. Josiah Royce, *Race Questions, Provincialism, and Other American Problems* (New York: Macmillan Co., 1908), p. 111. David Mark Chalmers, *The Social and Political Ideas of the Muckrakers* (New York: Books for Libraries Press, 1964), p. 105. On the national magazine market and reading public, see Christopher Wilson, *The Labor of Words: Literary Professionalism in the Progressive Era* (Athens: University of Georgia Press, 1985), pp. 2, 12. A good interpretation of the growing faith in public opinion during the Progressive Era is found in John Thompson, *Reformers and War: American Progressive Publicists and the First World War* (Cambridge: Cambridge University Press, 1987). See also Eldon Eisenach, *The Lost Promise of Progressivism* (Lawrence: University Press of Kansas, 1994), pp. 13–15 and chap. 3. On muckrakers' moral exhortation, see Stanley Schultz, "The Morality of Politics: The Muckrakers' Vision of Democracy," *Journal of American History* 52 (1965): 530. For an excellent essay on the failure of the muckrakers, see Richard McCormick, "The Discovery That Business Corrupts Politics: A Reappraisal of the Origins of Progressivism," *American Historical Review* 86 (1981): 247–74.

14. *Common Ground,* April 1910, pp. 1, 2. On the critique of the media being controlled by business interests, see "The Social Center as Mentor of the Press," *Survey,* 6 September 1913, p. 676. Henry Jackson wrote: "Ours is a government by public opinion. It is obvious that the public welfare requires that public opinion be informed and educated. The forum is an instrument fitted to meet this most urgent public need." See his *A Community Center: What It Is and How to Organize It* (New York: Macmillan Co., 1918), p. 10. Ward explained that one journalist who came to a social center in the hope of providing a journalistic account got so excited by the discussion that he joined in, illustrating the power of deliberation over the mere accounting of facts. Edward Ward, "The Rochester Movement," *Independent,* 14 October 1909, p. 861. For an interesting contemporary critique of the media from the same vantage point of social centers activists, see Daniel Yankelovich, *Coming to Public Judgment: Making Democracy Work in a Complex World* (Syracuse: Syracuse University Press, 1991).

15. The clearest statement on social centers and tolerance is "The Effect of a Social Center on a Community," *Settlement Bulletin* 2 (1908): 4. Ward's idea of synthesis in public can be seen in his explanation of how people synthesized different positions during a debate on the merits of saloons (*The Social Center,* pp. 63–65). On the idea that in public, citizens are not tolerant but respectful of another person's merits, see James Gouinlock, *Excellence in Public Discourse: John Stuart Mill, John Dewey, and Social Intelligence* (New York: Teachers College Press, 1986), p. 60. For more on the connections between deliberation and political equality, see Fishkin, *Democracy and Deliberation.*

16. Ward, *The Social Center,* p. 87. Stevens, "Social Centers, Politics, and Social Efficiency in the Progressive Era," p. 28. Walter Bagehot, *Physics and Politics* (1867; reprint, Boston: Beacon Press, 1956), pp. 117–18. George Forbes also argued that social centers tamed radical ideas: see *Democrat and Chronicle,* 16 December 1911, p. 14.

17. On creating a modern bricolage of pluralistic ethical beliefs, see Jeffrey Stout, *Ethics After Babel* (Boston: Beacon Press, 1988). On the communitarian tradition in America, see Robert Bellah et al., *Habits of the Heart: Individualism and Commitment in American Life* (New York: Harper and Row, 1985). On "public justification" and liberalism, see Stephen Macedo, *Liberal Virtues: Citizenship, Virtue, and Community in Liberal Constitutionalism* (Oxford: Clarendon Press, 1990). It is interesting to note that political scientists, who have examined citizens' contemporary outlooks, have found a thoughtful combination of communitarian and liberal beliefs. See the essay by Pamela Johnston Conover et al., "Duty is a Four-Letter Word," in *Reconsidering the Democratic Public,* ed. George E. Marcus and Russell Hanson (University Park: The Pennsylvania State University Press, 1993).

18. For contemporary thinking that stresses how the idea of a public draws one to a recognition of being a citizen, see Hannah Arendt's classic *The Human Condition* (Chicago: University of Chicago Press, 1958), especially p. 49. See also Bill Jordan, *The Common Good: Citizenship, Morality, and Self-Interest* (London: Basil Blackwell, 1989), pp. 69–70.

19. From a speech at the NEA in 1912, quoted in "Regulating the Use of Public School Buildings and Grounds in the District of Columbia," Report #389, *Senate Reports (Public),* 63d Cong., 2d sess., 1 December 1913–24 October 1914 (Washington, D.C.: Government Printing Office, 1914), p. 17.

20. J.G.A. Pocock, *The Machiavellian Moment: Florentine Political Thought and the Atlantic Republican Tradition* (Princeton: Princeton University Press, 1975), p. 49; Gordon Wood, *The Creation of the American Republic* (New York: Norton, 1969), p. 68.

21. For the elitist versus populist distinctions within republican thought, see J.G.A. Pocock's analysis of Guicciardini (an elitist thinker) versus Machiavelli (a more populist thinker) in his *The Machiavellian Moment.* See also Robert Shalhope, "Republicanism and Early American Historiography," *William and Mary Quarterly* 39 (1982): 352–53. Shalhope's article is an excellent source on republicanism.

22. Jefferson, *Writings* (New York: Library of America, 1984), p. 1380. For how Jefferson fit into the general republican framework, see Lance Banning, *The Jeffersonian Persuasion* (Ithaca: Cornell University Press, 1978). For more on Jefferson's radical democratic faith, see Richard Matthews, *The Radical Politics of Thomas Jefferson: A Revisionist View* (Lawrence: University Press of Kansas, 1984), especially pp. 87–88. For more on Jefferson's more modern enlightenment vision, see Joyce Appleby, *Capitalism and a New Social Order: The Republican Vision of the 1790s* (New York: New York University Press, 1984), pp. 79–81. The debates on Jefferson are too many to cite here in their entirety. For an understanding of Thomas Paine and his relation to a radical republican vision, see Eric Foner, *Tom Paine and Revolutionary America* (New York: Oxford University Press, 1976).

23. Recent political theorists argue that republican political thought cannot be renewed due to its ancient foundations. For a critique of republicanism's renewal based on its naive

idea that ownership of property and independence are synonymous, see Ian Shapiro, *Political Criticism* (Berkeley and Los Angeles: University of California Press, 1990), pp. 182–83. See also Stout's work, *Ethics After Babel*, for another criticism of the renewal of republicanism.

24. Ward, *The Social Center*, p. 179. Henry Campbell quoted in Edward Ward, "The Modern Social Center Revival," *Playground* 4 (1911): 403–4. William Pieplow, "Broader Use of School Buildings," *American School Board Journal*, January 1912, p. 15. Kelly, *The Community Capitol*, p. 58.

25. Henry Curtis, *Education Through Play* (New York: Macmillan Co., 1915), p. 323 (from his chapter on social centers). Eleanor Touroff Glueck, *The Community Use of Schools* (Baltimore: Williams and Wilkins Co., 1927), p. 1.

26. Kelly, *The Community Capitol*, pp. 25, 86.

27. Weet, "Citizenship and the Evening Use of School Buildings, II: The Social Center *and* the Civic Club," p. 8.

28. Forbes, "Buttressing the Foundations of Democracy," p. 8.

29. Ibid. (Forbes quoting Walsh).

30. Ibid., pp. 9–10.

31. George Forbes, "Relation of Playgrounds to Social Centers," *Playground* 2 (1909): 13. Ward, "Where Suffragists and Anti's Unite," p. 520.

32. Walsh is quoted in Edward Ward, "Permanent Primaries: Politics in the Social Center," *Common Good*, October 1913, p. 9. Frank Walsh's endorsement of direct primaries is noted in "The Social Centers—Center of Democracy," *Survey*, 6 September 1913, p. 676.

33. The argument to make citizens legislators through the initiative and referendum comes from Frank Walsh, quoted favorably by Ward, "Permanent Primaries," p. 9. Curtis, *Education Through Play*, p. 304. For the argument of many activists to have social centers accompany the initiative and referendum, see "The Social Centers—Center of Democracy," p. 676, and Kelly, *The Community Capitol*, p. 110. For Forbes's endorsement of commission government, see *Democrat and Chronicle*, 16 January 1911, p. 14. On those progressives who endorsed commission government for its initiative and referendum, see Bradley Rice, *Progressive Cities: The Commission Government Movement in America, 1901–1920* (Austin: University of Texas Press, 1977), pp. 72–73.

34. Kelly, *The Community Capitol*, p. 92. Forbes, "Buttressing the Foundations of Democracy," p. 11. Kelly, *The Community Capitol*, p. 83. Ward, *The Social Center*, p. 50.

35. Edward Ward, "Discovering the Public School," *New Boston*, March 1911, p. 493.

36. Pateman, *Participation and Democratic Theory*, p. 25. On this point, see also Hanna Fenichel Pitkin and Sara Shumer, "On Participation," *democracy*, Fall 1982, p. 44.

Chapter 5: Thinking Democratically

1. Mary Parker Follett, *The New State: Group Organization the Solution of Popular Government* (1918; reprint, Gloucester, Mass.: Peter Smith, 1965), p. 180.

2. John Collier, *From Every Zenith: A Memoir and Some Essays on Life and Thought* (Denver: Sage Books, 1963), p. 83.

3. Richard Cabot, "Mary Parker Follett, An Appreciation," *The Radcliffe Quarterly*, April 1934, p. 82. For dissertations on Follett, see Avrum Isaac Cohen, "Mary Parker Follett: Spokesman for Democracy, Philosopher for Social Group Work, 1918–1933" (D.S.W. diss., Tulane University, 1971); Elliot Milton Fox, "The Dynamics of Constructive Change in the Thought of Mary Parker Follett" (Ph.D. diss., Columbia University, 1970); Frances Ann Cooper, "Mary Parker Follett: The Power of Power-With" (Ph.D. diss., University of Southern California,

1980). Cohen's dissertation reprints certain letters of Follett's. Two helpful articles that include details on Follett's life are Eduard Lindeman, "Mary Parker Follett," *Survey Graphic*, February 1934, pp. 86–87, and Henry Metcalf and L. Urwick, "Introduction," in *Dynamic Administration: The Collected Papers of Mary Parker Follett*, ed. Henry Metcalf and L. Urwick (New York: Harper and Brothers, 1940).

4. Lindeman, "Mary Parker Follett," p. 86; Cohen, "Mary Parker Follett," p. 12. The influence of British political thought will reemerge when Follett writes *The New State*.

5. Mary Parker Follett, *The Speaker of the House of Representatives* (1896; reprint, New York: Longmans, Green and Co., 1909), pp. 307, 314.

6. Raymond Seidelman, *Disenchanted Realists: Political Science and the American Crisis* (Albany: SUNY Press, 1985), p. 7. A. D. Morse in *Political Science Quarterly* 12 (1897): 313; John Quincy Adams in *Annals of the American Academy of Political and Social Science* 9 (1897): 119. Theodore Roosevelt, the soon-to-be president who desired a very strong federal government and executive, gave the work a good review in the *American Historical Review* 2 (1896): 176–78. For an insightful and general work on professional political science, see David Ricci, *The Tragedy of Political Science: Politics, Scholarship, and Democracy* (New Haven: Yale University Press, 1984).

7. Fox, "The Dynamics of Constructive Change in the Thought of Mary Parker Follett," p. 33. For more on women's decisions to become active during the Progressive Era, see Christopher Lasch's chapter on Jane Addams in *The New Radicalism in America, 1889–1963* (New York: Norton, 1965), and Allen Davis, *American Heroine: The Life and Legend of Jane Addams* (New York: Oxford University Press, 1973).

8. On the period from 1900 to 1908 I rely on Cooper's and Fox's dissertations. On the idea of social control, see Christopher Lasch's chapter in *The New Radicalism in America* and William Muraskin, "The Social Control Theory," *Journal of Social History* 9 (1976): 559–69.

9. Mary Parker Follett, "Evening Recreation Centers," *Playground* 6 (1913): 387. For more on Follett's activities, see Cooper, "Mary Parker Follett," pp. 119–23, and Fox, "The Dynamics of Constructive Change in the Thought of Mary Parker Follett," pp. 34–39.

10. Follett quoted in Fox, "The Dynamics of Constructive Change in the Thought of Mary Parker Follett," p. 47. "Committee Report," *Women's Municipal League of Boston*, May 1912, p. 10. As seen in Chapter Two, Ford Hall Forum led the forum movement of the 1900s.

11. Follett, "Evening Recreation Centers," p. 392.

12. Follett, *The New State*, pp. 142, 147, 159. From now on quotes from this book will be followed by page numbers in parentheses.

13. For reviewers' complaints about Follett's enthusiasm, see Howard Lee McBain's review in *Political Science Quarterly* 34 (1919): 169; Charles Ellwood's review in the *American Journal of Sociology* 25 (1919): 97–99; Henry James Ford's review in the *American Political Science Review* 13 (1919): 494–95. On the excitement and pleasures of public life, see Hannah Arendt's classic, *The Human Condition* (Chicago: University of Chicago Press, 1958).

14. McBain in the *Political Science Quarterly*, p. 170. There are a number of sources on the social thought of the Progressive Era (far too many to cite here). A few key sources are Morton White, *Social Thought in America: The Revolt Against Formalism* (1947; reprint, New York: Oxford, 1976); David Noble, *The Progressive Mind, 1890–1917* (Chicago: Rand McNally and Co., 1970); James Kloppenberg, *Uncertain Victory: Social Democracy and Progressivism in European and American Thought, 1870–1920* (New York: Oxford University Press, 1986); and Part Two in Robert Westbrook, *John Dewey and American Democracy* (Ithaca: Cornell University Press, 1991).

15. For Kloppenberg's analysis, see his *Uncertain Victory*. For two examples of sociologists putting emphasis on intersubjectivity, see George Herbert Mead's *Mind, Self, and Society* (Chicago: University of Chicago Press, 1934), Part Three (Mead was a colleague of Dewey's), and Charles Horton Cooley, "Social Organization," in *The Two Major Works of Charles H. Cooley*

(Glencoe: The Free Press, 1956). Undoubtedly, the biggest influence on Follett (due to her background in British political theory) that helped her understand the importance of intersubjectivity was T. H. Green (a thinker studied by Kloppenberg). Writing during the late nineteenth century, Green developed a thorough critique of individualism and rights-based liberalism. See his *Lectures on the Principles of Political Obligation and Other Writings* (Cambridge: Cambridge University Press, 1986), especially his comments about "positive freedom" (p. 199) and his critique of liberal "rights" (p. 162).

16. Follett in a letter to H. A. Overstreet dated 23 September 1919, reprinted in Cohen, "Mary Parker Follett," p. 163. For William James's philosophy I rely on his classic *Pragmatism and the Meaning of Truth* (Cambridge, Mass.: Harvard University Press, 1975). For Royce I rely on the introductory essay and the works reprinted in *The Philosophy of Josiah Royce*, ed. John Roth (New York: Thomas Y. Crowell, 1971). For an excellent secondary work on James's philosophy, see George Cotkin, *William James, Public Philosopher* (Baltimore: The Johns Hopkins University Press, 1990). For more on the debates between James and Royce, see Bruce Kuklick, *The Rise of American Philosophy: Cambridge, Massachusetts, 1860–1930* (New Haven: Yale University Press, 1977). On the debate between Bosanquet and G.D.H. Cole, see F. M. Barnard and R. A. Vernon, "Pluralism, Participation, and Politics: Reflections on the Intermediate Group," *Political Theory* 3 (1975): 187. For a good analysis of Bosanquet's thought that shows the *similarity* between his and the pluralists' thought, see Andrew Vincent and Raymond Plant, *Philosophy, Politics, and Citizenship: The Life and Thought of the British Idealists* (Oxford: Basil Blackwell, 1984), pp. 120–32. On Laski's linking of pragmatism and pluralism together, see his *Studies in the Problem of Sovereignty* (New Haven: Yale University Press, 1917), p. 3, and "The Personality of the State," *Nation*, 22 July 1915, p. 115.

17. The classic work on the crowd was Gustave Le Bon's *The Crowd* (1895; reprint, New York: Viking Press, 1966). See also the rarely discussed but important early work by Robert Park, "The Crowd and the Public" (1904), in *The Crowd and the Public and Other Essays* (Chicago: University of Chicago Press, 1972). Park wrote: "If it is characteristic of the crowd that all its members are controlled by a common drive and that all purely individual impulses and interests are inhibited, then it is characteristic of the public that individual impulses arise out of the undefined basis of the common consciousness and develop further in a peculiar reciprocal interaction" (p. 50).

18. There are many sources on the communitarian criticism of liberalism. See here Christopher Lasch, "The Communitarian Criticism of Liberalism," in *Community in America: The Challenge of Habits of the Heart*, ed. Charles Reynolds and Ralph Norman (Berkeley and Los Angeles: University of California Press, 1988). Lasch mentions Follett as a communitarian critic of liberalism. See also Michael Walzer, "The Communitarian Critique of Liberalism," *Political Theory* 18 (1990): 6–23.

19. For a more recent account of urban neighborhoods akin to Follett's, see Jane Jacobs, *The Death and Life of Great American Cities* (New York: Vintage Books, 1963), especially chap. 6. Of course, Follett did not celebrate "Gemeinschaft" at a philosophical level since she believed in diversity and interpenetration. Her definition of community was based largely on the group process and interpenetration. See her article "Community Is a Process," *Philosophical Review* 28 (1919): 576–88.

20. John Neville Figgis, *Churches in the Modern State* (London: Longmans, Green and Co., 1913), pp. 51–52. On Cole's thought, see his *The World of Labour* (London: G. Bell and Sons, 1913), and *Self-Government in Industry* (London: G. Bell and Sons, 1918). For Laski's thought, see his *Studies in the Problem of Sovereignty* and "The Personality of Associations," *Harvard Law Review* 29 (1916): 404–26. See also here David Nicholls, *The Pluralist State* (New York: St. Martin's Press, 1975); Henry Meyer Magid, *English Political Pluralism* (New York: Columbia University Press, 1941); A. W. Wright, *G.D.H. Cole and Socialist Democracy* (Oxford: Oxford

University Press, 1979). For recent works that show how neighborhoods are inherently open (following Follett's arguments against the pluralists), see Matthew Crenson, *Neighborhood Politics* (Cambridge, Mass.: Harvard University Press, 1983), pp. 16–17, and Jeffrey Berry et al., *The Rebirth of Urban Democracy* (Washington, D.C.: The Brookings Institution, 1993), p. 168.

21. For Laski's thoughts on federalism, see his "The Personality of the State," pp. 115, 117; "The Personality of Associations," p. 425; and "The Pluralistic State," *Philosophical Review* 28 (1919): 570 (this article appeared alongside Follett's own "Community Is a Process"). See also Bernard Zylstra, *From Pluralism to Collectivism: The Development of Harold Laski's Political Thought* (Assen: Van Gorcum and Co., 1968), p. 51, and Herbert Deane, *The Political Ideas of Harold Laski* (New York: Columbia University Press, 1955), pp. 31–32. Laski included all sorts of different groups in his pluralist philosophy (he was famous for saying "There is not, as I can conceive, any fundamental difference, except in degree, between the nature of a state and the nature of a baseball club" ["The Personality of the State," p. 116]). This provided a problem: How to integrate all these groups together? Since Follett focused on the locale of the neighborhood and not every single existing group, she had a much clearer idea of how federalism could actually work.

22. Herbert Croly, *Progressive Democracy* (New York: Macmillan Co., 1914), p. 145. On the intellectuals at the *New Republic*, see Charles Forcey, *Crossroads of Liberalism: Croly, Weyl, Lippmann, and the Progressive Era* (New York: Oxford University Press, 1961). I especially rely on James Kloppenberg's thoughtful analysis of these intellectuals in *Uncertain Victory*, chap. 9. For a critique of intellectuals becoming enamored with those who hold political power, see Lasch, *The New Radicalism in America*, especially chap. 6.

23. For Croly's vision for a national school of political science, see Kloppenberg, *Uncertain Victory*, pp. 375–76.

24. R. Jeffrey Lustig, *Corporate Liberalism: The Origins of Modern American Political Theory, 1890–1920* (Berkeley and Los Angeles: University of California Press, 1982), pp. 134, 133, respectively. Lustig's desire to fit every single American thinker into a grand conception of "corporate liberalism" is what leads him to dismiss Follett's thought as conformist.

25. On the growing turn away from democratic socialism toward Leninism within the American left, see James Weinstein, *The Decline of Socialism in America, 1912–1925* (New York: Monthly Review Press, 1967).

26. James Tufts, review of *The New State*, *Ethics* 29 (1918–19): 376.

27. For some contemporary views on how communities retain their vitality, see Thomas Bender's theoretical work *Community and Social Change in America* (Baltimore: The Johns Hopkins University Press, 1978), and Harry Boyte's *Community Is Possible: Repairing America's Roots* (New York: Harper and Row, 1984). For other works making the argument that neighborhoods can still provide the basis of more participatory citizenship, see Crenson, *Neighborhood Politics*, and Berry et al., *The Rebirth of Urban Democracy*.

Chapter 6: The Waning of the Democratic Public

1. George Alger in "Where Are the Pre-War Radicals?" *Survey*, 1 February 1926, pp. 561–62.

2. For the original 1914 push in the national legislature, see "Regulating the Use of Public School Buildings in the District of Columbia," Report #389, in *Senate Reports (Public)*, 63d Cong., 2d sess., 1 December 1913–24 October 1914 (Washington, D.C.: Government Printing Office, 1914). Ward is mentioned here as an adviser, and one of his articles is reprinted. See also "Washington Schoolhouses for the People," *Survey*, 27 June 1914, p. 337. For Helen

Keller's speech, see "Opening School Doors to Popular Discussion," *Survey*, 8 April 1916, p. 61. On Ward's anger, see Thomas Marshall Todd, "Love, Science, and Social Justice: Voices and Conversations from the Urban Community Movement Before the Great War" (Ph.D. diss., University of Minnesota, 1981), p. 425. For more on the controversy over the D.C. forums, see *New York Times*, 27 March 1916, p. 4. For the quick raising of the bill and objections to it, see *Congressional Record*, vol. 54, pt. 2, 64th Cong., 2d sess., 1917 (Washington, D.C.: Government Printing Office, 1917), pp. 1972–73.

3. Wilson quoted in Stephen Vaughn, *Holding Fast the Inner Lines: Democracy, Nationalism, and the Committee on Public Information* (Chapel Hill: University of North Carolina Press, 1980), p. 4. Ronald Schaffer quoted on food production, *America in the Great War: The Rise of the War-Welfare State* (New York: Oxford University Press, 1991), p. 35. On the War Industries Board, see David Kennedy, *Over Here: The First World War and American Society* (New York: Oxford University Press, 1980), pp. 126–43, and Schaffer, *America in the Great War*, p. 45. For more on these sorts of initiatives, see Allen Davis, "Welfare, Reform, and World War I," *American Quarterly* 19 (1967): 516–33. For elementary and high schools, see Lewis Paul Todd, *Wartime Relations of the Federal Government and the Public Schools, 1917–1918* (New York: Teachers College, 1945). For universities, see Carol Gruber, *Mars and Minerva: World War I and the Uses of Higher Education* (Baton Rouge: Louisiana State University Press, 1975), and Kennedy, *Over Here*, pp. 57–59.

4. Kennedy's expression comes from the first chapter in his *Over Here*. George Creel, *How We Advertised America* (New York: Harper and Brothers, 1920), pp. 3, 5. For the growth in importance of "public opinion" and how it relates to the war, see John Thompson, *Reformers and War: American Progressive Publicists and the First World War* (Cambridge: Cambridge University Press, 1987). On George Creel's background, see Stephen Vaughn, *Holding Fast the Inner Lines*, pp. 19–20. On his endorsement of the social centers, see George Creel, "The Man Hunt," *McClure's*, November 1916, p. 34. Here he argued to turn to the school into a "headquarters for citizenship, an all-year round meeting-place of the community." See also here the *New York Times*, 27 March 1916, p. 4. On the activities of the CPI, see Creel, *How We Advertised America*, chap. 7, and Vaughn, *Holding Fast the Inner Lines*.

5. Barry Karl, *The Uneasy State: The United States from 1915 to 1945* (Chicago: University of Chicago Press, 1983), p. 46. Neil Wynn, *From Progressivism to Prosperity: World War I and American Society* (New York: Holmes and Meier, 1986), p. 81. On the localism of draft boards, see also Schaffer, *America in the Great War*, p. 176. For more on the general growth of the federal government during the Progressive Era, see Stephen Skorownek, *Building a New State: The Expansion of National Administrative Capacities, 1877–1920* (Cambridge: Cambridge University Press, 1982).

6. On local food drives and schools, see Todd, *Wartime Relations of the Federal Government and the Public Schools, 1917–1918*, chap. 6. On schools as places for propaganda and military training, see Kennedy, *Over Here*, p. 55, and Edward Krug, *The Shaping of the American High School*, 2 vols. (New York: Harper and Row, 1964), 2: 6. On the federal government's setting up its own towns around industries with community centers, see A. C. Calvert, "Public Schools in the New War Cities," *American City*, November 1918, especially p. 362. See also Richard Childs, "The Government's Model Villages," *Survey*, 1 February 1919, pp. 585–92. For a critique of the pseudo-community feel of towns created solely for business interests (and the case can be extended to government interests), see Arthur Evans Wood, "The Philosophy of Community Organization," *Papers and Proceedings of the 17th Annual Meeting of the American Sociological Society* 17 (1922): 182.

7. J. P. Lichtenberger, "The War Relief Work of the Council of National Defense," *Annals of the American Academy of Political and Social Science* 79 (1918): 230–31 (also quoted in Kennedy, *Over Here*, p. 116). *Survey*, 18 May 1918, p. 203.

8. The slogan of the NCD and Edward Burchard's words are quoted in Todd, "Love, Science, and Social Justice," pp. 532, 535. See also *Community Center*, November 1917, p. 1. For how the NCCA fought for the community councils idea, see John Collier, "Linking Centers with the Nation," *Community Center*, January 1918, p. 4. For more on the Council of National Defense, see William James Breen, "The Council of National Defense: Industrial and Social Mobilization in the United States, 1916–1920" (Ph.D. diss., Duke University, 1968).

9. John Collier, "Community Councils—Democracy Every Day: II," *Survey*, 21 September 1918, p. 689. For Ward's support of the war, see his avid nationalism and support for preparedness in the *New York Times*, 30 December 1915, p. 3. Here Ward tried to synthesize nationalism with democracy. M. Clyde Kelly said in 1917, "We are going to win [the war] by a mobilization of the public mind, so that they will stand back of everything that is done. Well, now that unification must come through these schoolhouse meetings." Quoted in Todd, "Love, Science, and Social Justice," p. 523.

10. Stuart Rochester, *American Liberal Disillusionment in the Wake of World War I* (University Park: The Pennsylvania State University Press, 1977), pp. 40–41. *New Republic* writer quoted in Charles Hirschfield, "Nationalist Progressivism and World War I," *Mid-America* 45 (1963): 146. For more on this move by nationalist progressives, see Kennedy, *Over Here*, pp. 39–44. For a good example of a progressive endorsement of the war, see John Dewey, "The Social Possibilities of War," in vol. 2 of *Characters and Events*, ed. Joseph Ratner (New York: Henry Holt and Co., 1929). See also Robert Westbrook, *John Dewey and American Democracy* (Ithaca: Cornell University Press, 1991), chap. 7. On Lippmann, see Ronald Steel, *Walter Lippmann and the American Century* (New York: Vintage Books, 1980), pp. 100–154. Some historians have challenged how much the war explains liberals' disillusionment. See, for instance, Christopher Lasch, *The New Radicalism in America, 1889–1963* (New York: Norton, 1965). But I would agree here with Stuart Rochester that although the war was not the only cause, it should not be understated (Rochester, *American Liberal Disillusionment*, pp. 100–101). This is especially true in the case of those who believed in the power of a democratic public, as we shall see.

11. Grosvenor Clarkson quoted in the *New York Times*, 12 January 1919, sec. 4, p. 11. Council of National Defense quoted in Todd, "Love, Science, and Social Justice," p. 555. L. J. Hanifan, *The Community Center* (Boston: Silver, Burdett, and Co., 1920), p. 7. Of previous activists studied, Charles Zueblin supported the war. See his "How the Forum May Serve America Today," *Open Forum*, May 1918, pp. 5–6. It should be noted that Frederic Howe never supported the war. See his "Democracy or Imperialism," *Annals of the American Academy of Political and Social Science* 66 (1916): 250–58.

12. John Collier, *From Every Zenith: A Memoir* (Denver: Sage Books, 1963), p. 90. Collier recognized the "rapidity" of the dismantling of community councils in 1918. See "Adaptation of Recreation and Community Service to Conditions of Peace," *Survey*, 7 December 1918, p. 313. For the challenge to free speech within social centers during the war, see "Radical Evictions," *Survey*, 19 February 1921, p. 719, and *New York Times*, 7 February 1921, p. 2. For the discontinuation of the Community Center Division within the Bureau of Education, see "National Community Board Organized," *American City*, October 1920, p. 421. For more on the fear of the federal government in terms of the local political initiatives as they relate to state councils, see Breen, "The Council of National Defense," p. 158. The gradual death of the community councils can be seen in articles from the *New York Times* that reported on the movement after the war. On 10 November 1918 the *Times* reported that people hoped the councils would continue after the war but that they were generally associated with the temporary crisis of World War I (sec. 4, p. 6). By 6 October 1919 the local community councils of New York City endorsed various plans of social justice (i.e., collective bargaining, worker self-management, social insurance) but seem to have lost sight of their localism (p. 3). By the mid-1920s reports on the community councils had died out.

13. For Dewey's vision of social centers, see Chapter Three. For a good argument that society and the state must be merged to a certain extent, see Nancy Fraser, "Rethinking the Public Sphere," in *The Phantom Public Sphere*, ed. Bruce Robbins (Minneapolis: University of Minnesota Press, 1993).

14. Wilson quoted in the *New York Times*, 19 March 1918, p. 6. Ward quoted in the *New York Times*, 30 December 1915, p. 3.

15. In many ways my criticism of the social centers movement leaders is akin to Randolph Bourne's critique of John Dewey's endorsement of World War I. Bourne argued that the war made liberals like Dewey lose sight of their more democratic ideals. See his "The War and the Intellectuals" (1917) and "Twilight of the Idols" (1917), in *The Radical Will: Randolph Bourne, Selected Writings, 1911–1918*, ed. Olaf Hansen (New York: Urizen Books, 1977).

16. "Unswerving loyalty" and the CPI comes from Vaughn, *Holding Fast the Inner Lines*, p. 103. The best source on nativism and 100 percent Americanism is still John Higham's *Strangers in the Land: Patterns of American Nativism, 1860–1925* (1955; reprint, New York: Atheneum, 1975). On the Espionage Act and Sedition Act, see Kennedy, *Over Here*, pp. 79–80. For two historical accounts that show how nationalism and patriotism transformed wartime conceptions of citizenship, see Carroll Engelhardt, "Citizenship Training and Community Civics in Iowa Schools," *Mid-America* 65 (1983): 60–61; Samuel Shermis, "World War I—Catalyst for the Creation of the Social Sciences," *Social Studies*, January–February 1989, p. 15. For an interesting contemporary analysis of differing conceptions of citizenship, see Michael Walzer, "Civility and Civic Virtue in Contemporary America," in his *Radical Principles: Reflections of an Unreconstructed Democrat* (New York: Basic Books, 1980).

17. John Collier, "School Buildings as Coordinating Places for the Civil Energies of the War," *American City*, June 1917, p. 588. Samuel Wilson, "The Community House—An Element in Reconstruction," *American City*, December 1918, p. 470. This losing sight of original visions is traced in a parallel way by Robert Westbrook in his analysis of John Dewey during World War I. Westbrook shows that Randolph Bourne pointed out how Dewey lost sight of his own democratic values. See his *John Dewey and American Democracy*, chap. 7.

18. George Creel, "The 'Lash' of Public Opinion," *Collier's*, 22 November 1924, p. 46. I am arguing here that intellectuals *believed* that public opinion could be manufactured. I am not arguing that this was actually the case. The arguments about the ability to manipulate public opinion still go on today. For an argument that public opinion cannot be so easily manipulated and one I largely agree with, see Michael Schudson, *Advertising: The Uneasy Persuasion* (New York: Basic Books, 1984).

19. The first Mencken quote is from Charles Fecher, *Mencken: A Study of His Thought* (New York: Knopf, 1978), p. 177 (see pp. 170–90 for more on Mencken's thought on democracy). The second is from H. L. Mencken, *A Mencken Chrestomathy* (New York: Vintage Books, 1992), p. 168. The term "civilized minority" comes from Christopher Lasch's *The True and Only Heaven* (New York: Knopf, 1991), chap. 10, especially p. 414. Steven Biel, *Independent Intellectuals in the United States, 1910–1945* (New York: New York University Press, 1992), p. 81. Before Mencken gained great fame prior to the 1920s Randolph Bourne understood the limits of his thinking. Bourne wrote: "Mr. Mencken . . . wastes away into a desert of invective." "H. L. Mencken," in *The Radical Will*, ed. Olaf Hansen (New York: Urizen Books, 1977), p. 472.

20. Edward Purcell, *The Crisis of Democratic Theory* (Lexington: University Press of Kentucky, 1973), p. 108.

21. Edward Bernays, "Manipulating Public Opinion," *American Journal of Sociology* 33 (1928): 971. For Edward Bernays's use of the term "public relations," see his *Crystallizing Public Opinion* (1923; reprint, New York: Horace Liveright, 1929), p. 11. On his love for Le Bon, see J. Michael Sproule, "Progressive Propaganda Critics and the Magic Bullet Myth," *Critical Studies in Mass Communication* 6 (1989): 232. On Bernays's life and thought I rely on

Vaughn, *Holding Fast the Inner Lines*, pp. 141–42; Marvin Olasky, "Bringing 'Order Out of Chaos': Edward Bernays and the Salvation of Society Through Public Relations," *Journalism History* 12 (1985): 17–21; and Bernays's autobiography, *Biography of an Idea: Memoirs of a Public Relations Counsel* (New York: Simon and Schuster, 1965).

22. Harold Laswell, *Propaganda Technique in the World War* (New York: Knopf, 1927), pp. 4, 5, 12. See also Harold Laswell, "The Theory of Political Propaganda," *American Political Science Review* 21 (1927): 627–31.

23. Details on Lippmann's life are found in Ronald Steel's excellent biography, *Walter Lippmann and the American Century*. For Lippmann's lack of trust in public opinion during the Progressive Era see his comments on political indifference in his introduction to *A Preface to Politics* (New York: Mitchell Kennerly, 1914). For Lippmann's reflection that World War I challenged the idea of public opinion, see his *Public Opinion* (New York: Harcourt, Brace and Co., 1922), pp. 46–47.

24. Lippmann quoted in Steel, *Walter Lippmann and the American Century*, p. 171.

25. Lippmann, *Public Opinion*, pp. 25, 248–49, 310. It is interesting to note that Lippmann's theory of knowledge and politics coalesced. He believed that politics needed to be based on objective knowledge. This is a crucial point and one drawn out by James Carey in his *Communication as Culture* (Boston: Unwin Hyman, 1989), especially pp. 74–82.

26. John Dewey, "Public Opinion," *New Republic*, 3 May 1922, p. 288. The arguments about what was needed to be done to evade Lippmann's pessimism can be found in Dewey's *The Public and Its Problems* (Denver: Swallow Press, 1927).

27. For similar points about Dewey's hope in democracy during the 1920s, see Lasch, *The True and Only Heaven*, pp. 367–68; and Westbrook, *John Dewey and American Democracy*, pp. 315–18. For a bit less pessimistic view, see James Kloppenberg, *Uncertain Victory: Social Democracy and Progressivism in European and American Thought, 1870–1920* (New York: Oxford University Press, 1986), pp. 390–94. It should be noted that John Dewey was involved in the community centers movement. He took part in the extremely important 1916 conference on "Community Centers and Related Problems" (see *American City*, April 1916, p. 407).

28. *Survey*, 21 January 1922, p. 637; Seba Eldridge, "Community Organization and Citizenship," *Social Forces* 7 (1928): 132; Roy Lubove, *The Professional Altruist* (Cambridge, Mass.: Harvard University Press, 1965), p. 180; Eleanor Touroff Glueck, *The Community Use of Schools* (Baltimore: Williams and Wilkins Co., 1927), p. 145. See also issues of the *Community Center*, 1918–1922, for this development. The one partial exception to this professionalization was the social unit plan in Cincinnati, Ohio. I do not deal with this effort here since it has already achieved great attention elsewhere. It was defeated during the Red Scare, making it quite short-lived, and it also oriented itself toward social work (though much more democratic forms of social work). On the social unit plan, see Patricia Mooney Melvin, *The Organic City: Urban Definition and Community Organization* (Lexington: University Press of Kentucky, 1987).

29. *Survey*, 15 February 1926, p. 569.

30. On the growth and modernization of advertising and the consolidation of a consumer culture during the 1920s, see Roland Marchand, *Advertising the American Dream: Making Way for Modernity, 1920–1940* (Berkeley and Los Angeles: University of California Press, 1985), and William Leach, *Land of Desire: Merchants, Power, and the Rise of a New American Culture* (New York: Pantheon, 1993).

31. Robert Park, "Community Organization and the Romantic Temper," *Journal of Social Forces* 3 (1925): 673, 675. For his argument to study community, see Robert Park, "The Problem of Community Organization," *Community Center*, July–August 1922, p. 80. Robert Park's involvement in the community center movement can be seen in his participation in a conference conducted by the National Community Center Association; see the conference schedule in the *Journal of Social Forces* 3 (1924): 101. See also conference reports found throughout the

Community Center. For Park's institutionalization of professional sociology at the University of Chicago, see Fred Matthews, *Quest for an American Sociology: Robert E. Park and the Chicago School* (Montreal: McGill-Queen's University Press, 1977), and Martin Bulmer, *The Chicago School of Sociology* (Chicago: University of Chicago, 1984). Both books are excellent sources on the professionalization of sociology and Park's conception of the modern city. For a good critique of modern sociological theory's treatment of community, see Thomas Bender, *Community and Social Change in America* (Baltimore: The Johns Hopkins University Press, 1978). For a nice analysis of "mobility," see Christopher Lasch, "Opportunity in the Promised Land: Social Mobility or the Democratization of Competence," in *The Revolt of the Elites and the Betrayal of Democracy* (New York: Norton, 1995). I should note here that Park's critique of community centers found its way into his most famous and classic work *The City.* Here he argued that city life was based on new forms of social control like advertising and on the "skating on thin surfaces and a scrupulous study of style and manners" (40). He did not celebrate this new form of social control. He believed it gave "city life a superficial and adventitious character" (41). Nonetheless, he accepted that "Our leisure is now mainly a restless search for excitement" (117). But unlike Follett who saw mass culture as growing out of a bored and tired city populace, Park attributed this new mass culture to "the romantic impulse" (117). Here Park's arguments fell apart. For though he argued that social centers philosophy was unrealistic because it did not take into account economic ideas about social mobility, he himself mistakenly believed that the new culture of consumption was based on a "romantic impulse," not the forces of industrial capitalism. Whatever the weaknesses of his case, Park saw no alternative to this new urban culture. All quotes here are from Robert Park et al., *The City* (1925; reprint, Chicago: University of Chicago Press, 1967).

32. Clarence Nickle, "Community Control," *Journal of Social Forces* 4 (1925): 347, 355.

33. W. S. Bittner, "The Relation of the Local Community to the Principal Factors of Public Opinion," *Journal of Social Forces* 7 (1928): 101. Compare this pessimism on the part of Bittner to C. H. Cooley's earlier faith in a healthy relation between communication on the local level and at the national level. On this point, see John Peters, "Satan and Savior: Mass Communication in Progressive Thought," *Critical Studies in Mass Communications* 6 (1989): 255. For Bittner's earlier endorsement of social centers, see his "Community Institutes," *Bulletin of the Extension Division, Indiana University* 2 (1917).

34. Dwight Sanderson, "Democracy and Community Organization," *Papers and Proceedings, 14th Annual Meeting of the American Sociological Society* 14 (1919): 85; Jesse Frederick Steiner, "Comments," *Papers and Proceedings, 14th Annual Meeting of the American Sociological Society* 14 (1919): 98.

35. Jesse Frederick Steiner, "Education for Social Work," *American Journal of Sociology* 26 (1921): 477.

36. Jesse Frederick Steiner, "Whither the Community Movement?" *Survey,* 15 April 1929, p. 130; Jesse Frederick Steiner, *Community Organization* (New York: Century Co., 1925), p. 57. Steiner's analysis is found in both these works. In many ways Steiner's work was part of mainstream social science during the late 1920s. This is seen in the ground-breaking work on social mobility done by the Lynds. See their *Middletown* (New York: Harcourt, Brace, and Co., 1929). For an interesting analysis of the Lynds' work, see Richard Wightman Fox, "Epitaph for Middletown: Robert S. Lynd and the Analysis of Consumer Culture," in *The Culture of Consumption: Critical Essays in American History, 1800–1980,* ed. Richard Wightman Fox and T. J. Jackson Lears (New York: Pantheon, 1983).

37. Le Roy Bowman, "Community Organization," *American Journal of Sociology* 35 (1930): 1008; Clarence Perry, "The Tangible Aspects of Community Organization," *Journal of Social Forces* 8 (1930): 560–61. Perry had many academic community studies to cite. There was one done by Ira Reid on Harlem and others such as Niles Carpenter and Daniel Katz, "The

Cultural Adjustments of the Polish Group in the City of Buffalo," *Journal of Social Forces* 6 (1927): 76–85. Many other studies like this one can be found in the *Journal of Social Forces* throughout the 1920s. On how the Lynds became "objective" social scientists as well, see Fox, "Epitaph for Middletown."

Conclusion: The Future of American Democracy

1. One of the first people to recognize the invasion of commercial advertising into politics was the journalist Joe McGinnis in his *The Selling of the President, 1968* (New York: Washington Square Press, 1969). See also the more historical work done by Robert Westbrook, "Politics as Consumption: Managing the Modern Election," in *The Culture of Consumption: Critical Essays in American History, 1890–1980*, ed. Richard Wightman Fox and T. J. Jackson Lears (New York: Pantheon, 1983), and Neil Postman, *Amusing Ourselves to Death: Public Discourse in the Age of Show Business* (New York: Penguin Books, 1985). Recent reform attempts such as "Free TV for Straight Talk Coalition" have tried to provide free airtime for rational debate between candidates. In addition, public journalists struggle to find ways to make written and television news less sensational and superficial and more meaningful for those concerned with the democratic activities of regular citizens.

2. For the term "emotivism," see Alasdair MacIntyre, *After Virtue: A Study in Moral Theory*, 2d ed. (Notre Dame: University of Notre Dame Press, 1984), chaps. 2 and 3; for "culture of complaint," see Robert Hughes, *The Culture of Complaint: The Fraying of America* (New York: Warner Books, 1993); for the "culture of narcissism," see Christopher Lasch, *The Culture of Narcissism* (New York: Warner Books, 1979), pp. 145–51 for interesting comments about politics, and Lasch, *The Minimal Self* (New York: Norton, 1984); on "therapeutic culture," see Phillip Rieff, *The Triumph of the Therapeutic* (New York: Harper and Row, 1966) (on p. 25 Rieff alludes to "I feel" replacing "I believe"), and Robert Bellah et al., *Habits of the Heart: Individualism and Commitment in American Life* (New York: Harper, 1985). It should be noted that many of these criticisms of American society can become overblown. On the other hand, as *Habits of the Heart* shows, a therapeutic culture has not completely dominated American culture. For a silly attempt to make talk shows into a sign of increasing democratic talk, see Paolo Carpignano et al., "Chatter in the Age of Electronic Reproduction: Talk Television and the "Public Mind,' " in *The Phantom Public Sphere*, ed. Bruce Robbins (Minneapolis: University of Minnesota Press, 1991). See my critique in Kevin Mattson, "The Phantom Public and Its Problems," *Telos* 26 (1993): 181–87.

3. There are many works about the civil rights movement, but the interpretation I rely on here is that of Aldon Morris, *The Origins of the Civil Rights Movement: Black Communities Organizing for Change* (New York: The Free Press, 1984). On the student left and its relation to democratic theory, see James Miller, *Democracy Is in the Streets: From Port Huron to the Siege of Chicago* (New York: Simon and Schuster, 1987), especially pt. 2.

4. Edward Chambers, "The Next Fifty Years," in *Organizing for Change: IAF, 50 Years of Power, Action, Justice*, Industrial Areas Foundation Report, 1990, p. 5. For more on Alinsky, see Sanford Horwitt, *Let Them Call Me Rebel: Saul Alinsky—His Life and Legacy* (New York: Knopf, 1989). For more on the contemporary work of the IAF, see Mary Beth Rogers, *Cold Anger: A Story of Faith and Power Politics* (Denton: University of North Texas Press, 1990). Harry Boyte's work is found in his *Commonwealth: A Return to Citizen Politics* (New York: The Free Press, 1989), and "The Growth of Citizen Politics," *Dissent*, Fall 1990, pp. 513–18. On cities incorporating participatory democracy into local government, see the excellent work done by Jeffrey Berry et al., *The Rebirth of Urban Democracy* (Washington, D.C.: The Brookings Institution, 1993).

5. For the work of the National Issues Forums, see David Mathews, *Politics for People: Finding a Responsible Public Voice* (Urbana: University of Illinois Press, 1994), pp. 108–9. For study circles, see *Planning Community-Wide Study Circle Programs,* Study Circles Resource Center Manual, Pomfret, Connecticut, 1996, sec. 1, p. 2, and Leonard Oliver's early work, *Study Circles* (Washington, D.C.: Seven Locks Press, 1987).

6. It should be noted that a consensus exists today among intellectuals on both the left and right that "civil society"—that realm between the state and the economy—matters for a healthy democratic politics (this is the realm in which Dewey located the social centers). See, for instance, the work of Peter Berger and Richard Neuhaus, *To Empower People: The Role of Mediating Structures in Public Policy* (Washington, D.C.: American Enterprise Institute, 1977), and many of the essays collected in Don Eberly, ed., *Building a Community of Citizens* (Lanham, Md.: University Press of America, 1994). For a more "left" appreciation of civic institutions, see Sarah Evans and Harry Boyte, *Free Spaces: The Sources of Democratic Change in America* (New York: Harper and Row, 1986).

7. As a side note, Senator Bill Bradley has argued that public schools could serve as "quality civic space" if used appropriately after hours. In this call Bradley echoes the call of social centers activists. See E. J. Dionne, *They Only Look Dead: Why Progressives Will Dominate the Next Political Era* (New York: Simon and Schuster, 1996), p. 311.

SELECT BIBLIOGRAPHY

"Introduction," "Conclusion," and General Works on Democracy

Ackerman, Bruce. "Why Dialogue?" *Journal of Philosophy* 86 (1989): 5–22.

Appadurai, Arjun, and Carol Breckenridge. "Why Public Culture?" *Public Culture Bulletin* 1 (1988): 5–9.

Arblaster, Anthony. *Democracy*. Minneapolis: University of Minnesota Press, 1987.

Arendt, Hannah. *The Human Condition*. Chicago: University of Chicago Press, 1958.

———. *On Revolution*. New York: Penguin, 1963.

Barber, Benjamin. *The Conquest of Politics: Liberal Philosophy in Democratic Times*. Princeton: Princeton University Press, 1988.

———. *Strong Democracy*. Berkeley and Los Angeles: University of California Press, 1984.

Bellah, Robert, et al. *Habits of the Heart: Individualism and Commitment in American Life*. New York: Harper and Row, 1985.

Bender, Thomas. *Community and Social Change in America*. Baltimore: The Johns Hopkins University Press, 1978.

———. *Intellect and Public Life: Essays on the Social History of Academic Intellectuals in the United States*. Baltimore: The Johns Hopkins University Press, 1993.

———. "Metropolitan Life and the Making of Public Culture." In *Power, Culture, and Place*, edited by John Mollenkompf. New York: Russell Sage Foundation, 1988.

———. "The New History: Then and Now." *Reviews in American History* 12 (1984): 612–22.

———. "New York in Theory." In *America in Theory*, edited by Leslie Berlowitz, Denis Donoghue, and Louis Menand. New York: Oxford University Press, 1988.

———. *New York Intellect*. Baltimore: The Johns Hopkins University Press, 1987.

———. *Toward an Urban Vision: Ideas and Institutions in Nineteenth-Century America*. Baltimore: The Johns Hopkins University Press, 1975.

———. "Wholes and Parts: Continuing the Conversation." *Journal of American History* 73 (1986): 120–36.

Berger, Peter, and Richard Neuhaus. *To Empower People: The Role of Mediating Structures in Public Policy*. Washington, D.C.: American Enterprise Institute, 1977.

Berman, Marshall. "Take It to the Streets: Conflict and Community in Public Space." *Dissent,* Fall 1986, pp. 476–85.

Berry, Jeffrey, et al. *The Rebirth of Urban Democracy.* Washington, D.C.: The Brookings Institution, 1993.

Boyte, Harry. *Commonwealth: A Return to Citizen Politics.* New York: The Free Press, 1989.

———. "The Growth of Citizen Politics." *Dissent,* Fall 1990, pp. 513–18.

Burnheim, John. *Is Democracy Possible?* Berkeley and Los Angeles: University of California Press, 1985.

Calhoun, Craig, ed. *Habermas and the Public Sphere.* Cambridge, Mass.: MIT Press, 1992.

Cohen, Mitchell. "Rooted Cosmopolitanism." *Dissent,* Fall 1992, pp. 478–83.

Coles, Robert. *The Call of Service: A Witness to Idealism.* Boston: Houghton Mifflin Co., 1993.

Crenson, Matthew. *Neighborhood Politics.* Cambridge, Mass.: Harvard University Press, 1983.

Crozier, Michel, et al. *The Crisis of Democracy.* New York: New York University Press, 1975.

Dagger, Richard. "Metropolis, Memory, and Citizenship." *American Journal of Political Science* 25 (1981): 715–37.

Dahl, Robert. *Democracy and Its Critics.* New Haven: Yale University Press, 1989.

Dallmayr, Fred. *Polis and Praxis.* Cambridge, Mass.: MIT Press, 1984.

Dewey, John. *The Public and Its Problems.* Denver: Swallow Press, 1927.

Dickstein, Morris. *Double Agent: The Critic and Society.* New York: Oxford University Press, 1992.

Dionne, E.J. *They Only Look Dead: Why Progressives Will Dominate the Next Political Era.* New York: Simon and Schuster, 1996.

———. *Why Americans Hate Politics.* New York: Simon and Schuster, 1991.

Dryzek, John. *Discursive Democracy.* Cambridge: Cambridge University Press, 1990.

Dunn, John. *Interpreting Political Responsibility.* Princeton: Princeton University Press, 1990.

Eberly, Don, ed. *Building a Community of Citizens.* Lanham, Md.: University Press of America, 1994.

Elshtain, Jean Bethke. *Democracy on Trial.* New York: Basic Books, 1995.

Entman, Robert. *Democracy Without Citizens.* New York: Oxford University Press, 1989.

Etzioni, Amitai. *The Spirit of Community.* New York: Crown, 1993.

Evans, Sarah, and Harry Boyte. *Free Spaces: The Sources of Democratic Change in America.* New York: Harper and Row, 1986.

Fishkin, James. *Democracy and Deliberation.* New Haven: Yale University Press, 1991.

———. *Voice of the People.* New Haven: Yale University Press, 1995.

Galston, William. "Liberal Virtues." *American Political Science Review* 82 (1988): 1277–90.

Gouinlock, James. *Excellence in Public Discourse: John Stuart Mill, John Dewey, and Social Intelligence.* New York: Teachers College Press, 1986.

Gould, Carol. *Rethinking Democracy: Freedom and Social Cooperation in Politics, Economy, and Society*. Cambridge: Cambridge University Press, 1988.

Habermas, Jürgen. *The Structural Transformation of the Public Sphere*. Cambridge, Mass.: MIT Press, 1989.

———. *Towards a Rational Society*. Boston: Beacon Press, 1970.

Hanson, Russell. *The Democratic Imagination in America*. Princeton: Princeton University Press, 1985.

Hausknecht, Murray. "On Politics and Trust." *Dissent*, Fall 1992, pp. 456–60.

Held, David. *Models of Democracy*. Stanford: Stanford University Press, 1987.

Horwitt, Sanford. *Let Them Call Me Rebel: Saul Alinsky—His Life and Legacy*. New York: Knopf, 1989.

Hughes, Robert. *The Culture of Complaint: The Fraying of America*. New York: Warner Books, 1993.

Jackson, J. B. "The American Public Space." *Public Interest*, Winter 1984, pp. 52–65.

Jacobs, Jane. *The Death and Life of Great American Cities*. New York: Vintage Books, 1963.

Jordan, Bill. *The Common Good: Citizenship, Morality, and Self-Interest*. London: Basil Blackwell, 1989.

Kariel, Henry, ed. *Frontiers of Democracy*. New York: Random House, 1970.

Kazin, Michael. *The Populist Persuasion*. New York: Basic Books, 1995.

Kemmis, Daniel. *Community and the Politics of Place*. Norman: University of Oklahoma Press, 1990.

Lasch, Christopher. *The Culture of Narcissism*. New York: Warner Books, 1979.

———. *The Revolt of the Elites and the Betrayal of Democracy*. New York: Norton, 1995.

Lennard, Suzanne, and Henry Lennard. *Public Life in Urban Places*. Southhampton: Gondolier Press, 1984.

Lummis, Charles Douglas. "The Radicalism of Democracy." *democracy*, Fall 1982, pp. 9–16.

Macedo, Stephen. *Liberal Virtue: Citizenship, Virtue, and Community in Liberal Constitutionalism*. Oxford: Clarendon Press, 1990.

MacIntyre, Alasdair. *After Virtue: A Study in Moral Theory*. 2d. ed. Notre Dame: University of Notre Dame Press, 1984.

Mansbridge, Jane. *Beyond Adversary Democracy*. New York: Basic Books, 1980.

Marcus, George, and Russell Hanson, eds. *Reconsidering the Democratic Public*. University Park: The Pennsylvania State University Press, 1993.

Mathews, David. *Politics for People: Finding a Responsible Public Voice*. Urbana: University of Illinois Press, 1994.

Miller, James. *Democracy Is in the Streets: From Port Huron to the Siege of Chicago*. New York: Simon and Schuster, 1987.

Mills, C. Wright. *Power, Politics, and People: The Collected Essays of C. Wright Mills*, edited by Irving Louis Horowitz. New York: Oxford University Press, 1967.

Miroff, Bruce. *Icons of Democracy*. New York: Basic Books, 1993.

Morone, James. *The Democratic Wish*. New York: Basic Books, 1990.

Morris, Aldon. *The Origins of the Civil Rights Movement: Black Communities Organizing for Change*. New York: The Free Press, 1984.

Oliver, Leonard. *Study Circles*. Washington, D.C.: Seven Locks Press, 1987.

Pateman, Carole. *Participation and Democratic Theory*. Cambridge: Cambridge University Press, 1970.

Pitkin, Hanna Fenichel, and Sara Shumer. "On Participation." *Democracy*, Fall 1982, pp. 43–54.

Postman, Neil. *Amusing Ourselves to Death: Public Discourse in the Age of Show Business*. New York: Penguin Books, 1985.

Pranger, Robert. *The Eclipse of Citizenship: Power and Participation in Contemporary Politics*. New York: Holt, Rinehart and Winston, 1968.

Putnam, Robert. "Bowling Alone: America's Declining Social Capital." *Journal of Democracy*, January 1995, pp. 65–78.

———. "Tuning In, Tuning Out: The Strange Disappearance of Social Capital in America." *PS: Political Science and Politics*, December 1995, pp. 664–83.

Robbins, Bruce, ed. *The Phantom Public Sphere*. Minneapolis: University of Minnesota Press, 1993.

Roelofs, H. Mark. *The Tension of Citizenship: Private Man and Public Duty*. New York: Rinehart and Co., 1957.

Rogers, Mary Beth. *Cold Anger: A Story of Faith and Power Politics*. Denton: University of North Texas Press, 1990.

Rustin, Michael. "The Fall and Rise of Public Space." *Dissent*, Fall 1986, pp. 486–94.

Sandel, Michael. *Democracy's Discontent: America in Search of a Public Philosophy*. Cambridge, Mass.: Harvard University Press, 1996.

———. *Liberalism and the Limits of Justice*. Cambridge: Cambridge University Press, 1982.

Schumpeter, Joseph. *Capitalism, Socialism, and Democracy*. 1942; Reprint, New York: Harper and Row, 1976.

Selznick, Philip. *The Moral Commonwealth*. Berkeley and Los Angeles: University of California Press, 1992.

Sennett, Richard. *The Fall of Public Man*. New York: Vintage, 1978.

———. *The Uses of Disorder*. New York: Vintage, 1970.

———, ed. *Classic Essays on the Culture of Cities*. New York: Meredith, 1969.

Shapiro, Ian. *Political Criticism*. Berkeley and Los Angeles: University of California Press, 1990.

Shklar, Judith. *American Citizenship*. Cambridge, Mass.: Harvard University Press, 1991.

Simmel, Georg. "The Metropolis and Mental Life." In *The Sociology of Georg Simmel*, edited by Kurt Wolff. New York: The Free Press, 1950.

Slater, Philip. *A Dream Deferred: America's Discontent and the Search for a New Democratic Ideal*. Boston: Beacon Press, 1991.

Smith, Michael. *The City and Social Theory*. New York: St. Martin's Press, 1979.

Smith, T. V., and Eduard Lindeman. *The Democratic Way of Life*. New York: Mentor Books, 1951.

"Special Issue on Universalism and Communitarianism." *Philosophy and Social Criticism* 14 (1988).

Stout, Jeffrey. *Ethics After Babel*. Boston: Beacon Press, 1988.

Sullivan, William. *Reconstructing Public Philosophy*. Berkeley and Los Angeles: University of California Press, 1982.

Thompson, Dennis. *The Democratic Citizen.* Cambridge: Cambridge University Press, 1970.
Tocqueville, Alexis de. *Democracy in America.* Garden City, N.Y.: Anchor Books, 1969.
Walzer, Michael. *The Company of Critics: Social Criticism and Political Commitment in the Twentieth Century.* New York: Basic Books, 1988.
———. "Pleasures and Costs of Urbanity." *Dissent,* Fall 1986, pp. 470–75.
———. "Political Decision-Making and Political Education." In *Political Theory and Political Education,* edited by Melvin Richter. Princeton: Princeton University Press, 1980.
———. *Radical Principles: Reflections of an Unreconstructed Democrat.* New York: Basic Books, 1980.
"Whatever Became of the Public Square?" *Harper's,* July 1990, pp. 49–60.
Wiebe, Robert. *Self-Rule: A Cultural History of American Democracy.* Chicago: University of Chicago Press, 1995.
Wolfe, Alan. *Whose Keeper? Social Science and Moral Obligation.* Berkeley and Los Angeles: University of California Press, 1989.
Yankelovich, Daniel. *Coming to Public Judgment: Making Democracy Work in a Complex World.* Syracuse: Syracuse University Press, 1991.

Chapter 1: Searching for a Public: From Beautifying Urban Space to Educating Citizens—The Work of Charles Zueblin

Manuscripts and Papers

Presidential Papers, 1889–1925, University of Chicago Library.

Primary and Secondary Sources

Adams, Brooks. "Public Art—The Test of Greatness." *Municipal Affairs* 5 (1901): 810–16.
Alling, Joseph. "Public Spirit Versus Selfishness." *American City,* August 1910, pp. 136–37.
American League for Civic Improvement. *The Twentieth-Century City: A Record of Work Accomplished for Civic Betterment.* Springfield: Home Florist, 1901.
American Park and Outdoor Art Association. Published Reports, 1897–1903.
"American Society of Landscape Architects, Minutes on the Life and Services of Charles Mulford Robinson, Associate Member." *Landscape Architecture* 9 (1919): 80–189.
Bartlett, Dana. *The Better City.* Los Angeles: Neuner Company Press, 1907.
Bell, Edward Hamilton. "Art in Municipal Decoration." *Harper's Weekly,* 28 April 1894, p. 401.
Bemis, Edward. "University Extension Among the Wage-Workers." *University Extension,* October 1894, pp. 97–102.
Bender, Thomas, and William Taylor. "Culture and Architecture: Some Aesthetic

Tensions in the Shaping of Modern New York City." In *Visions of the Modern City*, edited by William Sharpe and Leonard Wallack. New York: Heyman Center of the Humanities, 1983.

Benoit-Levy, Georges. "The Garden City." *Craftsman* 7 (1904–5): 284–93.

Bitter, Karl. "Municipal Sculpture." *Municipal Affairs* 2 (1898): 73–97.

Blashfield, Edwin. "Mural Painting." *Municipal Affairs* 2 (1898): 98–109.

———. "A Word for Municipal Art." *Municipal Affairs* 3 (1899): 582–93.

Bluestone, Daniel. "Denver: The City Beautiful Movement and the Problem of Commerce." *Journal of the Society of Architectural Historians* 47 (1988): 245–62.

Bogart, Michele. *Public Sculpture and the Civic Ideal in New York City, 1890–1930.* Chicago: University of Chicago Press, 1989.

Brunner, Arnold. "City and Town Planning Suggesting Beauty Based on Business Conditions." *Craftsman* 17 (1909–10): 657–67.

———. "Cleveland's Group Plan." *Proceedings of the 8th National Conference on City Planning*, New York, 5–7 June 1916.

Burnham, Daniel. "Plan of Chicago." In *The Urban Vision*, edited by Jack Tager and Park Dixon Goist. Homewood, Ill.: Dorsey Press, 1970.

Burton, Theodore. "Civic Betterment." *American City*, September 1909, p. 14.

Bush-Brown, H. K. "New York City Monuments." *Municipal Affairs* 3 (1899): 602–12.

———. "Parks." *Craftsman* 6 (1904): 115–24.

Cranston, Mary Ronkin. "The Garden as a Civic Asset." *Craftsman* 16 (1909): 205–10.

Croly, Herbert. "Art and Life." *Architectural Record* 1 (1891): 219–27.

———. " 'Civic Improvements': The Case of New York." *Architectural Record* 21 (1907): 347–52.

———. "The U.S. Post Office, Custom House, and Court House, Cleveland, Ohio." *Architectural Record* 29 (1911): 196.

———. "What Is Civic Art?" *Architectural Record* 16 (1904): 47–52.

Dannenberg, Joseph. "The Advance of Civic Art in Baltimore." *Craftsman* 9 (1905): 202–3.

Davis, Allen. "Continuing Education." *History of Education Quarterly* 20 (1980): 223–28.

Diner, Steven. *A City and Its Universities: Public Policy in Chicago, 1892–1919.* Chapel Hill: University of North Carolina Press, 1980.

Ferree, Barr. "The Lesson of Sculpture." *Craftsman* 7 (1904–5): 117–22.

Fleming, Ronald Lee, and Laura Halderman, eds. *On Common Ground: Caring for Shared Land from Town Common to Urban Park.* Cambridge, Mass.: Harvard Common Press, 1982.

Ford, Frederick C., comp. *The Grouping of Public Buildings.* Hartford, Conn.: Municipal Art Society, 1904.

Fowler, Frank. "Mural Painting, and a Word to Architects." *Architectural Record* 11 (1901): 510–24.

French, Lillie H. "Municipal Art." *Harper's Weekly*, 22 April 1893, p. 371.

Gillette, Howard. "White City, Capital City." *Chicago History* 28 (1989–90): 26–45.

Groves, Elma. "Municipal Art." *American Journal of Sociology* 6 (1901): 673–81.

"Growth and Beauty of Our American Cities." *Craftsman* 16 (1909): 399–413.

Harper, William Rainey. "The University Organization in Its Relation to University Extension." *Book News*, May 1891, pp. 343–45.

Hartman, Edward. "The Massachusetts Civic Conference." *American City*, January 1910, pp. 29–32.

Hill, Larry, and Robert Calvert. "The University of Texas Extension Services and Progressivism." *Southwestern Historical Quarterly* 86 (1982): 231–54.

Jensen, Jens. "Regulating City Building." *Survey*, 18 November 1911, pp. 1203–5.

Kantor, Harvey. "The City Beautiful Movement in New York." *New York Historical Society Quarterly* 57 (1973): 148–71.

Keeler, Charles. "Municipal Art in American Cities." *Craftsman* 8 (1905): 584–600.

Kriehn, George. "The City Beautiful." *Municipal Affairs* 3 (1899): 594–601.

———. "Digging Deeper into City Planning." *American City*, March 1912, pp. 557–62.

Lamb, Charles R. "The City Plan." *Craftsman* 6 (1904): 3–13.

———. "Civic Architecture." *Municipal Affairs* 2 (1898): 46–72.

Lamb, Frederick S. "The Beautifying of Our Cities." *Craftsman* 2 (1902): 172–88.

———. "Municipal Art." *Municipal Affairs* 1 (1897): 674–88.

Levy, David. *Herbert Croly of the New Republic.* Princeton: Princeton University Press, 1985.

Lopez, Charles. "Municipal Sculpture." *Municipal Affairs* 5 (1901): 696–720.

Manieri-Elia, Mario. "Toward an 'Imperial City': Daniel Burnham and the City Beautiful Movement." In *The American City from the Civil War to the New Deal*, edited by G. Ciucci et al. Cambridge, Mass.: MIT Press, 1973.

Marsh, Benjamin. "City Planning in Justice to the Working Population." *Charities and the Common*, 1 February 1908, pp. 1514–18.

———. *An Introduction to City Planning: Democracy's Challenge to the American City.* New York: Benjamin Marsh, 1909.

McCauley, L. M. "Municipal Art in Chicago." *Craftsman* 9 (1905): 321–40.

McFarland, J. Horace. "The Great Civic Awakening." *Outlook*, 18 April 1903, pp. 917–20.

———. "The Nationalization of Civic Improvement." *Charities and the Commons*, 3 November 1906, pp. 229–34.

McFarland, J. H., and Clinton Woodruff. "The Uplift in American Cities." *World's Work*, July 1904, pp. 4963–79.

"Mural Painting—An Art for the People and a Record of the Nation's Development." *Craftsman* 10 (1906): 54–66.

Nationwide Civic Betterment: A Report of the Third Annual Convention of the American League for Civic Improvement. Chicago: American League for Civic Improvement, 1903.

Peterson, Jon. "The City Beautiful Movement: Forgotten Origins and Lost Meanings." *Journal of Urban History* 2 (1976): 415–34.

Price, William. "The Beautiful City." *Craftsman* 17 (1909–10): 53–57.

"Public Art in American Cities." *Municipal Affairs* 2 (1898): 1–13.

Roberts, Edward. "Civic Art in Cleveland." *Craftsman* 9 (1905): 45–52.

Roberts, Kate. *The City Beautiful: A Study of Town Planning and Municipal Art.* White Plains, N.Y.: H. W. Wilson Co., 1916.
Robinson, Charles Mulford. *The Call of the City.* New York: Paul Elder and Co., 1908.
———. "Civic Improvements (A Reply)." *Architectural Record* 22 (1907): 117–20.
———. "Educational Value of Public Recreation Facilities." *Annals of the American Academy of Political and Social Science* 60 (1910): 134–40.
———. "Handicraft Workers and Civic Beauty." *Craftsman* 5 (1903): 235–39.
———. "Improvement in City Life: Part I, Philanthropic Progress." *Atlantic Monthly,* April 1899, pp. 772–85.
———. "Improvement in City Life: Part II, Educational Progress." *Atlantic Monthly,* May 1894, pp. 654–64.
———. "Improvement in City Life: Part III, Aesthetic Progress." *Atlantic Monthly,* June 1899, pp. 771–85.
———. *The Improvement of Towns and Cities; or, the Practical Basis of Civic Aesthetics.* New York: G. P. Putnam and Sons, 1901.
———. *Modern Civic Art.* New York: G. P. Putnam and Sons, 1904.
———. "New Dreams for Cities." *Architectural Record* 17 (1905): 410–21.
———. *Third Ward Traits.* Rochester, N.Y.: Genesee Press, 1899.
Ruckstuhl, Frederick. "Municipal Sculpture." *Craftsman* 7 (1904–5): 239–62.
Sargent, Irene. "Comments upon Mr. Shean's 'Mural Painting from the American Point of View.'" *Craftsman* 7 (1904): 28–34.
———. "Municipal Art: A Lesson from Foreign Towns." *Craftsman* 6 (1904): 321–28.
———. "The Mural Paintings of Robert Reid in the Massachusetts State House." *Craftsman* 7 (1904–5): 699–712.
———. "Prince Kropotkin's Economic Arguments." *Craftsman* 2 (1902): 157–71.
———. "Private Simplicity as a Promoter of Public Art." *Craftsman* 2 (1902): 209–21.
———. "A Second Lesson of Sculpture." *Craftsman* 7 (1904–5): 123–29.
Schopfer, Jean. "Art in the City." *Architectural Record* 12 (1902): 573–83.
———. "The Furnishing of a City." *Architectural Record* 13 (1903): 43–48.
———. "Greek Temples." *Architectural Record* 17 (1905): 441–70.
Sears, Charles. *The Redemption of the City.* Philadelphia: Griffith and Rowland Press, 1911.
Sharp, George. *City Life and Its Amelioration.* Boston: Richard Badger, 1915.
Shean, Charles. "The Decoration of Public Buildings." *Municipal Affairs* 5 (1901): 711–25.
———. "Mural Painting." *Craftsman* 7 (1904): 18–27.
Shillaher, Caroline. "The Charles Mulford Robinson Collection." *Harvard Library Bulletin* 15 (1967): 281–86.
Skolnik, Richard. "Civic Group Progressivism in New York City." *New York History,* July 1970, pp. 411–39.
Stickley, Gustav. "Thoughts Occasioned by an Anniversary: A Plea for Democratic Art." *Craftsman* 7 (1904): 42–60.
Stone, Susan. "The Town Beautiful." *Craftsman* 6 (1904): 125–29.

Storr, Richard. *Harper's University: The Beginnings.* Chicago: University of Chicago Press, 1966.

"Survey of Civic Betterment." *Chautauquan,* September 1903, pp. 69–79.

Underwood, Loring. "The City Beautiful: The Ideal to Aim At." *American City,* May 1910, pp. 214–18.

"Verdure for the City Streets: How the Municipal Art Society Is Working to Beautify New York with Plants and Flowers." *Craftsman* 16 (1909): 550–58.

Warner, John De Witt. "Civic Centers." *Municipal Affairs* 6 (1902): 1–23.

———. "The Importance of Municipal Improvement." *Craftsman* 5 (1904): 364–65.

———. "Matters That Suggest Themselves." *Municipal Affairs* 2 (1898): 123–32.

Watrous, Richard. "The American Civic Association." *American City,* October 1909, pp. 59–63.

White, Frank Ira. "Civic Art in Portland, Oregon." *Craftsman* 8 (1905): 796–803.

Wilson, Richard Guy. "Architecture, Landscape, and City Planning." In *The American Renaissance, 1876–1917.* New York: Pantheon Books, 1979.

Wilson, William. "The Billboard: Bane of the City Beautiful." *Journal of Urban History* 13 (1987): 394–425.

———. *The City Beautiful Movement.* Baltimore: The Johns Hopkins University Press, 1989.

———. "The Ideology, Aesthetics, and Politics of the City Beautiful Movement." In *The Rise of Modern Urban Planning,* edited by Anthony Sutcliffe. New York: St. Martin's Press, 1980.

———. "J. Horace McFarland and the City Beautiful Movement." *Journal of Urban History* 7 (1981): 15–334.

Woodruff, Clinton. "Annual Address." In American Park and Outdoor Art Association, *Year Book and Record of the Seventh Annual Meeting.* Rochester: Democrat and Chronicle Press, 1903.

———. "To Boycott the Billboard: The Right of the Citizen to an Unposted Landscape." *Craftsman* 13 (1907–8): 433–38.

———. *The City: As It Is and Is to Be.* Philadelphia: American Baptist Publication Society, 1910.

———. "The National Municipal League." *American City,* November 1909, 109–12.

———. "The Problem of the City." *American Journal of Politics* 9 (1896): 382–91.

———. "The Uplift in American Cities." *World's Work,* July 1904, pp. 4963–79.

Woytanowitz, George. *University Extension: The Early Years in America, 1885–1915.* Iowa City, Iowa: National University Extension Association, 1974.

Zueblin, Charles. *American Municipal Progress.* New York: Macmillan Co., 1916.

———. "The Chicago Ghetto." In *Hull House Maps and Papers.* Boston: Thomas Y. Crowell, 1895.

———. "The Chicago Society for University Extension." *University Extension,* March 1892, pp. 273–75.

———. "The City as Democracy's Hope." *Dial,* 1 April 1906, pp. 230–32.

———. "Civic Chronicle for 1903 and 1904." *Chautauquan,* June 1904, pp. 391–94.

———. *A Decade of Civic Development.* Chicago: University of Chicago Press, 1905.

———. *Democracy and the Overman.* New York: B. W. Huebsch, 1910.

———. "Greater New York." *Chautauquan,* February 1904, pp. 568–78.
———. "Harrisburg Plan of Municipal Improvement." *Chautauquan,* March 1904, pp. 60–68.
———. "The Lecturer and the Laborer." *University Extension,* January 1894, pp. 213–16.
———. "The Making of the City." *Chautauquan,* November 1903, pp. 267–75.
———. "Metropolitan Boston." *Chautauquan,* January 1904, pp. 478–86.
———. "Municipal Playgrounds in Chicago." *American Journal of Sociology* 4 (1898): 145–58.
———. "The New Civic Spirit." *Chautauquan,* September 1903, pp. 55–59.
———. *The Religion of a Democrat.* New York: B. W. Huebsch, 1908.
———. "Results and Prospects of University Extension." *Dial,* 1 April 1897, pp. 207–9.
———. "The Return to Nature." *Chautauquan,* May 1904, pp. 257–66.
———. "The Training of the Citizen." *Chautauquan,* October 1903, pp. 161–68.
———. "Washington Old and New." *Chautauquan,* April 1904, pp. 156–67.
———. " 'The White City' and After." *Chautauquan,* December 1903, pp. 373–84.
Zueblin, Rho Fisk. "Art Training for Citizenship." *Chautauquan,* April 1904, pp. 168–78.

Chapter 2: From Tent Meetings to the Forum Movement: Frederic Howe and the Democratic Public

Manuscripts and Papers

People's Institute Records, New York Public Library.

Primary and Secondary Sources:

Bemis, Edward. "The Cleveland Referendum on Street Railways." *Quarterly Journal of Economics* 23 (1908): 179–83.
———. "The Cleveland Street Railway Settlement." *Quarterly Journal of Economics* 24 (1910): 550–60.
———. "The Franchise Situation in Cleveland." *Municipal Affairs* 6 (1902): 261–67.
———. "Mayor Johnson." *Arena,* December 1905, pp. 576–77.
———. "The Significance of Mayor Johnson's Election." *Arena,* June 1903, pp. 582–85.
———. "The Street Railway Settlement in Cleveland." *Quarterly Journal of Economics* 22 (1908): pp. 543–75.
———. "Tom L. Johnson's Achievements as Mayor of Cleveland." *Review of Reviews,* May 1911, pp. 558–60.
Bremner, Robert. "The City, Hope of Democracy." *American Journal of Economics and Sociology* 12 (1953): 305–10.
———. "The Fight for Home Rule." *American Journal of Economics and Sociology* 11 (1951): 99–110.

———. "Honest Man's Story: Frederic Howe." *American Journal of Economics and Sociology* 8 (1949): 413–22.

———. "Self-Government." *American Journal of Economics and Sociology* 10 (1950): 87–91.

———. "The Single Tax Philosophy in Cleveland and Toledo." *American Journal of Economics and Sociology* 9 (1950): 369–76.

———. "The Street Railway Controversy in Cleveland." *American Journal of Economics and Sociology* 9 (1950): 185–206.

———. "Tom L. Johnson." *Ohio Archaeological and Historical Quarterly* 59 (1950): 1–13.

Briggs, Robert. "The Progressive Era in Cleveland, Ohio: Tom L. Johnson's Administration, 1901–1909." Ph.D. diss., University of Chicago, 1962.

Burnham, Daniel, et al. "The Grouping of Public Buildings at Cleveland." *Inland Architect and News Record* 42 (1903): 13–15.

"Burton and Johnson and Cleveland's Mayoralty." *Current Literature,* November 1907, pp. 473–80.

Campbell, Thomas F. *Daniel E. Morgan: 1877–1949, The Good Citizen in Politics.* Cleveland: Press of Western Reserve University, 1966.

Campbell, Thomas, and Edward Miggins, eds. *The Birth of Modern Cleveland, 1865–1930.* London: Associated University Presses, 1988.

Candeloro, Dominic. "The Single Tax Movement and Progressivism, 1880–1920." *American Journal of Economics and Sociology* 38 (1979): 113–27.

Child, Clinton. "A New York Social Center." *Survey,* 21 September 1912, pp. 769–70.

"Cleveland Street Railways." *Outlook,* 7 November 1908, pp. 508–9.

Coleman, George. "Legislators Learn About Forums." *Community Forum,* March 1918, p. 11.

———, ed. *Democracy in the Making: Ford Hall and the Open Forum Movement.* Boston: Little, Brown and Co., 1915.

Collier, John. "Charles Sprague Smith." *Survey,* 9 April 1910, p. 80.

———. *From Every Zenith: A Memoir and Some Essays on Life and Thought.* Denver: Sage Books, 1963.

———. "The People's Institute." *Independent,* 30 May 1912, pp. 1144–48.

Condon, George. *Cleveland, the Best Kept Secret.* Garden City, N.Y.: Doubleday and Co., 1967.

Cooley, Harris. "Tom Johnson's Full Day's Work." *Public,* 21 July 1911, pp. 685–87.

Crosby, Ernest. "Golden Rule Jones." *Craftsman* 7 (1904–5): 530–47, 679–88.

Crunden, Robert. *A Hero in Spite of Himself: Brand Whitlock in Art, Politics, and War.* New York: Knopf, 1969.

Cushing, G. C. "Mayor of Cleveland." *World Today,* July 1906, pp. 698–99.

Davis, Dwight. "The Neighborhood Center—A Moral and Educational Factor." *Charities and the Commons,* 1 February 1908, pp. 1504–6.

Dudden, Joseph. *Joseph Fels and the Single Tax Movement.* Philadelphia: Temple University Press, 1971.

"Ex-Mayor Johnson." *Outlook,* 22 April 1911, pp. 850–51.

"The Failure of Tom Johnson." *World's Work,* January 1909, pp. 11085–86.

Fairlie, John A. "The Municipal Crisis in Ohio." *Michigan Law Review* 1 (1903): 352–63.

Fisher, Robert Bruce. "The People's Institute of New York City, 1897–1934: Culture, Progressive Democracy, and the People." Ph.D. diss., New York University, 1974.

Flower, Benjamin. "The Field Against Mayor Johnson." *Arena,* August 1903, pp. 208–10.

———. "A New Champion for the People's Cause." *Arena,* November 1902, pp. 534–42.

———. "Two Notable Reform Victories in Ohio." *Arena,* June 1903, pp. 651–53.

Frank, Glenn. "The Parliament of the People." *Century,* July 1919, pp. 401–16.

Geiger, George Raymond. *The Philosophy of Henry George.* New York: Macmillan Co., 1930.

George, Henry, Jr. "Tom L. Johnson." *Twentieth-Century Magazine,* July 1911, pp. 291–98.

Grant, Percy Stickney. "The Open Forum Movement." *North American Review,* January 1916, pp. 81–92.

Haworth, Paul. "Mayor Johnson of Cleveland: A Study of Mismanaged Reform." *Outlook,* 23 October 1909, pp. 469–74.

Hines, Thomas. "The Paradox of 'Progressive' Architecture: Urban Planning and Public Building in Tom Johnson's Cleveland." *American Quarterly* 25 (1973): 426–48.

Holt, Byron. "The Single Tax Applied to Cities." *Municipal Affairs* 3 (1899): 328–49.

Howe, Frederic. "The Best-Governed Community in the World." *World's Work,* February 1902, p. 1726.

———. *The British City: The Beginnings of Democracy.* New York: Charles Scribner's Sons, 1907.

———. "The Case for Municipal Ownership." *Publications of the American Economics Association* 7 (1906): 113–33.

———. *The City: The Hope of Democracy.* New York: Charles Scribner's Sons, 1905.

———. "The City as a Socializing Agency." *American Journal of Sociology* 17 (1912): 590–601.

———. "A City in the Life-Saving Business." *Outlook,* 18 January 1908, pp. 123–27.

———. "City Sense." *Outlook,* 24 August 1912, pp. 944–53.

———. "Cleveland: A City 'Finding Itself.' " *World's Work,* October 1903, pp. 3988–99.

———. "Cleveland's Group Plan." *Charities,* 1 February 1903, p. 1548.

———. "Cleveland's Education Through Its Chamber of Commerce." *Outlook,* 28 July 1906, pp. 739–48.

———. *The Confessions of a Reformer.* 1925. Reprint, New York: Quadrangle Books, 1967.

———. "The Constitution and Public Opinion." *Proceedings of the Academy of Political Science* 5 (1914): 7–19.

———. "In Defence of the American City." *Scribner's Magazine,* April 1912, pp. 484–90.

———. "Democracy or Imperialism." *Annals of the American Academy of Political and Social Science* 66 (1916): 250–58.
———. *Denmark: A Cooperative Commonwealth.* London: George Allen and Unwin, 1922.
———. "Discovering the Schoolhouse." *Saturday Evening Post,* 1 June 1912, pp. 14–15, 54–56.
———. *European Cities at Work.* New York: Charles Scribner's Sons, 1913.
———. "The Garden Cities of England." *Scribner's Magazine,* July 1912, pp. 1–19.
———. "A Golden Rule Chief of Police." *Everybody's Magazine,* June 1910, pp. 814–23.
———. "Leisure." *Survey,* 3 January 1914, pp. 415–16.
———. "Milwaukee: A Socialist City." *Outlook,* 25 June 1910, pp. 411–22.
———. *The Modern City and Its Problems.* New York: Charles Scribner's Sons, 1915.
———. "Plans for a City Beautiful." *Harper's Weekly,* 23 April 1904, pp. 624–26.
———. *Privilege and Democracy in America.* New York: Charles Scribner's Sons, 1910.
———. "The Remaking of the American City." *Harper's Magazine,* July 1913, pp. 186–97.
———. *Socialized Germany.* New York: Charles Scribner's Sons, 1915.
———. *Taxation and Taxes in the United States Under the Internal Revenue System, 1791–1895.* New York: Thomas Crowell and Co., 1896.
———. "Tom Johnson and the City of Cleveland." *Reader Magazine,* October 1907, pp. 502–16.
———. "What to Do with Movies?" *Outlook,* 20 June 1914, pp. 412–16.
Huff, Robert Arthur. "Frederic C. Howe, Progressive." Ph.D. diss., University of Rochester, 1966.
Ivins, William. "Municipal Government." *Political Science Quarterly* 2 (1887): 291–312.
Johnson, Tom. "Address at the National Anti-Trust Conference, 1900." *Public,* 21 April 1911, pp. 373–79.
———. "The Ideal City." *Saturday Evening Post,* 9 November 1901, pp. 1–2, 5.
———. "Inequalities in Taxation." *Hampton's Magazine,* August 1911, pp. 195–205.
———. "Municipal Ownership for All Public Utilities." *Moody's Magazine,* November 1906, pp. 649–51.
———. "My Fight Against a Three-Cent Fare." *Hampton's Magazine,* September 1911, pp. 373–78.
———. *My Story.* New York: B. W. Huebsch, 1913.
——— "Nine Years' War with Privilege." *Hampton's Magazine,* July 1911, pp. 3–18.
———. "Our Leaders in Reform Are the Cities." *Smith's Magazine,* July 1906, unpaginated.
———. "The Three-Cent Fare Fight in Cleveland." *Hampton's Magazine,* October 1911, pp. 491–504.
———. "Three-Cent Fares in Cleveland." *Independent,* 8 August 1907, pp. 335–37.
"Johnsonism in Ohio." *Gunton's Magazine,* October 1903, pp. 283–94.
"Johnson's Appeal to the Farmers." *Gunton's Magazine,* November 1903, pp. 392–95.

Jones, Samuel. "American Workingmen and Religion." *Outlook*, 14 July 1900, p. 640.

———. "The New Patriotism." *Municipal Affairs*, 3 (1899): 455–76.

———. *The New Right*. New York: Eastern Book Concern, 1899.

Leckie, Shirley. "Brand Whitlock and the City Beautiful Movement in Toledo, Ohio." *Ohio History* 91 (1982): 5–36.

Lorenz, Carl. *Tom L. Johnson: Mayor of Cleveland*. New York: A. S. Barnes Co., 1911.

Lubove, Roy. "Frederic Howe and the Quest for Community." *Historian* 39 (1977): pp. 270–91.

Lurie, Reuben. *The Challenge of the Forum: The Story of Ford Hall and the Open Forum Movement*. Boston: Richard Badger, 1930.

Maltbie, Milo Ray. "Home Rule in Ohio." *Municipal Affairs* 6 (1902): 234–44.

Marcosson, Isaac. "A Practical School of Democracy." *World's Work*, July 1905, pp. 6414–17.

Massouh, Michael. "Innovations in Street Railways Before Electric Traction: Tom Johnson's Contributions." *Technology and Culture* 18 (1977): 202–17.

"Mayor Johnson and the Cleveland Clergy." *Arena*, April 1906, pp. 430–32.

"Mayor Johnson and the Traction Companies." *Outlook*, 4 August 1906, pp. 777–78.

"Mayor Johnson Again." *Outlook*, 24 July 1909, pp. 668–69.

"Mayor Johnson on Municipal Control of Vice." *Arena*, April 1906, pp. 400–409.

"Mayor Johnson's Latest Victory for Good Government." *Arena*, August 1903, pp. 208–10.

"Mayor Johnson's Victory and Its Significance in National Politics." *Arena*, December 1907, pp. 710–12.

McClure, Frank. "Cleveland's New Methods of Care for Her Wards." *Chautauquan*, December 1910, pp. 90–106.

Miller, Joseph. "Home Rule: A Plea for Free Cities." *American Journal of Politics* 4 (1894): 25–48.

———. "President Roosevelt and Mayor Johnson as Typical Representatives of Opposing Political Ideals." *Single Tax Review*, 3 January 1904, pp. 5–8.

"Millionaire Tax Reformer." *Review of Reviews*, June 1899, pp. 651–52.

Mullen, John. "American Perception of German City Planning at the Turn of the Century." *Urbanism Past and Present* 3 (1976–77): 5–15.

"The Municipal Problem." *Outlook*, 4 September 1909, pp. 13–14.

"The Municipal Problem." *Outlook*, 11 September 1909, pp. 55–56.

Murdock, Eugene. "Cleveland's Johnson." *Ohio Archaeological and Historical Quarterly* 62 (1953): 323–33.

———. "Cleveland's Johnson: At Home." *Ohio Historical Quarterly* 63 (1954): 319–35.

———. "Cleveland's Johnson: The Cabinet." *Ohio Historical Quarterly* 66 (1957): 375–90.

———. "Cleveland's Johnson: Elected Mayor." *Ohio Historical Quarterly* 65 (1956): 28–43.

———. "Cleveland's Johnson: First Term." *Ohio Historical Quarterly* 67 (1958): 35–49.

Noble, Ransom. "Henry George and the Progressive Movement." *American Journal of Economics and Sociology* 8 (1949): 259–69.

Norton, William. "Chief Kohler of Cleveland and His Golden Rule Policy." *Outlook*, 6 November 1909, pp. 537–42.

Oberholtzer, Ellis. "Home Rule for Our American Cities." *Annals of the American Academy of Political and Social Sciences* 3 (1892): 736–63.

Orth, Samuel P. "The Municipal Situation in Ohio." *Forum*, June 1902, pp. 430–37.

Patten, Simon. "The Decay of Local Government in America." *Annals of the American Academy of Political and Social Science* 1 (1890): 26–42.

"People's Institute Defining a Better New York." *Survey*, 22 November 1913, p. 198.

"The People's Institute of New York." *American City*, May 1910, p. 289.

Peyser, Nathan. "The School as the Community Center." *Survey*, 23 September 1916, pp. 621–23.

Pingree, Hazen. "The Problem of Municipal Reform: Contract By Referendum." *Arena*, April 1897, pp. 707–10.

Post, Louis. "Tom Johnson." *Public*, 21 July 1911, pp. 646–56.

"A Review of the World." *Current Literature*, November 1907, pp. 469–99.

Riis, Jacob. "The People's Institute of New York." *Century Magazine*, April 1910, pp. 850–63.

Roberts, Edward. "Civic Art in Cleveland." *Craftsman* 9 (1905): 45–52.

Rose, William Ganson. *Cleveland: The Making of a City*. Kent, Ohio: Kent State University Press, 1990.

Russell, Edgar Alexander. "Work of the People's Institute as Originated and Carried on by Charles Sprague Smith." *Craftsman* 10 (1906): 183–89.

"Self-Government in Public Recreation." *Survey*, 23 August 1913, pp. 638–39.

Shibley, George. "Referendum and Initiative in Relation to Municipal Ownership." *Municipal Affairs* 6 (1902–3): 781–86.

Sidlo, Thomas. "Centralization in Ohio Municipal Government." *American Political Science Review* 3 (1909): 591–97.

———. "Cleveland's Street Railway Settlement." *American Political Science Review* 4 (1910): 279–87.

———. "Ohio's First Step in Tax Reform." *Yale Review* 18 (1910): 413–17.

Sikes, George. "The City Government Questions in Ohio." *Outlook*, 23 August 1902, pp. 1008–10.

———. "Tom Johnson." *Outlook*, 16 November 1907, pp. 571–73.

———. "Tom L. Johnson, Mayor of Cleveland." *World Today*, July 1906, pp. 698–99.

Smith, Charles Sprague. "The People's Institute of New York and Its Work for the Development of Citizenship Along Democratic Lines." *Arena*, July 1907, pp. 49–52.

———. *Working with the People*. New York: A. Wessels Co., 1904.

Statement of Mayor Tom Johnson on Municipal Ownership. Cleveland: S. J. Monck Lithographs, n.d.

Steffens, Lincoln. *The Struggle for Self-Government*. New York: McClure, Phillips, and Co., 1906.

Suit, William. "Tom Loftin Johnson, Businessman Reformer." Ph.D. diss., Kent State University, 1988.

Thorburn, Neil. "A Progressive and the First World War: Frederic Howe." *Mid-America* 51 (1969): 108–18.
———. "A Public Official as a Muckraker: Brand Whitlock." *Ohio History* 78 (1969): 5–12.
———. "What Happened to Brand Whitlock's Progressivism?" *Northwest Ohio Quarterly* 40 (1968): 153–60.
"Tom Johnson to the Front." *Nation*, 11 September 1902, p. 201.
"Tom Johnson's Public Service." *Public*, 21 April 1911, pp. 363–65.
"Tom Johnson's Victory." *Nation*, 3 September 1903, pp. 183–84.
"Two Notable Victories." *Arena*, June 1903, pp. 651–53.
Walker, Joseph. "The Initiative, Referendum, and the Open Forum." *Community Forum*, November 1917, pp. 11–12.
Warner, Hoyt London. *Progressivism in Ohio, 1897–1917*. Columbus: Ohio State University Press, 1964.
"The Week." *Nation*, 13 April 1911, pp. 357–60.
Whipple, James. "Municipal Government in an Average City: Cleveland, 1876–1900." *Ohio Historical Quarterly* 62 (1953): 1–24.
Whitlock, Brand. "The City and Civilization." *Scribner's Magazine*, November 1912, pp. 623–33.
———. "The City and the Public Utility Corporation." *World Today*, September 1910, pp. 957–64.
———. *Forty Years of It*. New York: D. Appleton, 1914.
Wilcox, Delos. "How the Chicago and Cleveland Street Railway Settlements Are Working Out." *National Municipal Review*, April 1912, pp. 630–38.
Witt, Peter. "The Vision of Tom Johnson." *Public*, July 1911, pp. 684–85.
Wittke, Carl. "Peter Witt, Tribune of the People." *Ohio State Archaeological and Historical Quarterly* 58 (1949): pp. 361–67.
Woodruff, Clinton Rogers. "Growth of Demand for Municipal Ownership." *Municipal Affairs* 6 (1902–3): 787–90.

Chapters 3 and 4: "Buttressing the Foundations of Democracy": The Social Centers Movement/Envisioning Democracy: Social Centers and Political Thought

Bibliographical Note: I have condensed the bibliographies for these two chapters since there is much overlap between the two and since the fourth chapter grew organically out of the third.

Manuscripts and Papers

Charles Van Hise Papers, University of Wisconsin–Madison Library.
Local History Department, Rochester Public Library.

Primary and Secondary Sources

Andrews, Fannie. "Parents' Associations and the Public Schools." *Charities and the Commons,* 24 November 1906, pp. 335–43.

———. "Schoolhouses as Neighborhood Centers." *New Boston,* March 1911, pp. 490–92.

Bagehot, Walter. *Physics and Politics.* 1867. Reprint, Boston: Beacon Press, 1956.

Baker, Ray Stannard. "Do It for Rochester." *American Magazine,* September 1910, pp. 683–96.

Balliet, Thomas. "The Extension of the Public School: The Organization of a System of Evening Schools." In *Journal of Proceedings and Addresses of the 43rd Annual Meeting of the National Education Association.* Winona, Minn.: NEA, 1904.

Barclay, Lorne. "The Social Center and Democracy." *General Federation of Women's Club Magazine,* 19 October 1914, pp. 17–19.

Baxter, Sylvester. "Widening the Use of Public Schoolhouses." *World's Work,* March 1903, pp. 3247–48.

Berg, H. O. "The Public Schools as Municipal Neighborhood Recreation Centers." *American City,* January 1917, pp. 35–42.

Betten, Neil, and Michael Austin, eds. *The Roots of Community Organizing, 1917–1939.* Philadelphia: Temple University Press, 1990.

Bittner, W. S. "Community Institutes." *Bulletin of the Extension Division, Indiana University* 2 (1917): 3–27.

Bourne, Randolph. *The Gary Schools.* 1916. Reprint, Cambridge, Mass.: MIT Press, 1970.

Bulkley, William. "The School as a Social Center." *Charities and the Commons,* 7 October 1905, pp. 76–78.

Burns, Robert. "Schools as Community Centers." *Pennsylvania School Journal* 57 (1909): 490–500.

Bushnell, C. J. "The Community Center Movement as a Moral Force." *International Journal of Ethics* 30 (1920): 326–35.

Childs, Harriet Lusk. "The Rochester Social Centers." *American City,* July 1911, pp. 18–22.

"Civic Friendliness." *Outlook,* 28 August 1909, p. 966.

"Civic Nerve Centers." *New Boston,* May 1910, pp. 35–36.

Clark, E. P. "The Free Lecture Movement." *Nation,* 8 May 1902, p. 363.

"Clubbed into Democracy." *The Common Good of Civic and Social Rochester* 4 (1911): 3–4.

Coit, Stanton. *Neighborhood Guilds: An Instrument of Social Reform.* London: Sewan Sonneenschein and Co., 1891.

Collier, John. "Definitions and Debates of the Community Center Conference." *American City,* June 1916, pp. 572–74.

———. *From Every Zenith: A Memoir.* Denver: Sage Books, 1963.

———. "The Keystone of the Arch." *Survey,* 18 November 1911, p. 1200.

———. "Self-Determination in Community Enterprise." *Survey,* 20 September 1919, pp. 870–72.

———. "Social Centers." *National Municipal Review* 2 (1913): 455–60.

———. "The Spiritual Counterpart to the Social Center." *Survey*, 21 June 1913, pp. 416–17.

———. "The Stage, A New World." *Survey*, 3 June 1916, pp. 251–60.

Comey, Arthur Coleman. "Neighborhood Centers." In *City Planning*, edited by John Nolen. New York: D. Appleton and Co., 1929.

Crist, Raymond. "Cooperation of School Authorities and the Public in the Wider Use of School Buildings." In *Addresses and Proceedings of the 57th Annual Meeting of the National Education Association.* Washington, D.C.: NEA, 1919.

Curtis, Henry. *Education Through Play.* New York: Macmillan Co., 1915.

———. "The Neighborhood Center." *American City*, July 1912, pp. 14–17.

———. "The Neighborhood Center." *American City*, August 1912, pp. 133–37.

———. "The School Center." *Survey*, 19 April 1913, pp. 89–91.

Daggett, Mary Potter. "The City as a Mother." *World's Work*, November 1912, pp. 111–17.

Davis, Dwight. "The Neighborhood Center." *Charities and the Common*, 1 February 1908, pp. 1504–6.

De Bruyn, John. "Reviving the Spirit of the 'Little Red Schoolhouse.' " *New Boston*, February 1911, pp. 449–53.

Democrat and Chronicle, 1906–12.

Dewey, John. "Are the Schools Doing What the People Want Them To Do?" *Educational Review*, May 1901, pp. 459–74.

———. "The School as a Social Center." In *John Dewey: The Middle Works, 1899–1924*, edited by Jo Ann Boydston. Carbondale: Southern Illinois University Press, 1976.

———. "Schools of Tomorrow." In *The Middle Works, 1899–1924*, edited by Jo Ann Boydston. Carbondale: Southern Illinois University Press, 1979.

Dingwell, James. "The Civic Center and Better Citizenship." *Immigrants in America Review*, September 1915, pp. 84–87.

Downey, James. "Educational Progress in 1909." *School Review* (1910): 400–423.

"Dummerton's Grange Hall." *American City*, April 1910, p. 184.

Dutko, John. "Socialism in Rochester, 1900–1917." Master's thesis, University of Rochester, 1953.

"Echoes from the First National Conference of Social Centers." *Common Good*, December 1911, pp. 21–27.

Edwards, George. *The School as a Social Center.* Bulletin of the University of South Carolina, 1913.

"The Effect of a Social Center on a Community." *Settlement Bulletin* 2 (1908): 3–5.

Eliot, Charles. "Full Utilization of a Public School Plant." In *Journal of Proceedings and Addresses of the 42nd Annual Meeting of the National Education Association.* Winona, Minn.: NEA, 1903.

Evans, A. Grant. "Social Center Movement in Oklahoma." *Survey*, 18 May 1912, p. 297.

Felton, Ralph. *Serving the Neighborhood.* New York: Council of Women for Home Missions and Interchurch World Movement of North America, 1920.

Ferguson, Charles. *The University Militant.* New York: Mitchell Kennerley, 1911.

Fisher, Robert. "From Grass Roots Organizing to Community Service: Community

Organization Practice in the Community Center Movement." In *Community Organization for Urban Social Change,* edited by Robert Fisher and Peter Romanofsky. Westport, Conn.: Greenwood Press, 1981.

———. *Let the People Decide.* Boston: Twayne, 1984.

Fitzpatrick, Edward. "Political Aspects of the Community Center of the School Building as a Civic Center." *School and Society,* 29 July 1916, pp. 159–65.

Forbes, George. "Buttressing the Foundations of Democracy." *Common Good,* January 1912, pp. 8–13.

———. "Our University." *Common Good,* December 1912, pp. 75–77.

———. "The Relation of Playgrounds to Social Centers." *Playground* (1909): 12–15.

Ford, George. "Madison Conference on Social Centers." *Survey,* 18 November 1911, pp. 1229–31.

Forsyth, Anne. "Using the Schoolhouse Out of School Hours." *World Today,* January 1911, pp. 38–43.

Frankel, Ruth. *Henry Leipziger: Educator and Idealist.* New York: Macmillan Co., 1933.

Fuller, Wayne. "Changing Concepts of the Country School as a Community Center in the Midwest." *Agricultural History* 58 (1984): 423–41.

"Funds for Social Center Extension." *Survey,* 25 May 1912, pp. 328–29.

Gilbert, Charles. *The School and Its Life.* New York: Silver, Burdett, and Co., 1906.

Glueck, Eleanor Touroff. *The Community Use of Schools.* Baltimore: Williams and Wilkins Co., 1927.

———. "Description and Analysis of Dorchester School Center, Boston." *Journal of Social Forces* 3 (1925): 468–73.

Gove, Aaron. "The Proper Use of Schoolhouses." In *Journal of the Proceedings and Addresses of the 36th Annual Meeting of the National Education Association.* Chicago: University of Chicago Press, 1897.

Grice, Mary Van. *Home and School United in Widening Circles of Inspiration and Service.* Philadelphia: Christopher Sower Co., 1909.

Hall, G. Stanley. "Some Social Aspects of Education." *Educational Review,* May 1902, pp. 433–45.

Hanmer, Lee. "The Schoolhouse Evening Center—What It Is, What It Costs, and What It Pays." In *Journal of Proceedings and Addresses of the National Education Association.* Ann Arbor, Mich.: NEA, 1913.

Hebble, Charles, and Frank Goodwin, eds. *The Citizens' Book.* Cincinnati: Stewart and Kidd Co., 1916.

Henderson, William. "Back to the Little Red Schoolhouse." *World's Events,* August 1909, pp. 9–10, 24.

Holman, Charles. "Focusing Social Forces in the Southwest." *Survey,* 23 September 1911, pp. 866–68.

"How Grown-Ups Act in School." *Survey,* 6 May 1916, pp. 169–71.

Jerome, Amalie Hoffer. "The Playground as a Social Center." *Annals of the American Academy of Political and Social Science* 35 (1910): 345–49.

Jones, Richard Lloyd. "Social Centers and Hymns of Democracy." *Common Good,* December 1913, pp. 44–45.

Kelly, M. Clyde. *The Community Capitol: A Program For American Unity.* Pittsburgh: Mayflower Press, 1921.

King, Irving, ed. *Social Aspects of Education: A Book of Sources and Original Discussions.* New York: Macmillan Co., 1913.

Lang, Osian. "The Common School Community." *Journal of Proceedings and Addresses of the National Education Association.* Chicago: NEA, 1902.

Leipziger, Henry. "Adult Education." In *Journal of the Proceedings and Addresses of the 43rd Annual Meeting of the National Education Association.* Winona, Minn.: NEA, 1904.

———. "Free Lecture System for the People." *Municipal Affairs* 3 (1899): 462–72.

———. "Free Lectures to the People." *Critic,* 9 May 1896, pp. 329–30.

Lindeman, Eduard. *The Community: An Introduction to the Study of Community Leadership and Organization.* New York: Association Press, 1921.

Manny, Frank. "A Social Center in a Swiss Village." *Charities and the Commons,* 20 July 1907, pp. 437–38.

Margulies, Herbert. *The Decline of the Progressive Movement in Wisconsin, 1890–1920.* Madison: State Historical Society of Wisconsin, 1968.

Marsh, Benjamin. "The Unused Aspects of Our Public Recreation Facilities." *Annals of the American Academy of Political and Social Science* 35 (1910): 382–85.

Maxwell, William. "The Economical Use of School Buildings." In *Journal of Proceedings and Addresses of the 48th Annual Meeting of the National Education Association.* Winona, Minn.: NEA, 1910.

Mayer, Mary Josephine. "Our Public Schools as Social Centers." *American Review of Reviews,* August 1911, pp. 201–8.

McKelvey, Blake. "A History of City Planning in Rochester." *Rochester History* 6 (1944): 1–24.

———. "A History of the Rochester City Club." *Rochester History* 9 (1947): 1–24.

———. *Rochester: The Quest for Quality, 1890–1925.* Cambridge, Mass.: Harvard University Press, 1956.

———. "Rochester's Ethnic Transformations." *Rochester History* 25 (1963): 1–24.

———. "Rochester's Political Trends: A Historical Review." *Rochester History* 19 (1952): 1–24.

———. "Walter Rauschenbusch's Rochester." *Rochester History* 14 (1952): 1–27.

McLennan, William. "Democracy and the Settlement." *Journal of Social Forces* 4 (1926): 769–73.

Mero, Everett. "Recreation Advance in Milwaukee." *New Boston,* April 1911, pp. 520–23.

"Milwaukee's Recreation Movement." *Survey,* 18 February 1911, pp. 832–33.

Minus, Paul. *Walter Rauschenbusch: American Reformer.* New York: Macmillan Co., 1988.

Montgomery, Louise. "Social Work in the Hamline School." *The Elementary School Teacher,* November 1907, pp. 113–21.

Mowry, Duane. "Social and Recreational Activity in Milwaukee." *American City,* May 1912, pp. 748–50.

———. "The Use of School Buildings for Other Than School Purposes." *Education,* October 1908, pp. 92–96.

Munro, William Bennett. *Principles and Methods of Municipal Administration.* New York: Macmillan Co., 1916.

National Society for the Study of Education. *The Tenth Yearbook: Part I, The City School as a Community Center.* Chicago: University of Chicago Press, 1911.

"The Neighborhood Spirit and the Training for Citizenship." *Outlook,* 25 November 1911, pp. 700–701.

Neligh, Carl. "The School: A Social and Industrial Center." *Southern Workman* 36 (1907): 604–12.

Nye, Russell. *Midwestern Progressive Politics.* East Lansing: Michigan State College Press, 1951.

"Open Schools for Baltimore." *Charities and the Commons,* 29 February 1908, pp. 1641–47.

"Opening School Doors to Popular Discussion." *Survey,* 8 April 1916, p. 61.

"Opening the Doors of the Little Red Schoolhouse." *Survey,* 10 December 1910, p. 417.

"Organizing Social Center Work Under Paid Secretaries." *Survey,* 8 August 1914, p. 490.

"Our Evening Schools." *Bulletin* 3 (1910): 3.

Paulding, J. K. "The Public School as a Center of Community Life." *Educational Review* 15 (1898): 147–54.

Perry, Clarence. *Ten Years of the Community Center Movement.* New York: Russell Sage Foundation, 1921.

———. "Two Regrettable Events." *Survey,* 18 March 1911, pp. 996–97.

———. *Wider Use of the School Plant.* New York: Russell Sage Foundation, 1910.

Peyser, Nathan. "The School as the Community Center." *Survey,* 23 September 1916, pp. 621–23.

Pieplow, William. "Broader Use of School Buildings." *American School Board Journal,* January 1912, pp. 15–16, 37.

"The Political Use of School Buildings." *Outlook,* 14 September 1912, pp. 51–52.

Price, David. "Community and Control: Critical Democratic Theory in the Progressive Period." *American Political Science Review* 68 (1974): 1663–78.

Quandt, Jean. *From Small Town to the Great Community: The Social Thought of Progressive Intellectuals.* New Brunswick: Rutgers University Press, 1970.

Reese, William J. *Power and the Promise of School Reform: Grassroots Movements During the Progressive Era.* Boston: RKP, 1986.

Richard, Livy. "The Public Schools as Social Centers: Edward J. Ward's Work in Rochester, NY." *La Follette's Weekly Magazine,* 9 July 1910, p. 2.

———. "School Centers as 'Melting Pots.' " *New Boston,* April 1911, pp. 529–30.

Riley, Thomas. "Increased Use of Public School Property." *American Journal of Sociology* 11 (1906): 655–62.

Roark, Ruric Nevel. *Economy in Education.* New York: American Book Co., 1905.

Robbins, Jane. "The Settlement and the Public Schools." *Outlook,* 6 August 1910, p. 787.

Rochester Board of Education, *Proceedings,* 1908–14.

Rochester Social Centers and Civic Clubs. Rochester: League of Civic Clubs, 1909.

Rosenstein, David. "The Educational Function of the Social Settlement in a Democracy." *School and Society,* 29 September 1917, pp. 366–79.

Rumball, Edwin. "Are We Wrong in Using the School Buildings as Social Centers." *Common Good*, February 1914, pp. 74–77.

Schenck, Anna Pendleton. "The Need for Neighborhood Centers in American Cities." *American City*, April 1915, pp. 337–38.

"The School as a Social Center." *Independent*, 6 March 1902, pp. 583–84.

"The Schoolhouse for the People." *Independent*, 9 February 1911, pp. 317–18.

"Schools as Social Centers." *Independent*, 14 July 1904, pp. 110–11.

Scudder, Horace. "The Schoolhouse as a Centre." *Atlantic Monthly*, January 1896, pp. 103–9.

Search, Preston. *An Ideal School.* New York: D. Appleton and Co., 1902.

Shelby, Gertrude Matthews. "Extending Democracy: What the Cincinnati Social Unit Has Accomplished." *Harper's Magazine*, April 1920, pp. 688–95.

"Social Centers." *American City*, November 1911, p. 312.

"Social Centers and Schoolhouse Centers." *Common Good*, April 1914, pp. 99–100.

"Social Centers Begin." *Common Good*, December 1910, p. 3.

"The Social Centers—Center of Democracy." *Survey*, 6 September 1913, pp. 675–76.

"Social Centers in Columbus Schools." *Survey*, 12 February 1910, pp. 696–97.

"Social Centers in Wisconsin." *Survey*, 18 February 1911, p. 832.

"Some Social Aspects of the School." *Charities*, 18 July 1903, pp. 61–63.

Spargo, John. "The Social Service of a City School." *Craftsman*, August 1906, pp. 605–13.

Stevens, Edward. "Social Centers, Politics, and Social Efficiency in the Progressive Era." *History of Education Quarterly* 12 (1972): 16–33.

Stoddard, William Leavitt. "Democratizing Our Democracy." *Independent*, 18 May 1918, p. 279.

Stokes, J. G. Phelps. "Public Schools as Social Centers." *Annals of the American Academy of Political and Social Science* 23 (1904): 457–63.

Taylor, Graham. "The Public School as a Social Center." *Commons*, December 1901, p. 16.

Teller, Sidney. "The Temples of Democracy." *Common Good*, March 1912, pp. 27–29.

Ward, Edward. "Again, 'The Time Has Come for Rochester to Vote in Its Schools.' " *Common Good*, July 1912, pp. 25–26.

———. "The Community Secretary." *Education*, June 1916, pp. 666–68.

———. "Discovering the Public School." *New Boston*, March 1911, p. 493.

———. "The First Social Center Conference." *Survey*, 18 March 1911, pp. 1002–3.

———. "The Little Red Schoolhouse." *Charities and the Commons*, 7 August 1909, pp. 640–49.

———. "The Modern Social Center Revival." *Playground* 4 (1911): 404–6.

———. "Permanent Primaries: Politics in the Social Center." *Common Good*, October 1913, pp. 9–10.

———. "A Point of Agreement." *American City*, October 1912, pp. 325–28.

———. "Public Recreation in America." *La Follette's Weekly Magazine*, 25 June 1910, pp. 10–11.

———. "The Rochester Movement." *Independent*, 14 October 1909, pp. 860–61.

———. "School Extension." *Common Good*, January 1911, pp. 12–16.
———. "The Schoolhouse or the Saloon." *Outlook*, 2 August 1912, pp. 487–88.
———. *The Social Center.* New York: D. Appleton and Co., 1913.
———. "There Are Other Rochesters." *Common Good*, April 1914, pp. 101–2.
———. "Where Suffragists and Anti's Unite." *American City*, June 1914, pp. 519–24.
———. *Women Should Mind Their Own Business.* New York: National Woman Suffrage Association, n.d.
"Washington Schoolhouses for the People." *Survey*, 27 June 1914, p. 337.
Weet, Herbert S. "Citizenship and the Evening Use of School Buildings, I." *Common Good*, January 1911, pp. 5–7.
———. "Citizenship and the Evening Use of School Buildings, II." *Common Good*, February 1911, pp. 7–9.
Weston, Olive. "The Public School as a Social Center." *The Elementary School Teacher*, October 1905, pp. 108–16.
Wilson, Samuel. "The Community House—An Element in Reconstruction." *American City*, December 1918, pp. 467–70.
Wilson, Woodrow. "An Address in Madison, Wisconsin, on Community Centers." In *The Papers of Woodrow Wilson*, edited by Arthur Link. Vol. 23. Princeton: Princeton University Press, 1977.
Wood, Arthur Evans. "The Philosophy of Community Organization." *Papers and Proceedings of the 17th Annual Meeting of the American Sociological Society* 17 (1922): 178–84.
Woods, Robert. *The Neighborhood in Nation Building.* 1923. Reprint, New York: Arno Press, 1970.
Wright, Augustus, ed. *Who's Who in the Lyceum.* Philadelphia: Pearson Brothers, 1906.

Chapter 5: Thinking Democratically: The Political Thought of Mary Parker Follett

Barnard, F. M., and R. A. Vernon. "Pluralism, Participation, and Politics: Reflections on the Intermediate Group." *Political Theory* 3 (1975): 180–97.
Belloc, Hilaire. *The Servile State.* 1912. Reprint, New York: Henry Holt and Co., 1946.
Bosanquet, Bernard. *Aspects of the Social Problem.* 1895. Reprint, New York: Kraus Reprint Co., 1968.
———. *The Philosophical Theory of the State.* London: Macmillan Co., 1899.
Cohen, Avrum Isaac. "Mary Parker Follett: Spokesman for Democracy, Philosopher for Social Group Work, 1918–1933." D.S.W. diss., Tulane University, 1971.
Cole, G.D.H. *Self-Government in Industry.* London: G. Bell and Sons, 1918.
———. *The World of Labour.* London: G. Bell and Sons, 1913.
Collini, Stefan. "Hobhouse, Bosanquet, and the State: Philosophical Idealism and Political Argument in England, 1880–1918." *Past and Present* 72 (1976): 86–111.
"Committee Report." *Women's Municipal League of Boston*, May 1912, pp. 5–12.

Cooper, Frances Ann. "Mary Parker Follett: The Power of Power-With." Ph.D. diss., University of Southern California, 1980.

Cotkin, George. *Reluctant Modernism: American Thought and Culture, 1880–1900.* New York: Twayne, 1992.

———. *William James, Public Philosopher.* Baltimore: The Johns Hopkins University Press, 1990.

Deane, Herbert. *The Political Ideas of Harold Laski.* New York: Columbia University Press, 1955.

Dewey, John. "Green's Theory of the Moral Motive." In *Early Works, 1889–1892,* edited by Jo Ann Boydston. Carbondale: Southern Illinois University Press, 1969.

———. "The Philosophy of T. H. Green." *In Early Works, 1889–1892,* edited by Jo Ann Boydston. Carbondale: Southern Illinois University Press, 1969.

———. "Self-Realization as the Moral Ideal." *In Early Works, 1889–1892,* edited by Jo Ann Boydston. Carbondale: Southern Illinois University Press, 1969.

Dowler, Lawrence Earl. "The New Idealism and the Quest for Culture in the Gilded Age." Ph.D. diss., University of Maryland, 1974.

Figgis, John Neville. *Churches in the Modern State.* London: Longmans, Green and Co., 1913.

———. *Studies of Political Thought from Gerson to Grotius, 1414–1625.* 1907. Reprint, Cambridge: Cambridge University Press, 1931.

Follett, Mary Parker. "The Aims of Adult Education." *Playground* 7 (1913): 261–68.

———. "Community Is a Process." *Philosophical Review* 28 (1919): 576–88.

———. *Creative Experience.* New York: Longmans, Green and Co., 1924.

———. "Evening Recreation Centers." *Playground* 6 (1913): 384–92.

———. *The New State: Group Organization the Solution of Popular Government.* 1918 Reprint, Gloucester, Mass.: Peter Smith, 1965.

———. "Placement Bureau." *Women's Municipal League Committees (Boston) Bulletin,* May 1917, p. 10.

———. *The Speaker of the House of Representatives.* 1896. Reprint, New York: Longmans, Green and Co., 1909.

Fowler, W. S. "Neo-Hegelianism and State Education in England." *Educational Theory* 9 (1959): 55–61.

Fox, Elliot Milton. "The Dynamics of Constructive Change in the Thought of Mary Parker Follett." Ph.D. diss., Columbia University, 1970.

Freeden, Michael. *The New Liberalism: An Ideology of Social Reform.* New York: Oxford University Press, 1986.

Garson, G. David. "On the Origins of Interest Group Theory." *American Political Science Review* 68 (1974): 1505–19.

Glass, S. T. *The Responsible Society: The Ideas of the English Guild Socialist.* London: Longmans, Green and Co., 1966.

Goetzman, William. "Introduction: The American Hegelians." In *The American Hegelians.* New York: Knopf, 1973.

Green, T. H. *Lectures on the Principles of Political Obligation and Other Writings.* Cambridge: Cambridge University Press, 1986.

———. "The Philosophy of Aristotle." In *Works,* edited by R. L. Nettleship. Vol. 3. London: Longmans, Green and Co., 1911.

———. "Popular Philosophy in Its Relation to Life." In *Works,* edited by R. L. Nettleship. Vol. 3. London: Longmans, Green and Co., 1911.

Greengarten, I. M. *Thomas Hill Green and the Development of Liberal-Democratic Thought.* Toronto: University of Toronto Press, 1981.

Greenleaf, W. H. *The British Political Tradition.* Volume 2, *The Ideological Heritage.* London: Methuen, 1983.

———. "Laski and British Socialism." *History of Political Thought* 2 (1981): 573–91.

Harris, Paul, and John Morrow, eds. *T. H. Green, Lectures on the Principles of Political Obligation and Other Writings.* Cambridge: Cambridge University Press, 1986.

Holt, Edwin. *The Freudian Wish.* New York: Henry Holt and Co., 1915.

Hsiao, Kung Chuan. *Political Pluralism.* New York: Harcourt, Brace and Co., 1927.

Kariel, Henry. "The New Order of Mary Parker Follett." *Western Political Quarterly* 8 (1955): 425–40.

Kuklick, Bruce. *The Rise of American Philosophy: Cambridge, Massachusetts, 1860–1930.* New Haven: Yale University Press, 1977.

Laski, Harold. "The Apotheosis of the State." *New Republic,* 22 July 1916, pp. 302–4.

———. "The Justification of History." *Dial,* 25 January 1917, pp. 59–60.

———. "The Literature of Politics." *New Republic,* 17 November 1917, pp. 6–8.

———. "The Literature of Reconstruction." *Bookman,* October 1918, pp. 215–20.

———. "The Means and the End." *New Republic,* 4 September 1915, pp. 133–34.

———. "The Personality of Associations." *Harvard Law Review* 29 (1916): 404–26.

———. "The Personality of the State." *Nation,* 22 July 1915, pp. 115–17.

———. "A Philosophy Embattled." *Dial,* 8 February 1917, pp. 96–98.

———. "The Pluralistic State." *Philosophical Review* 28 (1919): pp. 562–75.

———. "The Responsibility of the State in England." *Harvard Law Review* 32 (1919): 447–72.

———. *Studies in the Problem of Sovereignty.* New Haven: Yale University Press, 1917.

Le Bon, Gustave. *The Crowd.* 1895. Reprint, New York: Viking Press, 1966.

Lindeman, Eduard. "Mary Parker Follett." *Survey Graphic,* February 1934, pp. 86–87.

Lustig, R. Jeffrey. *Corporate Liberalism: The Origins of Modern American Political Theory, 1890–1920.* Berkeley and Los Angeles: University of California Press, 1982.

MacIver, R. M. *Community.* 1917. Reprint, London: Macmillan Co., 1924.

Magid, Henry Meyer. *English Political Pluralism.* New York: Columbia University Press, 1941.

Martin, Kingsley. *Harold Laski.* London: Victor Gollancz, Ltd., 1953.

McDougall, William. *An Introduction to Social Psychology.* Boston: John W. Luce Co., 1921.

Metcalf, Henry, and L. Urwick, eds. *Dynamic Administration: The Collected Papers of Mary Parker Follett.* New York: Harper and Brothers, 1940.

Morrow, John. "Liberalism and British Idealist Political Philosophy." *History of Political Thought* 5 (1984): 81–108.

Nicholls, David. *The Pluralist State.* New York: St. Martin's Press, 1975.

———. *Three Varieties of Pluralism.* New York: St. Martin's Press, 1974.

Park, Robert. *The Crowd and the Public and Other Essays.* Chicago: University of Chicago Press, 1972.

Pocock, J.G.A. *The Machiavellian Moment.* Princeton: Princeton University Press, 1975.

Pound, Roscoe. "The Scope and Purpose of Sociological Jurisprudence." *Harvard Law Review* 24 (1911): 591–619.

———. "The Scope and Purpose of Sociological Jurisprudence." *Harvard Law Review* 24 (1911): 140–68.

———. "The Scope and Purpose of Sociological Jurisprudence." *Harvard Law Review* 25 (1912): 489–516.

Richter, Melvin. *The Politics of Conscience: T. H. Green and His Age.* Lanham, Md.: University Press of America, 1983.

Robbins, Peter. *The British Hegelians, 1875–1925.* New York: Garland, 1982.

Robinson, Lilian. "The Larger Use of a Boston School." *Charities,* 1 April 1905, pp. 652–53.

Simhony, Avital. "T. H. Green's Theory of the Morally Justified Society." *History of Political Thought* 10 (1989): 481–98.

Smith, Craig. "The Individual and Society in T. H. Green's Theory of Virtue." *History of Political Thought* 2 (1981): 187–201.

Soffer, Reba. *Ethics and Society in England: The Revolution in the Social Sciences, 1870–1914.* Berkeley and Los Angeles: University of California Press, 1978.

Stener, James. "Mary Parker Follett and the Quest for Pragmatic Administration." *Administration and Society* 18 (1986): 159–77.

Vincent, Andrew. "Classical Liberalism and Its Crisis of Identity." *History of Political Thought* 11 (1990): 143–61.

Vincent, Andrew, and Raymond Plant. *Philosophy, Politics, and Citizenship: The Life and Thought of the British Idealists.* Oxford: Basil Blackwell, 1984.

Women's Municipal League of Boston (Education Department). *Handbook of Opportunities for Vocational Training in Boston.* Boston: Women's Municipal League of Boston, 1913.

Wood, Gordon. *The Creation of the American Republic.* New York: Norton, 1969.

Worrell, Dorothy. *The Women's Municipal League of Boston: A History of Thirty-Five Years of Civic Endeavor.* Boston: Women's Municipal League Committees, Inc., 1943.

Wright, A. W. *G.D.H. Cole and Socialist Democracy.* Oxford: Oxford University Press, 1979.

Zylstra, Bernard. *From Pluralism to Collectivism: The Development of Harold Laski's Political Thought.* Assen: Van Gorcum and Co., 1968.

Chapter 6: The Waning of the Democratic Public: World War I, Social Centers, and America

"Adaptation of Recreation and Community Service to Conditions of Peace." *Survey,* 7 December 1918, pp. 313–14.

Baker, Sibyl. "The Adaptation of School Centers in Washington to Changing Urban Needs." *Journal of Social Forces* 9 (1930): 229–31.

Beard, Charles. "A Declaration of Independence for the Public Forum." *Community Center*, 17 March 1917, 10–11.

Bernays, Edward. *Biography of an Idea: Memoirs of a Public Relations Counsel.* New York: Simon and Schuster, 1965.

———. *Crystallizing Public Opinion.* 1923. Reprint, New York: Horace Liveright, 1929.

———. "Manipulating Public Opinion." *American Journal of Sociology* 33 (1928): 958–71.

———. "Our Debt to Propaganda." *Forum*, March 1929, pp. 146–48.

———. "Rebuttal." *Forum*, March 1929, p. 149.

Bestor, Arthur. "The Making of Public Opinion in War Time." *Open Forum*, May 1918, pp. 3–4, 15.

Bittner, W. S. "The Relation of the Local Community to the Principal Factors of Public Opinion." *Journal of Social Forces* 7 (1928): 98–101.

Bowman, Le Roy. "Community Organization." *American Journal of Sociology* 35 (1930): 1002–9.

———. "Notes on the Community Conference." *Journal of Social Forces* 4 (1926): 576–78.

Breen, William James. "The Council of National Defense: Industrial and Social Mobilization in the United States, 1916–1920." Ph.D. diss., Duke University, 1968.

Bulmer, Martin. *The Chicago School of Sociology.* Chicago: University of Chicago Press, 1984.

Calvert, A. C. "Public Schools in the New War Cities." *American City*, November 1918, pp. 360–62.

Carey, James. *Communication as Culture.* Boston: Unwin Hyman, 1989.

———. "Communications and Progressives." *Critical Studies in Mass Communications* 6 (1989): 264–82.

Childs, Richard. "The Government's Model Villages." *Survey*, 1 February 1919, pp. 585–92.

Clarke, Ida Clyde. *The Little Democracy: A Textbook on Community Organization.* New York: D. Appleton and Co., 1918.

Collier, John. "Community Councils—Democracy Every Day." *Survey*, 31 August 1918, pp. 604–6.

———. "Community Councils—Democracy Every Day: II." *Survey*, 21 September 1918, pp. 689–91.

———. "Community Councils—Democracy Every Day: III." *Survey*, 28 September 1918, pp. 709–11, 725.

———. "The Crisis of Democracy." *Community Center*, June 1917, pp. 3–4, 23.

———. "Democracy Every Day." *Journal of the Proceedings and Addresses of the National Education Association of the U.S.* 56 (1918): 53–54.

———. "School Buildings as Coordinating Places for the Civil Energies of the War." *American City*, June 1917, pp. 588–91.

Creel, George. *How We Advertised America.* New York: Harper and Brothers, 1920.

———. "The 'Lash' of Public Opinion." *Collier's*, 22 November 1924, pp. 8–9, 46.

Dahir, James. *Community Centers as Living War Memorials.* New York: Russell Sage Foundation, 1946.

Daniels, John. *America Via the Neighborhood.* New York: Harper and Brothers, 1920.

Davis, Allen. "Welfare, Reform, and World War I." *American Quarterly* 19 (1967): 516–33.

Dewey, John. "Public Opinion." *New Republic,* 3 May 1922, pp. 286–88.

———. "The Social Possibilities of War." In *Characters and Events,* edited by Joseph Ratner. Vol. 2. New York: Henry Holt and Co., 1929.

Dinwiddie, Courtenay. *Community Responsibility: A Review of the Cincinnati Social Unit Experiment.* New York: New York School of Social Work, 1921.

Earle, Genevieve. "Meaning of the Community Center Movement." *Journal of Social Forces* 3 (1925): 294.

Eldridge, Seba. "Community Organization and Citizenship." *Social Forces* 7 (1928): 132–40.

Engelhardt, Carroll. "Citizenship Training and Community Civics in Iowa Schools." *Mid-America* 65 (1983): 55–69.

Fecher, Charles. *Mencken: A Study of His Thought.* New York: Knopf, 1978.

Glad, Paul. "Progressives and the Business Culture of the 1920s." *Journal of American History* 53 (1966): 75–89.

Gruber, Carol. *Mars and Minerva: World War I and the Uses of Higher Education.* Baton Rouge: Louisiana State University Press, 1975.

Hanifan, L. J. *The Community Center.* Boston: Silver, Burdett, and Co., 1920.

Hawley, Ellis. *The Great War and the Search for a Modern Order.* New York: St. Martin's Press, 1979.

Hiebert, Ray Elbon. *Courtier to the Crowd: The Story of Ivy Lee and the Development of Public Relations.* Ames: Iowa State University Press, 1966.

Hirschfield, Charles. "Nationalist Progressivism and World War I." *Mid-America* 45 (1963): 139–56.

Jackson, Henry. *A Community Center.* New York: Macmillan Co., 1918.

Karl, Barry. *The Uneasy State: The United States from 1915 to 1945.* Chicago: University of Chicago Press, 1983.

Kennedy, David. *Over Here: The First World War and American Society.* New York: Oxford University Press, 1980.

Laswell, Harold. *Propaganda Technique in the World War.* New York: Knopf, 1927.

———. "The Theory of Political Propaganda." *American Political Science Review* 21 (1927): 627–31.

Lichtenberger, J. P. "The War Relief Work of the Council of National Defense." *Annals of the American Academy of Political and Social Science* 79 (1918): 229–32.

Link, Arthur. "What Happened to the Progressive Movement in the 1920s?" *American Historical Review* 64 (1959): 833–51.

Lippmann, Walter. *Public Opinion.* New York: Harcourt, Brace and Co., 1922.

Lowrie, Gale. "The Social Unit." *National Municipal Review,* September 1920, pp. 553–66.

Lubove, Roy. *The Professional Altruist.* Cambridge, Mass.: Harvard University Press, 1965.

Martin, Everett Dean. "Our Invisible Masters." *Forum*, March 1929, pp. 142–45.

Matthews, Fred. *Quest for an American Sociology: Robert E. Park and the Chicago School.* Montreal: McGill-Queen's University Press, 1977.

McClymer, John. *War and Welfare: Social Engineering in America, 1890–1925.* Westport, Conn.: Greenwood Press, 1980.

Mencken, H. L. *A Mencken Chrestomathy.* New York: Vintage Books, 1992.

"National Community Board Organized." *American City*, October 1920, p. 421.

"Newton Baker, Secretary of War, Speaks on War Camp Community Recreation Service." *American City*, November 1917, p. 403.

Nickle, Clarence. "Community Control." *Journal of Social Forces* 4 (1925): 345–55.

Noggle, Burl. *Into the Twenties: The United States from Armistice to Normalcy.* Urbana: University of Illinois Press, 1974.

Olasky, Marvin. "Bringing 'Order Out of Chaos': Edward Bernays and the Salvation of Society Through Public Relations." *Journalism History* 12 (1985): 17–21.

Pangburn, Weaver. "The War and the Community Movement." *American Journal of Sociology* 26 (1920): 82–95.

Park, Robert. "Community Organization and the Romantic Temper." *Journal of Social Forces* 3 (1925): 673–77.

———. "The Problem of Community Organization." *Community Center*, July–August 1922, pp. 73, 80.

Park, Robert, et al., *The City.* 1925. Reprint, Chicago: University of Chicago Press, 1967.

Perry, Clarence. "The Rehabilitation of the Local Community." *Journal of Social Forces* 4 (1926): 558–62.

———. "The Tangible Aspects of Community Organization." *Journal of Social Forces* 8 (1930): 558–61.

Peters, John. "Satan and Savior: Mass Communication in Progressive Thought." *Critical Studies in Mass Communications* 6 (1989): 247–63.

Purcell, Edward. *The Crisis of Democratic Theory.* Lexington: University Press of Kentucky, 1973.

Rochester, Stuart. *American Liberal Disillusionment in the Wake of World War I.* University Park: The Pennsylvania State University Press, 1977.

Sanderson, Dwight. "Democracy and Community Organization." *Papers and Proceedings, 14th Annual Meeting of the American Sociological Society* 14 (1919): 83–99.

Schaffer, Ronald. *America in the Great War: The Rise of the War-Welfare State.* New York: Oxford University Press, 1991.

Schlesinger, Arthur, and Erik McKinley Eriksson. "The Vanishing Voter." *New Republic*, 15 October 1924, pp. 162–67.

Shermis, Samuel. "World War I—Catalyst for the Creation of the Social Sciences." *Social Studies*, January–February 1989, pp. 11–15.

Sproule, J. Michael. "Progressive Propaganda Critics and the Magic Bullet Myth." *Critical Studies in Mass Communication* 6 (1989): 229–46.

Steel, Ronald. *Walter Lippmann and the American Century.* New York: Vintage Books, 1980.

Steiner, Jesse Frederick. "An Appraisal of the Community Movement." *Social Forces* 7 (1929): 333–42.

———. "Comments." *Papers and Proceedings, 14th Annual Meeting of the American Sociological Society* 14 (1919): 98.

———. *Community Organization.* New York: Century Co., 1925.

———. "Education for Social Work." *American Journal of Sociology* 26 (1921): 475–518.

———. "Whither the Community Movement?" *Survey*, 15 April 1929, pp. 130–31.

Thompson, John. *Reformers and War: American Progressive Publicists and the First World War.* Cambridge: Cambridge University Press, 1987.

Todd, Lewis Paul. *Wartime Relations of the Federal Government and the Public Schools, 1917–1918.* New York: Teachers College, 1945.

Todd, Thomas Marshall. "Love, Science, and Social Justice: Voices and Conversations from the Urban Community Movement Before the Great War." Ph.D. diss., University of Minnesota, 1981.

Vaughn, Stephen. *Holding Fast the Inner Lines: Democracy, Nationalism, and the Committee on Public Information.* Chapel Hill: University of North Carolina Press, 1980.

Ward, Edward. "Bringing the Franchise to the National Capitol." *Community Center*, June 1917, pp. 7, 23.

Wood, Arthur Evans. "The Philosophy of Community Organization." *Papers and Proceedings of the 17th Annual Meeting of the American Sociological Society* 17 (1922): 178–84.

Wynn, Neil. *From Progressivism to Prosperity: World War I and American Society.* New York: Holmes and Meier, 1986.

Zueblin, Charles. "How the Forum May Serve America Today." *Open Forum*, May 1918, pp. 5–6.

General Primary Works

Abbot, Lyman. "Local Option by Popular Vote." *Municipal Affairs* 5 (1901): 859–66.

Addams, Jane. "Problems of Municipal Administration." *American Journal of Sociology* 10 (1905): 425–44.

———. "Recreation in Urban Communities." *American Journal of Sociology* 17 (1912): 615–19.

———. *Twenty Years at Hull-House.* 1910. Reprint, New York: Signet Classics, 1960.

Bourne, Randolph. *The Radical Will: Randolph Bourne, Selected Writings, 1911–1918,* edited by Olaf Hansen. New York: Urizen Books, 1977.

Burleigh, Louise. *The Community Theatre.* Boston: Little, Brown and Co., 1917.

Croly, Herbert. *Progressive Democracy.* New York: Macmillan Co., 1914.

———. *The Promise of American Life.* New York: Macmillan Co., 1909.

Dewitt, Benjamin Parke. *The Progressive Movement.* New York: Macmillan Co., 1915.

Eldridge, Seba. *Problems of Community Life.* New York: Thomas Cromwell Co., 1915.

Lilly, W. S. "The Shibboleth of Public Opinion." *Forum*, November 1890, pp. 256–63.

MacKaye, Percy. *Community Drama: Its Motive and Method of Neighborliness.* Boston: Houghton Mifflin Co., 1917.
———. *The Playhouse and the Play.* New York: Macmillan Co., 1909.
Overstreet, H. A. "Arousing the Public Interest in City Planning." *American City,* June 1928, pp. 85–89.
Parsons, Frank. *The City for the People (or the Municipalization of the City-Government and of Local Franchises).* Philadelphia: C. F. Taylor, n.d.
———. *Direct Legislation or the Veto Power in the Hands of the People.* Philadelphia: C. F. Taylor, n.d.
Royce, Josiah. *The Philosophy of Loyalty.* New York: Macmillan Co., 1908.
———. *Race Questions, Provincialism, and Other American Problems.* New York: Macmillan Co., 1908.
Sheffield, Alfred Dwight. *Joining in Public Discussion.* New York: George Doran Co., 1922.
Steffens, Lincoln. *The Autobiography of Lincoln Steffens.* New York: Harcourt, Brace and Co., 1931.
Stewart, Herbert L. "Some Ambiguities in 'Democracy.' " *American Journal of Sociology* 26 (1920): 545–57.
Sullivan, J. W. *Direct Legislation by the Citizenship Through Initiative and Referendum.* New York: Twentieth-Century Publishing Co., 1892.
Tager, Jack, and Park Dixon Goist, eds. *The Urban Vision.* Homewood, Ill.: Dorsey Press, 1970.
Tucker, William Jewett. *Public Mindedness.* Concord: Rumford Press, 1910.
Weber, Adna Ferrin. *The Growth of Cities in the 19th Century: A Study in Statistics.* 1899. Reprint, Ithaca: Cornell University Press, 1963.
Weeks, Arland. *The Psychology of Citizenship.* Chicago: A. C. McClurg Co., 1917.
Weyl, Walter. *The New Democracy.* New York: Harper and Row, 1914.
White, Bouck. *The Free City: A Book of Neighborhood.* New York: Moffet, Yard, and Co., 1919.
Wilcox, Delos. *American City: A Problem in Democracy.* New York: Macmillan Co., 1909.
Woolston, Howard. "The Urban Habit of Mind." *American Journal of Sociology* 17 (1912): 602–14.

General Secondary Works

Akam, Everett. "Pluralism and the Search for Community: The Social Thought of American Cultural Pluralists." Ph.D. diss., University of Rochester, 1989.
Anderson, Charles. *Pragmatic Liberalism.* Chicago: University of Chicago Press, 1990.
Anderson, Stanford, ed. *On Streets.* Cambridge, Mass.: MIT Press, 1978.
Appleby, Joyce. *Capitalism and a New Social Order: The Republican Vision of the 1790s.* New York: New York University Press, 1984.
Banning, Lance. *The Jeffersonian Persuasion.* Ithaca: Cornell University Press, 1978.
Bender, Thomas, ed. *The University and the City.* New York: Oxford University Press, 1988.

Berman, Marshall. *All That Is Solid Melts into Air: The Experience of Modernity.* New York: Simon and Schuster, 1982.

Biel, Steven. *Independent Intellectuals in the United States, 1910–1945.* New York: New York University Press, 1992.

Blake, Casey Nelson. *Beloved Community: The Cultural Criticism of Randolph Bourne, Van Wyck Brooks, Waldo Frank, and Lewis Mumford.* Chapel Hill: University of North Carolina Press, 1990.

Bledstein, Burton. *The Culture of Professionalism.* New York: Norton, 1978.

Bode, Carl. *The American Lyceum: Town Meeting of the Mind.* New York: Oxford University Press, 1956.

Bodnar, John. *The Transplanted: A History of Immigrants in Urban America.* Bloomington: Indiana University Press, 1985.

Boris, Eileen. *Art and Labor: Ruskin, Morris, and the Craftsman Ideal.* Philadelphia: Temple University Press, 1986.

Boyer, Paul. *Urban Masses and Moral Order in America, 1820–1920.* Cambridge, Mass.: Harvard University Press, 1978.

Braeman, John, et al., eds. *Change and Continuity in Twentieth-Century America: The 1920s.* Columbus: Ohio State University Press, 1968.

Brandes, Stuart. *American Welfare Capitalism, 1880–1940.* Chicago: University of Chicago Press, 1970.

Bridges, Amy. *A City in the Republic: Antebellum New York and the Origins of Machine Politics.* Cambridge: Cambridge University Press, 1984.

Buenker, John. *Urban Liberalism and Progressive Reform.* New York: Charles Scribner's Sons, 1973.

Carlson, Robert. *The Quest for Conformity: Americanization Through Education.* New York: John Wiley and Sons, 1975.

Carter, Paul. *The Twenties in America.* Arlington Heights, Ill.: AHM Publishing, 1975.

Cavallo, Dominick. *Muscles and Morals: Organized Playgrounds and Urban Reform, 1880–1920.* Philadelphia: University of Pennsylvania Press, 1981.

Chalmers, David Mark. *The Social and Political Ideas of the Muckrakers.* New York: Books for Libraries Press, 1964.

Chambers, John Whiteclay. *The Tyranny of Change: America in the Progressive Era, 1900–1917.* New York: St. Martin's Press, 1980.

Cooper, John Milton. *Pivotal Decades: The United States, 1900–1920.* New York: Norton, 1990.

———. *The Warrior and the Priest: Woodrow Wilson and Theodore Roosevelt.* Cambridge, Mass.: The Belknap Press of Harvard University Press, 1983.

Crunden, Robert. *Ministers of Reform: The Progressives' Achievement in American Civilization, 1889–1920.* Urbana: University of Illinois Press, 1982.

Danbom, David. *"The World of Hope": Progressives and the Struggle for an Ethical Public Life.* Philadelphia: Temple University Press, 1987.

Davis, Allen. *Spearheads for Reform: The Social Settlements and the Progressive Movement.* New York: Oxford University Press, 1967.

Dumenil, Lynn. *The Modern Temper: American Culture and Society in the 1920s.* New York: Hill and Wang, 1995.

Eisenach, Eldon. *The Lost Promise of Progressivism.* Lawrence: University Press of Kansas, 1994.

Ekirch, Arthur. *Progressivism in America.* New York: New Viewpoints, 1974.

Farmer, Rod. "Direct Democracy in Arkansas, 1910–1918." *Arkansas Historical Quarterly* 40 (1981): 99–118.

———. "The Maine Campaign for Direct Democracy, 1902–1908." *Maine Historical Society Quarterly* 23 (1983): 13–27.

Filene, Peter. "An Obituary for the Progressive Movement." *American Quarterly* 22 (1970): 20–34.

Fisher, Philip. "Appearing and Disappearing in Public." *Amerikastudien* 31 (1986): 81–100.

Folsom, Burton. "Tinkerers, Tipplers, and Traitors: Ethnicity and Democratic Reform in Nebraska During the Progressive Era." *Pacific Historical Review* 50 (1981): 53–75.

Foner, Eric. *Tom Paine and Revolutionary America.* New York: Oxford University Press, 1976.

Forcey, Charles. *Crossroads of Liberalism: Croly, Weyl, Lippmann, and the Progressive Era.* New York: Oxford University Press, 1961.

Fox, Richard Wightman, and T. J. Jackson Lears, eds. *The Culture of Consumption: Critical Essays in American History, 1880–1980.* New York: Pantheon, 1983.

Frisch, Michael. "Urban Theorists, Urban Reform, and American Political Culture in the Progressive Period." *Political Science Quarterly* 97 (1982): 295–315.

Furner, Mary. *Advocacy and Objectivity: A Crisis in the Professionalization of American Social Science, 1865–1905.* Lexington: University Press of Kentucky, 1975.

Ginger, Ray. *Altgeld's America: 1890–1905.* Chicago: Quadrangle Books, 1958.

Glassberg, David. *American Historical Pageantry: The Uses of Tradition in Early Twentieth-Century America.* Chapel Hill: University of North Carolina Press, 1990.

Goist, Paul Dixon. *From Main Street to State Street: Town, City, and Community.* Port Washington, N.Y.: Kennikat Press, 1977.

Goodwyn, Lawrence. *The Populist Moment: A Short History of the Agrarian Revolt in America.* New York: Oxford University Press, 1978.

Gorrell, Donald. *The Age of Social Responsibility: The Social Gospel in the Progressive Era, 1900–1920.* Macon: Mercer University Press, 1988.

Gould, Lewis, ed. *The Progressive Era.* Syracuse: Syracuse University Press, 1974.

Green, Martin. *The Problem of Boston.* New York: Norton, 1966.

Griffen, Clyde. "The Progressive Ethos." In *The Development of an American Culture,* edited by Stanley Coben and Corman Ratner. Englewood Cliffs, N.J.: Prentice-Hall, 1970.

Haber, Samuel. *Efficiency and Uplift: Scientific Management in the Progressive Era, 1890–1920.* Chicago: University of Chicago Press, 1964.

Hall, Peter. *Cities of Tomorrow: An Intellectual History of Urban Planning and Design in the Twentieth Century.* Oxford: Basil Blackwell, 1988.

Handlin, Oscar, and John Burchard, eds. *The Historian and the City.* Cambridge, Mass.: MIT Press, 1963.

Harris, Neil. *Cultural Excursions.* Chicago: University of Chicago Press, 1990.

Hays, Samuel. "The Politics of Reform in Municipal Government in the Progressive Era." *Pacific Northwest Quarterly* 55 (1964): 157–69.

Heckscher, August. *Open Spaces: The Life of American Cities.* New York: Harper and Row, 1977.

Hobson, Wayne. "Professionals, Progressives, and Bureaucratization: A Reassessment." *Historian* 39 (1977): 639–58.

Hofstadter, Richard. *The Age of Reform.* New York: Vintage, 1955.

Hollinger, David. *In the American Province: Studies in the Historiography of Ideas.* Baltimore: The Johns Hopkins University Press, 1989.

Horowitz, Daniel. *The Morality of Spending: Attitudes Toward the Consumer Society in America, 1875–1940.* Baltimore: The Johns Hopkins University Press, 1985.

Jones, Howard Mumford. *Ideas in America.* Cambridge, Mass.: Harvard University Press, 1944.

Kaus, Mickey. *The End of Equality.* New York: Basic Books, 1992.

Kennedy, David. "An Overview: The Progressive Era." *Historian* 37 (1975): 453–68.

Kenyon, Cecelia, ed. *The Anti-Federalists.* Indianapolis: Bobbs-Merrill, 1966.

Kirschner, Donald. "The Ambiguous Legacy: Social Justice and Social Control in the Progressive Era." *Historical Reflections* 2 (1975): 69–88.

Kloppenberg, James. *Uncertain Victory: Social Democracy and Progressivism in European and American Thought, 1870–1920.* New York: Oxford University Press, 1986.

Krug, Edward. *The Shaping of the American High School.* 2 vols. New York: Harper and Row, 1964.

Lasch, Christopher. *The New Radicalism in America, 1889–1963.* New York: Norton, 1965.

———. *The True and Only Heaven.* New York: Knopf, 1991.

Leach, William. *Land of Desire: Merchants, Power, and the Rise of a New American Culture.* New York: Pantheon, 1993.

Lears, Jackson. *No Place of Grace: Antimodernism and the Transformation of American Culture, 1880–1920.* New York: Pantheon, 1981.

Lees, Andrew. *Cities Perceived: Urban Society in European and American Thought, 1820–1940.* New York: Columbia University Press, 1985.

Leuchtenberg, William. *The Perils of Prosperity: 1914–1932.* Chicago: University of Chicago Press, 1958.

Link, Arthur, and Richard McCormick. *Progressivism.* Arlington Heights: Harlan Davidson, 1983.

Lubove, Roy. *Community Planning in the 1920s: The Contribution of the Regional Planning Association of America.* Pittsburgh: University of Pittsburgh Press, 1963.

Mann, Arthur. "British Social Thought and American Reformers of the Progressive Era." *Mississippi Valley Historical Review* 42 (1956): 672–92.

———. *Yankee Reformers in the Urban Age.* Cambridge, Mass.: Belknap Press, 1954.

Marchand, Roland. *Advertising the American Dream: Making Way for Modernity, 1920–1940.* Berkeley and Los Angeles: University of California Press, 1985.

Marsh, Margaret. *Suburban Lives.* New Brunswick: Rutgers University Press, 1990.

Matthews, Richard. *The Radical Politics of Thomas Jefferson: A Revisionist View.* Lawrence: University Press of Kansas, 1984.

Mattson, Kevin. "American Communitarianism Reconsidered." *Telos* 24 (1991): 181–86.

———. "The Phantom Public and Its Problems." *Telos* 26 (1993): 181–87.

———. "The Struggle for an Urban Democratic Public: Harlem in the 1920s." *New York History* 76 (1995): 291–318.

May, Henry. *The End of American Innocence: A Study of the First Years of Our Own Time, 1912–1917.* New York: Knopf, 1959.

May, Lary. *Screening Out the Past: The Birth of Mass Culture and the Motion Picture Industry.* New York: Oxford University Press, 1980.

McCarthy, Michael. "Urban Optimism and Reform Thought in the Progressive Era." *Historian* 51 (1989): 239–62.

McCormick, Richard. "The Discovery That Business Corrupts Politics: A Reappraisal of the Origins of Progressivism." *American Historical Review* 86 (1981): 247–74.

McFarland, Gerald. *Mugwumps, Morals, and Politics.* Amherst: University of Massachusetts Press, 1975.

McGerr, Michael. *The Decline of Popular Politics: The American North, 1865–1928.* New York: Oxford University Press, 1986.

Melvin, Patricia Mooney. *The Organic City: Urban Definition and Community Organization, 1880–1920.* Lexington: University Press of Kentucky, 1987.

Meyer, Stephen. *The Five Dollar Day: Labor Management and Social Control in the Ford Motor Company, 1908–1921.* Albany: State University of New York Press, 1981.

Mohl, Raymond. *The New City: Urban America in the Industrial Age, 1860–1920.* Arlington Heights: Harlan Davidson, 1985.

Morrison, Theodore. *Chautauqua: A Center for Education, Religion, and the Arts in America.* Chicago: University of Chicago Press, 1974.

Muraskin, William. "The Social Control Theory." *Journal of Social History* 9 (1976): 559–69.

Nash, Roderick. *The Nervous Generation: American Thought, 1917–1930.* Chicago: Ivan R. Dee, 1970.

Pease, Otis. "Urban Reformers in the Progressive Era." *Pacific Northwest Quarterly* 62 (1971): 49–58.

Ricci, David. *The Tragedy of Political Science: Politics, Scholarship, and Democracy.* New Haven: Yale University Press, 1984.

Rice, Bradley. *Progressive Cities: The Commission Government Movement in America, 1901–1920.* Austin: University of Texas Press, 1977.

Rodgers, Daniel. *Contested Truths: Keywords in American Politics Since Independence.* New York: Basic Books, 1987.

———. "In Search of Progressivism." *Reviews in American History* 10 (1982): 113–32.

Rosenzweig, Ray. "Middle-Class Parks and Working-Class Play." *Radical History Review,* Fall 1979, pp. 31–46.

Ross, Dorothy. *The Origins of Social Science.* Cambridge: Cambridge University Press, 1991.

———. "Socialism and American Liberalism: Academic Social Thought in the 1890s." *Perspectives in American History* 11 (1977–78): 1–79.

Rybczynski, Witold. *City Life: Urban Expectations in a New World.* New York: Charles Scribner's Sons, 1995.

Schiesl, Martin. *The Politics of Efficiency: Municipal Administration and Reform in America, 1800–1920.* Berkeley and Los Angeles: University of California Press, 1977.

Schultz, Stanley. "The Morality of Politics: The Muckrakers' Vision of Democracy." *Journal of American History* 52 (1965): 527–47.

Schultz, Stanley, and Clay McShane. "To Engineer the Metropolis: Sewers, Sanitation, and City Planning in Late Nineteenth-Century America." *Journal of American History* 65 (1978): 389–411.

Schuyler, David. *The New Urban Landscape: The Redefinition of City Form in Nineteenth-Century America.* Baltimore: The Johns Hopkins University Press, 1986.

Scott, Donald. "The Popular Lecture and the Creation of a Public in Mid-Nineteenth-Century America." *Journal of American History* 60 (1980): 791–809.

Scott, Mel. *American City Planning Since 1890.* Berkeley and Los Angeles: University of California Press, 1971.

Seidelman, Raymond. *Disenchanted Realists: Political Science and the American Crisis.* Albany: State University of New York Press, 1985.

Shalhope, Robert. "Republicanism and Early American Historiography." *William and Mary Quarterly* 39 (1982): 334–56.

———. "Toward a Republican Synthesis: The Emergence of an Understanding of Republicanism in American Historiography." *William and Mary Quarterly* 29 (1972): 49–80.

Sklar, Martin. *The Corporate Reconstruction of American Capitalism, 1890–1916.* Cambridge: Cambridge University Press, 1988.

Skorownek, Stephen. *Building a New State: The Expansion of National Administrative Capacities, 1877–1920.* Cambridge: Cambridge University Press, 1982.

Smith, Michael. *The City and Social Theory.* New York: St. Martin's Press, 1979.

Sullivan, William. *Work and Integrity: The Crisis of Professionalism in America.* New York: HarperBusiness, 1995.

Sussman, Warren I. *Culture as History: The Transformation of American Society in the Twentieth Century.* New York: Pantheon, 1984.

Tager, Jack. "Progressives, Conservatives, and the Theory of the Status Revolution." *Mid-America* 48 (1966): 162–75.

Taylor, William. "The Evolution of Public Space in New York City." In *Consuming Visions,* edited by Simon Bronner. New York: Norton, 1989.

Teaford, John. *The Municipal Revolution in America.* Chicago: University of Chicago Press, 1975.

Thelen, David. "Lincoln Steffens and the Muckrakers." *Wisconsin Magazine of History* 58 (1975): 313–17.

———. *The New Citizenship: Origins of Progressivism in Wisconsin, 1885–1900.* Columbia: University of Missouri Press, 1972.

———. *Robert M. La Follette and the Insurgent Spirit.* Boston: Little, Brown and Co., 1976.

Thomas, John. *Alternative America: Henry George, Edward Bellamy, Henry Demarest Lloyd, and the Adversary Tradition.* Cambridge, Mass.: The Belknap Press of Harvard University Press, 1983.

Trachtenberg, Alan. *The Incorporation of America: Culture and Society in the Gilded Age.* New York: Hill and Wang, 1982.

Trolander, Judith Ann. "Hull House and the Settlement House Movement." *Journal of Urban History* 17 (1991): 410–20.

Tropea, Joseph. "Rational Capitalism and Municipal Government: The Progressive Era." *Social Science History* 13 (1989): 137–58.

Veysey, Laurence. *The Emergence of the American University.* Chicago: University of Chicago Press, 1965.

Warner, Sam Bass. *The Urban Wilderness: A History of the American City.* New York: Harper and Row, 1972.

Weiner, Howard. "The Response to the American City (1885–1915) as Reflected in Writings Dealing with the City in Scholarly and Professional Serial Publications." Ph.D. diss., New York University, 1972.

Weinstein, James. *The Corporate Ideal in the Liberal State: 1900–1918.* Boston: Beacon Press, 1968.

Westbrook, Robert. *John Dewey and American Democracy.* Ithaca: Cornell University Press, 1991.

White, Dana Francis. "The Self-Conscious City." Ph.D. diss., George Washington University, 1969.

White, Morton. *Social Thought in America: The Revolt Against Formalism.* 1947. Reprint, New York: Oxford University Press, 1976.

White, Morton, and Lucia White. *The Intellectual Versus the City.* Cambridge, Mass.: Harvard University Press, 1962.

Wiebe, Robert. "The Progressive Years." In *The Reinterpretation of American History and Culture,* edited by William Cortwright and Richard Watson. Washington, D.C.: National Council for the Social Studies, 1973.

———. *The Search for Order, 1877–1920.* New York: Hill and Wang, 1967.

Wilson, Christopher. *The Labor of Words: Literary Professionalism in the Progressive Era.* Athens: University of Georgia Press, 1985.

Wilson, R. Jackson. *In Quest of Community: Social Philosophy in the United States, 1860–1920.* New York: John Wiley and Sons, 1968.

Index